Front endpaper photograph: *East Dorset, Vermont, at turn of the century was a tiny hamlet with marble sidewalks and tree-lined streets.* Back endpaper photograph: *In his Bedford Hills studio, Wit's End, Bill spent hours "just sitting" and thinking.*

'PASS IT ON'

The story of Bill Wilson
and how the A.A. message
reached the world.

'PASS IT ON'

The story of
Bill Wilson and how
the A.A. message
reached the world

1984
Alcoholics Anonymous World Services, Inc., New York, N.Y.

First Printing 1984
Nineteenth Printing 2002

Grateful acknowledgment is made for permission to reprint the following:

Material from the A.A. Grapevine (see "Sources," page 410)
is copyrighted by the A.A. Grapevine, Inc.,
reprinted by permission of the publisher.

Material from "Lois Remembers," copyrighted 1979 by Al-Anon
Family Group Headquarters, Inc., reprinted by permission of the publisher.

Letter from C.G. Jung to Bill Wilson (pages 383-385), C.G. Jung,
"Letters," eds. Gerhard Adler and Aniela Jaffe, trans. R.F.C. Hull,
Bollingen Series 95, Vol. II: 1951-1961. Copyright 1953, 1955, (c) 1961,
1963, 1968, 1971, 1972, 1974, 1975 by Princeton University Press.
Excerpt pp. 623-25. Reprinted by permission of Princeton University Press.

This is A.A. General Service Conference-approved literature

Library of Congress Catalog Card No. 84-072766

A.A. and Alcoholics Anonymous are registered trademarks of A.A. World
Services, Inc.

ISBN 0-916856-12-7

Printed in the United States of America

". . . I'll never forget the first time I met Bill Wilson. I was a couple of months sober and so excited, so thrilled to actually meet the co-founder that I gushed all over him with what my sobriety meant to me and my undying gratitude for his starting A.A. When I ran down, he took my hand in his and said simply, 'Pass it on.' "

— *from a letter to the A.A. General Service Office*

Foreword

Bill told his story countless times. He himself dubbed it "the bedtime story," and this name quickly caught on in the groups, as the story acquired a comforting familiarity. As many times as he told it, A.A. never tired of listening to it.

This is a detailed retelling of the bedtime story. Bill's life was so full of adventure, experiment, thought, and invention that to report it all would require much more space than a single volume affords. Bill showed us how to receive the gift of life. This is our gift to him — his life, as we see it. We like to think he would enjoy this telling of his tale.

Contents

Chapter One

William Griffith Wilson was born on November 26, 1895, in East Dorset, Vermont — in a room behind a bar. The bar was in the Wilson House, the village hotel run by the widow Wilson, who was Bill's grandmother. Bill's mother and father had come to live there after their marriage in 1894.

Bill was born about 3:00 a.m. on a wintry morning. His birth was difficult. Emily, his mother, said, "When they brought you to me, you were cold and discolored and nearly dead, and so also was I, you from asphyxiation and I from painful lacerations and loss of blood, but I held you to me, close in my arms, and so we were both warmed and comforted — and so we both lived, but the memory of it all could not be clearer in my consciousness if it had been seared into my brain with a red-hot branding iron, for I was given no anesthetic while those huge instruments were clamped onto your head."

During the early months of her pregnancy, Emily had written a poem, which she addressed to her mother and her sister Millie. She titled it "A Welcome Guest":

"When baby comes! The earth will smile / And with her wintry arts beguile / The frost sprites and the fairies blest, / All in pure snowy garments drest / To greet my guest. / When baby comes! Now fades from mind / All thought of self. The world grows kind, / Old wounds are healed, old wrongs forgot, / Sorrow and pain not, / Earth holds no blot. / When baby comes! Methinks I see / The winsome face that is to be, / And old-time doubts and haunting fears / Are lost in dreams of happier years / Smiles follow tears. / When baby comes! God make me good / And rich in grace of motherhood, / Make white this woman's soul of mine / And meet for this great gift of Thine / In that glad time."

With an attention to detail that was characteristic of her, Emily recorded all her baby's statistics: Bill weighed 6³/₄ pounds at birth. He gained rapidly: 26 pounds at six months, 32 pounds at one year. He walked at 15 months, and got his first tooth at ten months. He learned his letters and words quickly: "He finds G on his blocks and says, 'That's G. See his tail.' Afterwards, he says, 'It's Q.' We say, 'No, it's G.' Then he says, 'We'll call it Q,' with a very roguish twinkle in his eyes."

Bill's father, Gilman Barrows Wilson, was an immensely likable man, known as an excellent storyteller with a fine voice that got even better with a few drinks. "How jolly Gilly was," said one of the old neighbors. "I remember how he'd always say, 'Darn the little ones and damn the big ones.' " He managed a marble quarry near East Dorset, and he was so highly regarded as a leader that later, when he went off to work in British Columbia, a number of old East Dorset quarrymen pulled up stakes to follow him.

During Bill's early childhood, he had a fine companionship with his father, who would play ball in the yard with him every night. "On Sundays, we would rent a covered buggy, with a flat top with tassels all around," Bill remembered. "We would drive about in some style and with a great deal of satisfaction."

Gilman's people, the Wilsons, were amiable and noted for

their humanity: easygoing, tolerant people, who were also good managers and organizers. There is evidence of alcoholism in the family. Bill's paternal grandfather had been a serious drinker who got religion at a revival meeting and never touched another drop. Gilman was "a pretty heavy drinker, but not an alcoholic." But, said Bill, his father did get into more than one scrape because of liquor.

His mother's family were different. The Griffiths were teachers, lawyers, and judges. The Griffiths were hard-driving and strong-willed, with courage and fortitude. Emily had taught school before she married. She had intelligence, determination, ambition — and immense courage. She would later become successful in a profession, long before most career fields were open to women. But the Griffiths also had some difficulty forming close relationships with people outside their own family. "They were always highly respected, but scarcely dearly loved" was the way Bill put it.

Although Bill never made any real effort to trace his roots — he was Scots-Irish on his father's side and primarily Welsh on his mother's — he believed himself to be a distant relative of Woodrow Wilson. "Thanks for your all-too-flattering comparison between me and cousin Woodrow!" he once wrote to a friend. "As a matter of fact, he is a fourth cousin, about once removed. Years ago, some member of the Wilson family — now so large as to be the leading name in the Chicago telephone book — visited my father and told him this. I guess there is a certain amount of resemblance, when one stops to think about it." In fact, as an adult, he did have a facial and physical resemblance to President Wilson.

Bill's sister, Dorothy Brewster Wilson, born in 1898, re-

Next two pages: Left, *Bill's mother, Emily Griffith Wilson, succeeded professionally long before most careers were open to women.* Right, *Gilman Barrows Wilson, who came from an easygoing, tolerant family, was an affectionate companion for his young son.*

searched their genealogy in order to qualify for membership in the Daughters of the American Revolution (DAR). When asked what her ancestor had done in that war, she answered that he led American troops at the Battle of Monmouth. But, she added with amusement, he was not a general, but a drummer boy.

Dorothy remembered the East Dorset of her turn-of-the-century childhood as a small village of "about 20 homes on two main streets with marble sidewalks and many beautiful trees, mostly sugar maples. There were two general stores, two marble mills, a cheese factory, a blacksmith shop, and a cobbler shop; also a public school and two churches." Today, with a population of about 300, East Dorset has scarcely more than 50 houses. Tucked away in the Vermont Valley against the western slopes of the Green Mountains, Bill's home village is one of a number of small hamlets that make up the township of Dorset.

From his window, Bill could see Mount Aeolus rising above the town. Said Bill: "An early recollection is one of looking up and seeing that vast and mysterious mountain and wondering whether I would ever climb that high." Named for the wind-god of Greek mythology, Mount Aeolus is known for the gusts that sweep around its summit and howl over the pits left by East Dorset's now-defunct marble quarrying industry.

Marble quarrying had died out in the area by the end of World War I, but it was still an active industry in Bill's childhood. "My people always were operators of marble quarries, that is, on the Wilson side, and my father inherited the tradition," Bill recalled. "I can remember, as a small boy, seeing him set off in a gig for the so-called north quarry, and it was out of this quarry that many noted memorials, I think Grant's Tomb, perhaps the New York Public Library and other buildings in New York City were fashioned." Dorset marble is white, with light blue-gray shadings.

Bill was a precocious child. When he was very young, his father gave him a large illustrated dictionary to look at, and he would ask what the pictures were. Among other things, he learned the looks of a cantilever bridge. When his mother took him on the train to New York City, the route lay along the Hudson River with its several bridges. Standing up in the seat, he called in a loud voice: "Oh Mom, there is a cantilever bridge." The other passengers gazed at this smart little boy.

Bill started school in the two-room schoolhouse at East Dorset. His early letters to his mother show a good imagination and an active mind. In a letter probably sent from East Dorset in February 1902, when he was about six years old, to Emily and Dorothy, who were in Florida, he wrote:

"Dear Mama, Please will you send me some oranges. I hope you will have a good time. How are you, Mama? Is it nice place? I would like to go too. If Papa would let me go with you."

On March 9, Bill wrote again: "Dear Mama, How are you and Dorothy? Papa just brought Dorothy's picture. We think it is very nice. Grandma got the flowers you sent us last night.

The Wilson house in East Dorset, Vermont, tucked away on the western slopes of the Green Mountains.

They are lovely. Has Dorothy got any alligator? How did Dorthy like the boat? William Griffith Wilson''

In yet another letter, Bill announced that he was wearing 11-year-old pants. "I guess you will not know me when you come home," he added. "When are you coming home? I am having school vacation until the first of April. I will be glad to see you." This was signed, "From Willie.''

Emily and Dorothy were still away from East Dorset when Bill wrote on September 21, 1902: "Dear Mama, School has begun and we are in the second reader. I have a brand new arithmetic. We have the same teacher that was here before. I have two new under teeth. They look just like little saws. Granpa and I went to Captain Thomases show. The Cap is a slick one. When are you and Dorothy coming home? I want to see you ever so much. I try to be a good boy. Grandpa says I am. I am learning to read and do numbers very fast. From your little son Willie. P.S. Kiss sister for me.''

In 1903, the Wilson family moved to Rutland, 25 miles north, where Bill's father took over management of the Rutland-Florence quarry. They lived at 42 Chestnut Avenue, and Bill attended the Church Street School.

Compared to East Dorset, Rutland was a metropolis, and Bill found his new school threatening: "I well recall how overcome I was by the large number of children around me and how I began to develop a great shyness," he said. "Because of my shyness and awkwardness, I began to work overtime to be a baseball player. . . . In sports, I . . . alternated between feeling extremely competitive and elated upon success, and deeply discouraged and timid in defeat." A defeat was particularly painful if it took the shape of a physical trouncing by some smaller schoolmate. Bill (who would reach a height of six feet two inches) was already tall for his age, as was indicated by the "11-year-old

Young Bill worked hard to excel at school sports in an effort to overcome his "shyness and awkwardness."

pants" at age six. He remembered that his shyness and awkwardness prevented him from developing close friendships as a child.

Bill did have one childhood friend who remained close throughout his life. Mark Whalon was nine years older than Bill and actually remembered hearing Emily's cries on the morning Bill was born. (He later appears in Bill's letters and recollections as "my friend the postman," because he became the rural letter carrier in East Dorset.)

Although there were inner conflicts developing in Bill's childish heart, he was hardly regarded as a troublesome or unfriendly youngster. On the contrary, "I never heard anyone say they didn't like Bill," a former classmate recalled. "He was a mighty nice fellow, very popular. He was very tall and well built, with broad shoulders — a nice-looking boy."

Bill showed an early interest in science, and while they were living in Rutland, he made himself a chemistry laboratory in the woodshed. He almost blew up the shed — and himself. "I remember how horrified my father was, when coming home one night, he found that I had mixed certain acids — I should imagine sulphuric and nitric — to make actual nitroglycerin in the back shed, and when he arrived, I was dipping strips of paper in the nitroglycerin and burning them. You can imagine what a sensation this made with a man accustomed, as he was in his quarry business, to the use of dynamite, which is but a pale imitation of the real stuff. I remember how very gingerly Dad lifted that dish, dug a very large hole, which he wet, and gingerly spread the evil stuff about it, and just as gingerly covered it up."

Another experiment Bill tried was a telegraph set. He and his friend Russ communicated by Morse code with a set Bill made.

In 1906, Emily, Bill, and Dorothy moved back to East Dorset. Some of Bill's letters from that period have survived:

"Nov. 12, 1906: Dear Mama, It snowed today quite hard and at school there was a great deal of snowballing. Dorothy is well and so am I and I hope you are well too. We got our 'jacks' haloween and I called mine Punch and Dorothy called hers Judy.

"You were asking me when you make N what happens after you light the P. The fumes of phosphoric anhydride, P_2O_5, at once rise and fill the jar with dense white fumes which after standing the H_2O absorbs the P_2O. As the P burns it consumes the oxygen of the jar, thus leaving the nitrogen nearly pure. Air is composed of 1/5 oxygen, 4/5 nitrogen. As the oxygen is consumed by the burning P the water rises 1/5 the height of the jar. So that is what happens." . . .

"Nov. 13: On haloween night they had a haloween party at the hall. They had shadow pictures and all sorts of games. Had refreshments. The room was entirely lit by 'jacks' and 'Jap' lanterns. Had a great time. I can't think of any more. Your loving son, Willie Wilson. P.S. I have not yet been to Rutland to see Rus."

A note on the letter carries the comment: "He happens to know what happens, doesn't he? Isn't this too funny? I think he can beat his mother in the art of letter writing." That may have been written by Emily or by one of Bill's grandparents in enclosing the letter for mailing.

There is no date on the following letter, although the reference to Valentines suggests it may have been February or March 1907.

"Dear Mama, We are well and I hope you are. Have not found time to write. We have to study day and night. Can just pinch along and so can the rest.

"Today I wrote a composition on the 'iron and steel industry.'

"The valentines you sent were all gone before breakfast the next morning. We got them at night. We could have sold 50 more if we had had them. Dorothy says she wants you to send some Easter cards.

"Do you remember Mr. Parent?, the little girls father her name was Lillie, she used to come to play with Dorothy. Well the mill shut down here. Lillie's father went to work at West Rutland. He was going across the crossing. He had his cap pulled over his ears, so he didn't hear the train that was coming that killed him. It was to bad.

"About that medicine. When I came from Russels house I came down Centre Street. I got Dorothy a set of doll dishes. I thought there was something more I had to buy but couldn't think of it. I got to the depot in time to catch the train and never thought of it till I got home. I am sorry. Your loving son Will."

There was a reason for Emily's prolonged absences. "All unbeknown to Dorothy and me, a rift was developing between my mother and my father," Bill recalled. "I recollect, too, my mother was having what they said were nervous breakdowns, sometimes requiring that she go away for extended periods to the seashore, and on one occasion to the sanitarium.

"Though I did not know it, and though my father never became an alcoholic, he was at times a pretty heavy drinker. Like me, he was a person to be pretty much elated by success and, together with some of his marble quarry friends and their financial backing in New York, would have extended sprees. Though I never knew the details, I think one of these episodes had consequences that greatly affronted my mother and increased the strain between them."

Shortly after they returned to East Dorset, the rift between Emily and Gilman became an open break. "Mother took Dorothy and me on what we thought was to be a picnic at beautiful North Dorset Pond, now called Emerald Lake. We sat on the southwest shore under a shade tree, and Mother seemed very quiet, and I think we both had a sense of foreboding.

"Then it was that Mother told us that Father had gone for good. To this day, I shiver every time I recall that scene on the grass by the lakefront. It was an agonizing experience for one who apparently had the emotional sensitivity that I did. I hid the wound, however, and never talked about it with anybody, even my sister."

His parents' divorce was a shock Bill never forgot. The pain was heightened by the fact that he did not see his father again for nine years. After the separation, Gilman left Vermont. He eventually settled in western Canada, continuing his work as a quarryman in High River, Alberta, and around Marblehead, British Columbia.

Bill's strong-willed mother lacked the warmth and understanding that might have stood her son in good stead at such a difficult time. "My mother was a disciplinarian, and I can remember the agony of hostility and fear that I went through when she administered her first good tanning with the back of a hairbrush. Somehow, I never could forget that beating. It made an indelible impression on me."

Emily settled Bill and Dorothy in with her own parents, Gardner Fayette Griffith and Ella Griffith, in East Dorset. She remained there with them for a time, recovering from an unidentified illness and completing arrangements for the divorce.

"By this time, I was ten or 11, still growing (even more rapidly), still suffering from my physical awkwardness and from my mother's and father's separation and divorce," Bill said. "I remember hearing Mother and Grandfather talking about this divorce and how it could be brought about. I recall Mother's covert trip to Bennington, Vermont, to see a man called Lawyer Barber. Then I learned that the divorce was complete. This certainly did something to me which left a deep mark."

For young Bill, the divorce must have been painful beyond imagining. He was being separated from a father he adored, at a difficult time in the life of a young boy — the beginning of puberty. To compound the injury, divorce in a small New England town at the beginning of the century — 1906 — was virtually unheard-of; it may have aroused feelings of shame and disgrace that the child of divorced parents today would not understand or share.

Bill said he remained depressed for almost a year following his parents' divorce.

Of this time in her husband's childhood, Lois Wilson later wrote: "Although Bill and Dorothy loved their grandparents, who were very good to them, they felt abandoned. Bill was especially devoted to his father and badly missed him after he moved to the West. . . . The separation made him feel set apart and inferior to youngsters who lived with a mother and father."

And now Emily, too, went away from East Dorset. Leaving Bill and Dorothy in the full-time care of their grandparents, she moved to Boston to go back to school — specifically, osteopathic college. The effect on her family notwithstanding, this was a courageous undertaking for a woman of her age, in her time.

Fayette Griffith, Bill's grandfather, now became his substitute father. All accounts show that it was a warm and complex relationship. "My grandfather loved me deeply, and I loved him as I have few other people," Bill said.

The Griffiths "were capable of great love for their own, and this [was] certainly a factor in my grandfather's relation to me, but somehow they were not overpopular people."

"People didn't like Fayette particularly," Lois said, "because he was almost everybody's landlord. He had ideas of his own; he was a very opinionated gentleman. He owned property; he owned the waterworks. When it was time to be paid, he wanted to be paid."

A cousin, Robert Griffith of Brattleboro, had a similar perception: "Uncle Fayette was not a humble man," he said. "Though I always found him kindly, he was popularly considered a rather smug person.

"Once when he was driving a team of spirited horses, the horses balked and threw him from the seat. He landed on his head just inches from a block of marble used as a step when alighting from a carriage. Somebody said, 'You were lucky you didn't break your head on that horse block.' 'Humph!' grunted

Bill and his younger sister, Dorothy, "felt abandoned" after their parents' divorce, in spite of loving grandparents.

Uncle Fayette. 'Jolly well knew where I was going to land!'

"He was known behind his back as 'Jolly' Griffith — not because he was jolly, but because he used the word colloquially."

Fayette had been reared in Danby, about nine miles north of East Dorset, and was a Civil War veteran who had returned to Vermont to farm after serving as an ambulance driver at the Battle of Gettysburg. "He had chipped out a precarious living until he got the notion of lumbering and then, importing many French woodchoppers, had begun to aggregate a comfortable competence," Bill said.

Fayette had married Ella Brock, a woman as passive and gentle as he was forceful and opinionated. It was said of her that "she took up very little room in anybody's life."

Like many of the other Griffiths, Fayette was a shrewd businessman, and there were probably several reasons why he became interested in lumbering. For one thing, while the marble industry around Dorset was in decline, the mountains had an abundance of choice hardwoods, and it was not too difficult to take them out. Fayette's cousin Silas Griffith had become Vermont's first millionaire by lumbering the mountains around Danby, and had helped endow the S. L. Griffith Memorial Library in that town. Bill remembered that Silas had been "a super businessman for those days."

As East Dorset's most prosperous citizen, Fayette provided well for his family. He paid for Emily's education at the osteopathic college and was generous with Bill and Dorothy. Fayette's only son, Clarence, had died in Colorado the year before Bill's birth; having a grandson may have helped to soften Fayette's grief. Bill was considered a rather privileged boy in the village. "He had a motorcycle at one time and a saddle horse, the equipment necessary to his wireless set, along with his violins and cello. In those days, a kid who owned a fielder's glove, or a ball and bat, a .22 rifle, and a bicycle was considered well-off," said Robert Griffith.

Fayette was proud of Bill and had great expectations for him. "Uncle Fayette thought Will was the smartest person that ever was," an aged cousin recalled. "He *was* smart. He made that radio!" she added, referring to Bill's experiments with a wireless set.

Since Fayette read a great deal himself, he probably helped encourage Bill's early interest in reading. He read travel books to Bill, and that spurred a strong interest in other kinds of reading: "The Heidi books and the Alger books, and all kinds of things that kids used to read in that time," Bill said.

A neighbor, Rose Landon, installed a circulating library in her father's deserted cobbler shop. "I began to be a voracious reader myself as quickly as I got the ability, reading anything and everything that came into that library. In fact, I used to sleep very little when on these reading sprees. I would seemingly go to bed after being sent there rather sternly by my grandfather, and then I would wait until I felt they wouldn't notice the light, light up the old kerosene lamp, place it on the floor, and lay a book alongside and hang off the edge of my bed to read, sometimes all night."

Encouraged by his grandfather, Bill plunged into a succession of activities with single-minded determination — a trait that remained with him throughout his life. One project that stood out in his memory was the boomerang project.

"My grandfather got in the habit of coming to me with what he thought were impossible projects," Bill recalled. "One day, he said to me, 'Will' — for that's what he called me — 'Will, I've been reading a book on Australia, and it says that the natives down there have something they call boomerangs, which is a weapon that they throw, and if it misses its mark, it turns and returns to the thrower. And Will,' he said very challengingly, 'it says in this book that nobody but an Australian can make and throw a boomerang.'

"My hackles rose when he said that nobody but an Australian could do it. I can remember how I cried out, 'Well, I will be

the first white man ever to make and throw a boomerang!' I
suppose at this particular juncture I was 11 or 12."

For most children, Bill later reflected, such an ambition
might have lasted a few days or at most a few weeks. "But mine
was a power drive that kept on for six months, and I did nothing
else during all that time but whittle on those infernal
boomerangs. I sawed the headboard out of my bed to get just the
right piece of wood, and out in the old workshop at night by the
light of the lantern I whittled away."

Finally, the day came when Bill made a boomerang that
worked. He called his grandfather to watch as he threw the
boomerang. It circled the churchyard near their house and almost struck Fayette in the head as it came back.

"I remember how ecstatically happy and stimulated I was
by this crowning success," Bill said. "I had become a Number
One man."

Success with the boomerang now set Bill to proving himself
a Number One man in other activities. He decided that with
enough perseverance and determination, he could do anything
he set his mind to. With surprising tenacity and fierce concentration, he began to excel in scientific endeavors, in baseball, and in
music. "In my schoolwork, if my interest was high (as it was in
chemistry, physical geography, and astronomy), my marks
would range from 95 to 98 percent. Other subjects, including
English and algebra, caused me trouble, and I received poor
grades."

Bill later described himself as extremely happy during this
period of his life, because he was succeeding on all fronts that
mattered to him. "It was during this period that I can see how
my willpower and yearning for distinction, later to keynote my
entire life, were developed. I had many playmates, but I think I
regarded them all as competitors. At everything, I must excel. I
felt I had to be able to wrestle like Hackensmith, bat like Ty
Cobb, walk the tightrope like the folks in the circus, and shoot
like Buffalo Bill, who I had seen at the circus riding a horse and

breaking glass balls thrown in the air.

"My attempt to make a replica of this performance consisted in taking out a hod of coal and holding my rifle in one hand and tossing a lump of coal into the air with the other. I would try to break the lumps with the rifle, and got so good that I could do about two out of three, although it was a wonder I didn't kill some of the farmers about, as it was a very high-powered gun."

He turned his room into a chemical laboratory for a while. Then, he started experimenting with radio, a brand-new invention at the time. "I believe I had one of the first wireless-reception sets in Vermont. I studied Morse code and was always amazed that I never could keep up with the fast operators. But my radio adventures created quite a sensation in the town and marked me out for distinction, something which, of course, I increasingly craved, until at last it became an obsession."

Bill's grandfather challenged him to learn the violin — so he did, first rebuilding an old fiddle that he found in the attic; it had once belonged to his Uncle Clarence. He taught himself to play by pasting a diagram on the fingerboard and then sawing away until the right notes emerged, whereupon he announced his intention to become the leader of the school orchestra. He spent hours listening to the Victrola, after which he would return to his fiddle practice, neglecting all else.

Nearly accomplishing his announced ambition, Bill became first violin in the high school orchestra. He would later downplay this by describing himself as a very bad first violin and the orchestra as very poor. Although he would dismiss his achievement as just another bid for recognition, music would nonetheless provide him a satisfying outlet all his life.

In the period when the Wright brothers first proved their ideas about heavier-than-air flying machines, Bill built a glider. "Like many of his other projects, it didn't exactly work out," his sister Dorothy said — Bill had given her the dubious privilege of piloting the craft off the roof of a building. Fortunately, it plummeted softly into a haystack.

"He did a great many useful things, too," Dorothy said. "He made maple syrup every year out in the backyard, using a huge iron kettle." She remembered the dogged way he stayed with the job. "It didn't matter if it got dark or if he had to get more wood. The sap was running, and he would keep at it. That was the way he was built."

Was he merely stubborn? Dorothy didn't think so. "Persistent is a better word," she said. "People who are stubborn are apt to be disagreeable. And I never remember Bill being disagreeable."

Bill also made bows and arrows, an iceboat, jackjumpers (a jackjumper is a one-legged stool mounted on a short ski), skis, and sleds. His grandfather insisted that he learn how to do farm work. He spent sweaty afternoons in the cornfields, getting in the fodder, milking the cows.

Of all Bill's adolescent activities, it was probably baseball that claimed most of his physical energies and brought him the recognition he craved. In primary school, he excelled at baseball but later declared that the other players there had not been much good. It was a different matter in secondary school, where he found real competition on the baseball field.

It started badly for him. "On my very first appearance on the field, someone hit a fly ball," Bill recalled. "I put up my hands and somehow missed catching it, and it hit me on the head. It knocked me down, and I was immediately surrounded by a crowd of concerned kids. But the moment they saw I wasn't hurt, they all started to laugh at my awkwardness, and I remember the terrible spasm of rage that came up in me. I jumped up and shook my fist and said, 'I'll show you! I'll be captain of your baseball team.' And there was another laugh. This started a terrific drive on my part to excel in baseball, a desperate struggle to be Number One."

Bill eventually did become the best baseball player at the school. Pursuing this goal with the same fierce, single-minded determination he had demonstrated in making the boomerang, he practiced every spare moment. ''If I could not get anybody to play with me, I'd throw a tennis ball up against the side of a building. Or I'd spend hours and hours heaving rocks at telephone poles to perfect my arm, so that I could become captain of that baseball team. . . . I did develop a deadly aim and great speed with a baseball and had a high batting average. So, in spite of my awkwardness, I became Number One man on the baseball field. The pitcher was the hero in those days. I became pitcher, and I finally made captain.''

The school was Burr and Burton Seminary, in Manchester, Vermont, and when Bill started there in 1909, a new world opened for him. Established in 1829 as a training school for ministers, Burr and Burton quickly became a coeducational institution for general education. The semiprivate academy still serves as the main high school for the Manchester-Dorset area. The main building, with its load-bearing walls of thick gray limestone, was already more than 75 years old when Bill attended the school, and is still in service.

Bill traveled from East Dorset to Manchester by train, boarded at school five days a week, and went home for weekends. As one of Bill's classmates remembered, Bill ''had to hike [about two miles] to Burr and Burton from the station. That was a jaunt. The kids won't do it nowadays.''

Manchester, just south of East Dorset on the Rutland Railroad, had long been a fashionable resort town; its famous Equinox House could rival similar grand hotels in Saratoga or Newport. Manchester is built on the foothills of Mount Equinox and is still known for its marble sidewalks and streets shaded with stately maples and elms. Summer tourists have been coming to Manchester ever since the post-Civil War era. They have included Mrs. Abraham Lincoln and later her son Robert Todd Lincoln, who established his summer home, Hildene, there. One of Manchester's two country clubs is the elegant Ekwanok Country Club; its 1899 founders included the fathers of Lois Burnham and Ebby T., two important people in Bill's life.

Ebby T. was the son of a family that had been prominent in Albany for three generations and kept a summer home in Manchester. He and Bill first met in 1911, when Bill played ball in Manchester. Later, Ebby was a classmate of Bill's for one season at Burr and Burton. Their friendship was a significant one for Bill and for Ebby.

Bill's years at Burr and Burton were happy and successful. Popular with his schoolmates, he was elected president of the senior class. He was fullback on the football team, and became the school's best punter and drop kicker. He was first violin in the orchestra. His academic record was good, and he was proving that he could be Number One in almost anything he set his mind to.

A few items from the Manchester *Journal* of that period:

April 18, 1912 — "*Shakespeare in Manchester* — Pleasing rendition of 'As You Like It' by students of Burr and Burton. The audience surely showed their appreciation of the singing of William Wilson, appearing as Jaques."

April 25, 1912 — "*Gymnasium Exhibit at Burr and Burton Seminary* — The fourth number was the high jumping by the boys. The top mark was set by William Wilson, followed by Derwin and Bennett. Wilson's mark was four feet and six inches."

May 9, 1912 — "*Burr and Burton Seminary Notes* — On Wednesday last, as announced, Burr and Burton played Proctor, and was defeated 4 to 0. The game was a good one, being a pitchers' battle, Eskaline having 15 strikeouts and Wilson 14. The pitcher whom the Burr and Burton boys faced was the hardest one they will meet this year."

May 16, 1912 — "*Burr and Burton Seminary Notes* — On Saturday the Seminary team played Bennington High at that village and suffered defeat, its worst one so far this season. The score was 13 to 1 for the home team. Wilson pitched his worst game of the season and his support the poorest yet displayed by the team. The poor pitching was due to a lame arm and was a misfortune rather than a fault."[1]

Bill's life now had everything — except romance. "At this juncture, despite my homely face and awkward figure,[2] one of the girls at the seminary took an interest in me," he recalled. "They had been very slow to do that when I first appeared, and I had a terrific inferiority respecting the gals. But now came the minister's daughter, and I suddenly found myself ecstatically in love.

"Well, you see, at this period, now that I am in love, I am fully compensated on all these primary instinctual drives. I have all the prestige there is to have in school. I excel — indeed, I'm Number One where I choose to be. Consequently, I am emotionally secure; my grandfather is my protector and is generous with my spending money; and now, I love and am loved completely for the first time in my life. Therefore, I am deliriously happy and am a success according to my own specifications."

The girl was Bertha Bamford, daughter of Manchester's Episcopal minister. A beautiful, popular girl, Bertha was senior class treasurer at Burr and Burton and president of the Y.W.C.A. As Bill remembered, Bertha "made a profound influence on everyone." It was a mutual love, and Bertha's parents also liked Bill and welcomed him in their home. Bertha made the summer and early fall of 1912 one of the happiest, most ecstatic periods in Bill's life.

Then came a blow as cruel and unexpected as the separation of his parents. On the morning of November 19, a Tuesday, Bill hurried into chapel and took his place with the other students. Bertha was away in New York City with her family. There was nothing to prepare him for what was to come:

"The principal of the school came in and announced with a very grave face that Bertha, the minister's daughter and my beloved, had died suddenly and unexpectedly the night before. It was simply a cataclysm of such anguish as I've since had but two or three times. It eventuated in what was called an old-fashioned nervous breakdown, which meant, I now realize, a tremendous depression."

Bertha's death was reported in the Manchester *Journal* on Thursday, November 21: "The many friends of the Rev. and Mrs. W. H. Bamford of this village learned with great sorrow on Tuesday morning of the death of their daughter, Miss Bertha D. Bamford, following an operation at the Flower Hospital in New York City. The removal of a tumor was successful, but the young lady died during the night from internal hemorrhage. Her untimely death at the early age of 18 has thrown the school into mourning. The funeral will be held at Zion Church on Friday afternoon at two-thirty, and the remains will be placed in the receiving vault, to be taken on to Jeffersonville, Ind., Mrs. Bamford's home, for interment."

The details of the funeral were reported in the *Journal* a week later: "The funeral of Miss Bertha Bamford was held from Zion Episcopal Church Friday afternoon. The remains were placed in the vault at Center Cemetery. The ceremony was particularly impressive because of the attendance in a body and the marching to the cemetery of more than 70 students of Burr and Burton Seminary. The bearers were Principal James Brooks and W. H. Shaw of the Seminary faculty, William Wilson and Roger Perkins of the senior class, of which Miss Bamford was a member, and Clifford Wilson and John Jackson."

The loss of Bertha marked the beginning of what Bill remembered as a three-year depression, the second such period in his life. "Interest in everything except the fiddle collapsed. No athletics, no schoolwork done, no attention to anyone. I was utterly, deeply, and compulsively miserable, convinced that my whole life had utterly collapsed." His depression over Bertha's death went far beyond normal human grief. "The healthy kid would have felt badly, but he would never have sunk so deep or stayed submerged for so long," Bill later commented.

With the onset of depression, his academic performance dropped. "The upshot was that I failed German and, for that reason, could not graduate. Here I was, president of my senior class . . . and they wouldn't give me a diploma! My mother arrived, extremely angry, from Boston. A stormy scene took place in the principal's office. Still, I didn't get that diploma.''

He failed to graduate with his class (although school records now list him with the group). Following a summer of agonizing depression, he went to live with his mother near Boston and completed makeup work that qualified him for college.

What had caused Bill to change from a high achiever to a helpless depressive? As he saw it, the major problem was that he could no longer be Number One. ''I could not be *anybody* at all. I could not win, because the adversary was death. So my life, I thought, had ended then and there.''

---

1. The lame arm may have been from too much practice. See his own description, page 33. Said Lois: ''I saw this game, and although I didn't know Bill yet, I nevertheless felt sorry for the pitcher, who was evidently rattled by something.''

2. Early pictures of Bill show that he had anything but a homely face, and his awkwardness was clearly well under control, if one is to judge from his athletic record.

Chapter Two

"I don't know how I ever got through the next summer," said Bill of the period following Bertha's death. "It was spent in utter apathy, often running into anguish, in compulsive reflection, all centering around the minister's daughter."

Yet the summer of 1913 was more active than his memory of it suggests. He made up his German class work. He met Lois Burnham (although their courtship would not begin until the following summer). And he went with his grandfather to Gettysburg, Pennsylvania, for the 50th anniversary of the Civil War battle.

The Gettysburg reunion was a spectacular undertaking, directed with meticulous care and efficiency by the state of Pennsylvania with the cooperation of the War Department. Bill and Fayette probably stayed in the Great Camp, a tented city that the War Department had erected on farmlands leased near the battlefield to house the thousands of aged Union and Confederate veterans who poured in for the event. Bill toured the battlefield with Fayette, who showed him where Vermonters had outflanked Pickett's charge and helped determine the outcome of the battle. The hot days at Gettysburg were packed with speeches and exhibitions, climaxed by President Woodrow Wilson's address on Friday, July 4.

Meeting Lois was the high point of that summer. The oldest daughter of a respected New York physician, she and her family took their summer vacations a few miles from Bill's home, at Emerald Lake in North Dorset. She was not only attractive, intelligent, and charming, she was, to Bill, a member of a different social class: "She represented areas in which I had always felt a great inferiority. Her people were of a fine family in Brooklyn. They were what we Vermonters called city folks. She had social graces of which I knew nothing. People still ate with their knives around me; the back door step was still a lavatory. So her encouragement of me and her interest in me did a tremendous amount to buck me up."

As Lois remembered their first meeting, her brother Rogers had been talking enthusiastically about his friend Bill. She found Bill to be tall and lanky, but hardly much more — after all, he was a mere boy of 18, and she was a young lady, four years older than he.

Bill and Lois shared friendly times that summer, usually in a group that included her brother and his sister. In the fall, she returned to Brooklyn with her family. The following spring, in 1914, the Burnhams returned to the lake. That summer, the relationship between Bill and Lois changed. They had what she remembered as "a glorious vacation picnicking, hiking, and taking all-day drives. Long before the end of the season," Lois said, she thought Bill "the most interesting, the most knowledgeable, and the finest man I knew." She had forgotten all about the difference in their ages.

The timing of their romance was providential, because the summer of 1914 was a bad time for Bill. She listened sympathetically as he told her he was no good, couldn't face returning to school, couldn't bear to leave her.

He gave Lois credit for helping him out of his depression. "She lifted me out of this despond, and we fell very deeply in love, and I was cured temporarily, because now I loved and was loved and there was hope again.

"At the unconscious level, I have no doubt she was already becoming my mother, and I haven't any question that that was a very heavy component in her interest in me." Whatever the individual needs that sparked their early courtship, Bill and Lois were drawn together. Said Bill, "I think Lois came along and picked me up as tenderly as a mother does a child."

Lois was the oldest of six children. She said her childhood had been so happy that she had hated to grow up. "Mother and Dad truly loved one another and openly showed their affection to each other and to us children," she wrote. "They taught us never to be afraid to tell of our love, never to go to sleep angry with anyone, always to make peace in our hearts before closing our eyes at night, and never to be ashamed to say, 'I'm sorry. I was wrong.' "

At the time Lois met Bill, she had already completed school at Brooklyn's Packer Collegiate Institute, and two terms of drawing at the New York School of Fine and Applied Art. Still living at home, she was working in the employment department of the Y.W.C.A.

Meanwhile, Bill's post-high-school education had followed an uneven path. In the 1913-14 school year, he had gone to live with his mother and sister Dorothy in Arlington, Massachusetts, a Boston suburb. "I was entered in the Arlington High School and barely got through some courses there," Bill said. "The idea of this was to prepare me for the examinations for the Massachusetts Institute of Technology. Because of my scientific interests, it was supposed that I should be an engineer. I took the examinations and could hardly pass a one of them."

Three generations of the Wilson and Griffith families sat for this family portrait.

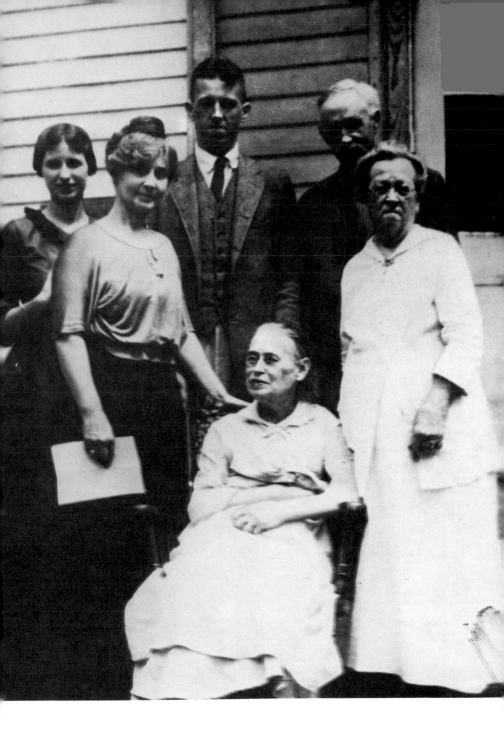

He had enrolled at Norwich University, which had entrance requirements far easier than M.I.T.'s. Called "The Hill," Norwich, in Northfield, Vermont, is a military college with discipline as strict as at West Point. In the midsummer of 1914, Europe was on the verge of war, and there was a possibility — albeit slight — that the United States might be drawn into it.

In August, just prior to the start of his first year at Norwich, Bill went to visit his father. It was the first time he had seen Gilman since the divorce eight years previous.

Bill made the long journey to British Columbia on a transcontinental train that he boarded in Montreal. His letters home, written to his Grandmother Wilson, describe the journey west in striking detail:

"I woke up with a ringing in my ears and feeling a peculiar exhilaration. This was my first view of the Rockies. The mountains rise straight up and are clothed about the bases with scrub evergreens excepting when great slides have torn paths down the sides. The mountains are formed of many colored shales lying in strata sometimes tilted, sometimes horizontal. Everything is jagged and angular, showing marks of sudden and violent changes, a great contrast to the smooth, gentle curves of our mountains.

"Great number of streams rush down the sides fed from the perpetual snows above the timber line. Every high valley above the snow line has its glacier. The ice is a beautiful deep blue covered here and there with great white patches of newly fallen snow. The sky is cloudless and almost matches the ice in color. We pass through miles of such scenery as this. On one side of the road the peaks rise up like a wall. So straight and abrupt that it seems that their snows would slide off onto the train. To preclude any possibility of this, miles and miles of snowsheds have been built. On the other side, one looks down into the river gorge sometimes deep enough to be called a canyon. There is always the deep, narrow, swift-flowing river with numerous falls and splendid rapids. Forever tearing at its banks it undermines great rocks and cedars which falling in are swept away like toothpicks on the dark flood.''

Already showing the powers of observation that would later serve him so well on Wall Street, Bill remarked on the oil field discoveries and natural gas developments in Alberta. He noted that in Medicine Hat, Alberta, the streetlights operated on natural gas that was never turned off, since the gas flowed as strongly as the day it was found 22 years before.

Bill's letters were written on his father's office stationery from Marblehead, British Columbia, a small community high in the Canadian Rockies. The letterhead listed G. B. Wilson as manager of the Marblehead Quarries of Canadian Marble Works, Ltd., quarry owners and manufacturers of Kootenay marbles. Its main offices were in Nelson, British Columbia.

For all Bill's detailed descriptions of his surroundings, there was nothing in his letters about his reunion with his father. Father and son apparently got along well, although Gilman seems to have made little effort to keep in touch with his children.

A month later, Bill was an entering freshman at Norwich, which at that time had a total enrollment of 145. Bill was miserable during his first semester there: ''Again, I felt I was nobody. I couldn't even begin to compete in athletics, in music, or even for popularity with the people around me. I so keenly remember when the rush for the fraternities was on, and I didn't get a bid to a single one. I tried out for baseball and football and wasn't good enough for either first team. I remember how there was a fellow who played the violin so much better than I that I could not even get into the dance orchestra. I remember how I produced an old cello that I had and somehow scraped up a part in the glee club with that. But I was very second-rate. Some of my studies, I handled very well; others, I began to fail in.''

However, a letter to his mother written shortly after he arrived paints a very different picture: ''There are four fraternities here, have been to all several times to dinner and have had 'bids' to join three which is quite an honor for a rook. However, I figure that if one is going to join a frat, it might be good to take a year to

size up the bunches who belong." Some months later, he
brought up the fraternity matter again: "Can't seem to get away
from being popular. Have had second invitations to all the frats.
But think it policy to stall. Just the minute you join a frat, you
join more or less of a clique. In spite of all that's done to prevent
it, the frats can pull strings in the military business and by keeping out of them I think one will stand more on his own merits. As
it is now, I am popular with men of the strongest frats here. If I
join one, I lose my influence with all the rest. So me for the
Commons."[1]

During that first semester, Bill received 94 in chemistry, 86
in French, 75 in drawing, 68 in English, 61 in trigonometry, and
53 in algebra. He had an outstanding rating of 98 in military
duty and 100 in deportment. His final average of 86 gave him a
standing of fifth in his class. If he was not leading the pack, he
was certainly holding his own.

From a letter to his mother, written in February: "Am glad
to know that you were pleased with at least a part of my marks.
The week preceding midyears, I was laid up with a touch of the
grippe and thus missed the general review which is held at the
time. So my exams were not what they should have been. Algebra was the first exam and I got out of bed to take it. For the rest
of them I had a whole day preparation. My exams fortunately
coming one every other day, I took a makeup exam Saturday
and passed with 65%. Could I have done that in the first place I
should have ranked third or fourth in the class. At any rate, I do
not compare unfavorably with the others. I am confident of rank-
ing in second place next semester as I expect to get over 90% in
four subjects."

But it did not turn out that way. On a morning early in his
second semester, he fell on his way to class and injured his elbow.
He insisted on going to Boston to be treated by his mother, who
by now was a practicing osteopath.

He had no desire to return to school. "How terribly reluctant I was to face that discipline, and that idea of being no good

and second-rate. As I got on the train going from Boston back to Northfield, I began to have terrible sensations in the solar plexus. I felt like the world was coming to an end.'' Short of breath, having heart palpitations, ''I was in stark panic that I had heart trouble and was going to die. Back at school, as soon as I would attempt a few simple exercises, this terrible palpitation would set in, and I would collapse.''

Following these attacks, Bill would be taken to the college infirmary, but no physical cause could be found for his troubles. ''This happened again and again, until, at the end of a couple of weeks, I was sent to my grandfather in East Dorset, which was just exactly where I wanted to go.'' He was overcome by inertia, unable to do anything. ''I used to go into fits of palpitations and cry to see the doctor,'' he said. The doctor gave him a bromide and tried to persuade him that there was nothing wrong with his heart.

Bill stayed with his elderly grandparents that spring and summer, and gradually recovered enough to consider returning to Norwich for the fall semester. An April letter to his mother shows how preoccupied he was with his health problems:

''Up to the time Dr. Grinell made his second visit, I had been miserable. Some days eating nothing and the most a few slices of soft toast. Terribly sour stomach, consequent heart burn and palpitation. This last of course scares me to death. Makes me mad to think I am scared but I am just the same.

''Dr. Grinell came about six p.m. I was feeling awfully. He applied a stethoscope and said at once that I had the best valve action he had seen for some time. Desired me to listen. I did so. Sounded just the same as it did last time. I registered immediate relief. He said that the large intestine was rather inactive, causing sour stomach, and gas. Gave me a mild physic to take after eating. Did not seem to think my stomach was out of order. Grandpa and grandma think so. Hence they pursued him until he said, 'I don't think diet has anything to do with this case.' He saw that he said the wrong thing so he afterward qualified the statement, by saying, 'Of course, he mustn't eat too much,' a very definite statement, you see.''

Bill's ''heart'' problems were clearly temporary; he soon recovered and had no difficulty either in passing the Army's physical examination in 1917 or in performing his military duties.

Another letter, also written that spring, indicates that Bill was feeling better, and had his mind on other things. He wanted an automobile:

''I looked over the catalogue you sent with some interest and threw it aside. Grandpa picked it up and began to look it over. Pretty soon he began to talk about the machine some. Grandma remarked that it must be hard to learn to run a machine in view of this fact that Jim Beebe wouldn't learn to run his. Grandpa at once 'waxed enthusiastic' and said he guessed there wasn't much to it. Said he bet he could learn in short order.

''Heard no more about autos for a couple days. One morn he came in from the garden and said, 'Better send and get one of those, hadn't we? Seems as if we might get the agency perhaps. Guess *I* could sell those things. Never saw anything I couldn't sell yet.'

''Naturally I was interested. We got the terms for agents through Will Griffith (who has been offered the agency) and Grandpa had me go to Manchester and talk up the machine. I went, and banking on your consent have practically disposed of one to the Bamfords. As to the financial risk, there is none, I think. This is also Grandpa's opinion for the selling of one machine excludes the risk element and Grandpa has a sneaking notion that he wants one anyway. We figure that there is about $85 profit on a machine.

''Now to come to my present condition. Am glad to say that sinking spells and dizziness have totally disappeared. I have palpitation on a strenuous exertion. Am yet nervous. Am convinced that will disappear as soon as I convince myself that nothing ails my heart. I have no stomach symptoms, am able to eat everything. Am physically myself as regards weight and strength. Obviously a diversion of the mind will now effect a cure.

"I know of no subject upon which I can discourse with greater intelligence or enthusiasm than automobiles.

"Consider the body risks. There are chances to be taken. Accidents occur daily. I should say the risks encountered in autos are considerably less than those Grandpa has taken taming kicking horses or that tunnel workers have of a scale dropping on their head or that you took as a child in running around on the edge of a flume or on narrow beams in the top of the barn or that I have taken every day at school with bucking horses. Consider the number of accidents also the number of autos. H. Ford runs off 1800 of them a day. If this amounts [to a] nervous strain to which I should be subjected in driving perhaps you are the better judge. Certainly not more than steering a horse over a three-foot hurdle. Certainly no more demand upon concentrative faculties than as much violin practice. Certainly a more healthful occupation. I have heard you say that no more exhilarating and yet mild form of exercise existed than motoring.

"Now as to the danger which would be peculiar to me. Perhaps at this moment I am not fit to operate a machine because I am too nervous. But I'm not going to be this way all summer. At the present rate of improvement, shall be restored in another month.

"Normally, you know I am about as excitable as a mud turtle. It cuts me to think you have not enough confidence in my judgment to allow me to do what Jamie Beebe, Clifford Copping, Francis Money, David Cochran, Lyman Burnham are allowed to do without the parents entertaining grave fears as to their safety.

"Rogers [Burnham] has driven since he was 14. I should hate to think my judgment at present is not the equal of his at that time.

"Again, autos have come to stay. They will soon be as common as horses.

"You consider yourself competent to drive a machine with safety. You even would like to have ridden the motorcycle. You certainly could do both. But I should be fearful of your trying the motorcycle as you are that I attempt the auto. Love from Will."

In a later letter to his mother, there is no reference to illness or doctors. He had been hired to play the fiddle for ten dances, for which he was to receive five dollars per dance. His confidence in his own playing had clearly risen, as he told his mother:

"I do think that I can put myself through school with it. Have played enough for money now so that the thing has lost its glamor and it really seems like work. Have improved a lot since you were here."

During the summer of 1915, Bill had a job peddling burners for kerosene lamps in nearby villages. That summer, Lois had opened a small tea arbor at the north end of Emerald Lake. Bill found a number of reasons to turn up at the tea arbor during the day. "He didn't sell many burners and I didn't sell much tea; but we had wonderful visits," Lois said. "Often I would give him a treat of wild strawberries or fried picked-on-the-hill mushrooms on toast."

By late summer, their courtship had become serious. But Bill had competition: Several years earlier, Lois had met a young Canadian named Norman Schneider at a young people's church convention. Norman's family owned a meat packing firm in Kitchener, Ontario. Lois and Norman had dated; he was a good person, nice-looking and intelligent. She had enjoyed being with him. Now, he came to the lake for a week's visit, and just before he left to return to Canada, he asked Lois to marry him.

Lois, who had longed to be with Bill every minute she was with Norman, had her answer. "Just as Norman stepped on the train for Montreal, Bill jumped off," she wrote. "We walked back to the lake together. But somehow our fingers often seemed to brush against each other."

That same evening, they told each other of their love and became engaged. (When asked many years later whether she had any regrets, Lois replied: "Never, never, never, never. It never occurred to me. I never dreamt about anybody but Bill Wilson.")

At first, Bill and Lois kept their betrothal a secret from everybody except Mark Whalon, in whom Bill did confide. Mark was a "sort of uncle or father" to Bill. They had worked together on summer jobs and helped string the first telephone lines into East Dorset. They also hunted and fished together, and they shared an interest in Vermont history. Later, they would drink together, although Mark's drinking never progressed into alcoholism.

During the fall of 1915, Bill made an effort to compensate for past failures at school. His course of study was electrical engineering, which he chose because of his interest in science. Some of his old drive had finally returned, and he began to become popular on campus. Several of his classmates found themselves involved in a hazing incident. Because no one would name names, the whole class was suspended for a full term. The hazing scandal and the suspension happened to coincide in time with the Mexican border troubles. (The following year, U.S. troops under General Pershing were sent into Mexico in a vain attempt to capture Pancho Villa.) Because the Norwich cadets were part of the Vermont National Guard, they were mobilized — although they never were sent to the border. The mobilization was fortuitous for Bill, because it meant that he was reinstated at Norwich.

He continued to be driven by a need to stand out, to do something unique. He found such an opportunity, he believed, in a calculus course.

"I was failing miserably in calculus," Bill recalled. He had had difficulty memorizing formulas in algebra, and he was encountering similar problems in calculus. "I realized that I was going to be an absolutely flat failure in calculus. In fact, the professor promised me that I would get zero."

Then Bill discovered that his professor had certain shortcomings in his own understanding of the subject. "He was a

catalog of formulas; he could apply the formulas; he was glib; but deep down, he didn't know how the thing worked,'' Bill said. ''And I made up my mind I would learn.''

At the library, he studied the history of mathematics and the evolution of calculus. Finally, he grasped the concept sufficiently to discuss it. He had developed considerable talents in argument.

''I got the professor over a barrel, and I made a fool out of him before his class,'' Bill said. ''He did give me zero, but I had

Bill, stretched out at a picnic with Mark Whalon (center foreground), in a pose many remember as characteristic.

won one battle. In other words, I was the only one on the school grounds — the Number One man again — the only one who deeply understood the underlying principles of calculus.''

The incident did nothing to help him academically, but it did make him the center of attention. It was a rerun of the boomerang project. His drive for prestige was reasserting itself, making him a sort of hero to his classmates — but a brash upstart in the eyes of his calculus professor.

Bill was an unusually gifted young man, although he was often hypercritical of himself. He possessed a native talent for leadership, which was finally recognized in the military program at Norwich.

"I had been made a corporal or a sergeant in the corps," Bill said, "and then it was discovered that I had talent for instructing people. Curiously enough, though awkward myself, I had talent for drilling people. I had a voice and I had a manner that would compel a willing obedience, and so much so that the attention of the commandant was drawn to it." This talent for leadership would serve him well on active duty in the Army. And, he assumed, it would serve him equally well when, upon leaving military service, he would find himself "at the head of vast enterprises," which he "would manage with utmost assurance."

Bill had mixed feelings about military service. It was honor, glory, and duty, but it was also danger and death. Growing up in East Dorset, Bill had spent countless hours target-shooting with old Bill Landon, Civil War veteran and "great character" who lived next door. Grandfather Griffith never talked about the Civil War, but old Bill Landon "would spin me yarns by the hour. He had been sergeant on Sheridan's staff, and he used to tell me how, on a charge, a minié ball had struck his musket butt, and it passed through and stuck in his skull just over the eye; how he plucked it out and continued his charge. And old Bill had a drooping eye, a scar, and poor sight to prove all this."

Landon, reliving the glories of the Civil War, also spoke with great scorn of those who had managed to avoid active service. "One of the worst forms of opprobrium that could be cast on anybody when I was a kid was to be called a slacker," Bill re-

As a young officer, Bill anticipated honor and glory, feared danger— and had his first drink.

membered. "Those who failed to go to the Civil War, evaded
service, or got some sort of an easy job got a stigma that they
carried all their lives." Old Landon had told Bill about a wealthy
and respected East Dorset citizen who carried this stigma. "All
during the Civil War, he was ill and used to toddle down to the
village with a long shawl over his shoulders, very much stooped,
with a bottle of smelling salts, and all during that period, no one
would speak to him," said Landon.

But in the cemetery south of East Dorset is a marker for
Waldo Barrows, Bill's great-uncle, killed in the 1864 Battle of
the Wilderness. And the Gettysburg battlefield, which Bill had
visited with his grandfather, also had a cemetery. "Neurotic that
I was, I was ambivalent," he said. "The great upwellings of
patriotism would overtake me one day — and the next day, I
would just be funked and scared to death. And I think that the
thing that scared me most was that I might never live my life out
with Lois, with whom I was in love."

The tradition of military service, however, was deeply em-
bedded in Bill. When America entered World War I in 1917, he
was called up by the military and never graduated from Norwich.

When he was called, he chose to serve in the Coast Artillery.
The decision later caused him guilt, because that was considered
one of the safer branches of military service.

From Norwich, Bill was sent to the new officers training
camp at Plattsburgh, New York. Here, he discovered that the
Norwich cadets' military training had given them a head start on
the others in the camp, and he moved rapidly through the training. His flair for leadership brought him further recognition, and
after additional training at Fort Monroe, Virginia, he was commissioned a second lieutenant. It was a heady experience for a
21-year-old who only a few years earlier had been in deepest
depression. Then, he was sent to Fort Rodman, just outside New
Bedford, Massachusetts. "Here was all the tradition of the old
Army, seasoned regular officers and noncoms, along with the

drafted men and volunteers,'' he remembered. ''How I enjoyed that atmosphere, encouraged as I was by actually being put in command of soldiers. But still there crept into me at times that nagging undertone of fear about going abroad.''

Lois, accompanied by Bill's grandmother and his sister Dorothy, had visited him at Plattsburgh. She and Bill had now been engaged for almost two years; it was clear that they would marry. Lois's parents approved of Bill so completely that she was actually permitted to visit him unchaperoned. ''Their understanding and their trust in Bill and me were very unusual during that conventional era,'' Lois wrote. She was 25 years old; her comment clearly illustrates how young women of her day continued to answer to their parents, even when they were no longer living at home. At this time, Lois had a teaching position in Short Hills, New Jersey, and was living with the aunt who operated the school where she taught.

It was at Fort Rodman, New Bedford, that Bill's life took a new course. He learned about liquor.

Until that time, he had never had a drink. The Griffiths did not drink, and there was a family memory of what alcohol had done to some of the Wilsons. Bill, who thought it may have been one of the reasons for his parents' divorce, was afraid of liquor. He was critical —specifically of Norwich students who sneaked off to Montpelier to drink beer and consort with ''loose women.''

New Bedford was different. Bill would later remember the charged atmosphere of the town in that wartime period: ''moments sublime with intervals hilarious.'' He also remembered the social circles that opened to young officers like him. ''The society people in town began to invite the young officers to their homes,'' he recalled. ''One of the great fortunes and one of the leading families of New Bedford was the Grinnell family. They were very rich and very much socialites. I remember so well Emmy and Catherine Grinnell. Emmy's husband had gone off to the wars; Katy had lost hers; and the two of them used to entertain a group of us kids at their house. This was the first time in my life that I had ever been out in society. This was the first time in my life that I had ever seen a butler. And a great rush of fear, ineptitude, and self-consciousness swept over me. In conversation, I could hardly say two words. The dinner table was just a terrible trial.''

At the Grinnells', Bill was offered a Bronx cocktail (usually concocted of gin, dry and sweet vermouth, and orange juice). Despite all the warnings, despite all his training, despite all his fears about drinking, he found himself accepting it.

''Well, my self-consciousness was such that I simply had to take that drink,'' he recalled. ''So I took it, and another one, and then, lo, the miracle! That strange barrier that had existed between me and all men and women seemed to instantly go down. I felt that I belonged where I was, belonged to life; I belonged to the universe; I was a part of things at last. Oh, the magic of those first three or four drinks! I became the life of the party. I actually could please the guests; I could talk freely, volubly; I could talk well. I became suddenly very attracted to these people and fell into a whole series of dates. But I think, even that first evening, I got thoroughly drunk, and within the next time or two, I passed out completely. But as everybody drank hard, nothing too much was made of that.''

By his own account, Bill was an excessive drinker from the start. He never went through any moderate stage or any period of social drinking. Bill's inner warning system must have told him his drinking was unusual, because he ''kept the lid on'' when Lois came to visit him and was invited to meet his friends. But he did not stop altogether. Without liquor, Bill again felt inferior.

It was now early 1918; the United States was fully at war; and Bill could be shipped out at any time. He and Lois had set

Meeting Lois, here in her wedding dress, lifted Bill out of deep depression and into love and renewed hope.

their wedding day for February 1. There was a rumor that Bill was to be sent overseas soon; so they decided to push the wedding date up to January 24 and change the invitations to announcements. They chose to go ahead with the big church wedding they had planned, and everyone pitched in to help. It was all done in such a rush that the best man, Lois's brother Rogers, arrived from Camp Devens too late to change his heavy-duty boots, and had to stomp down the aisle.

In Brooklyn for the wedding, Bill was again conscious of those horribly familiar feelings of inferiority. He even imagined that some of Lois's family and friends were asking, ''Where did Lois get *that* one?'' In contradiction, he also remembered that they went out of their way to make him feel comfortable. Lois, on her part, was clearly delighted with her new husband, and with the ''great welcome'' that waited for the couple at the furnished apartment Bill had rented for them in New Bedford. ''Flowers and plants were everywhere, and people dropped in continuously to congratulate us,'' she recalled. ''Bill was very popular on the post.''

One aspect of his new social life had been unknown to Lois, but she discovered it while they were in New Bedford. Bill remembered that during this period, he must have passed out at about every third party. At a party one evening, Lois was shocked to hear Bill's Army buddies tell how they had dragged him home and put him to bed. Still, she was not terribly perturbed about it, confident that she could persuade him to return to his former abstinence. ''Living with me would be such an inspiration, I was sure, he would not need alcohol!''

In his recollections of that period, Bill referred frequently to his fear of going to war, and his shame about that fear. He even felt that he was letting his Vermont ancestors down: ''None of those who came across the mountains with rifles and axes would have acted like that!''

He was sent to Fort Adams near Newport, Rhode Island, to await orders. Finally, the dreaded day arrived. On an August night just a few hours before he was to ship out for England, he and Lois climbed one of the beautiful Newport cliffs that overlook the sea. Their mutual gloom and depression of a sudden lifted, and was replaced by a feeling of patriotism and duty. "She and I gazed out over the ocean, wondering. The sun was just setting, and we talked about the future with joy and optimism. There, I felt the first glimmerings of what I was to later understand as a spiritual experience . . . I shall never forget it."

Aboard the British ship Lancashire in the North Atlantic, two significant things happened to Bill. The first was that he met a ship's officer, who shared his brandy with Bill. The second was that in a brief encounter with danger, Bill discovered, to his great relief, that he was a man of courage after all. The prospect of this test, which he knew he must sooner or later face, had made him apprehensive, pessimistic, and occasionally sick with self-doubt.

The Lancashire was a troop transport; her decks were packed solid with bunks and, in the middle of the night, sleeping men. Officers were stationed at every hatch on every deck. Bill was on night watch belowdecks, "practically on the keel," where the men would be the last to be rescued in an emergency. The Lancashire was not far from the British coast. Bill was trying to stay awake. Suddenly, there was a huge thud against the hull of the ship. The men were instantly awake and, in the same instant, headed in a panic for the ladder at the base of which Bill was stationed.

He pulled out his gun; he had orders to shoot any who tried to climb out without permission. But instead of using the gun, he used his voice. In a few minutes, he found that he was able to calm the men, to reassure them, and to prevent panic without his having any information about what had actually happened. In turn, he was as reassured as they were, because the incident gave proof of the courage that he had so sorely doubted.

There had been no real danger. An American depth charge, a so-called ashcan intended for an enemy ship, had exploded so close to the Lancashire that it had made a shattering noise against the ship's hull.

The Lancashire reached England safely. It was shortly after landing there that Bill had another soul-shaking experience. As the experience aboard ship had, it revealed an inner resource that he had never recognized before.

An epidemic kept Bill and his regiment detained at a camp near Winchester. Depressed, lonely, and apprehensive about what lay ahead, Bill went to visit Winchester Cathedral. Inside the great cathedral, the atmosphere impressed itself so deeply upon him that he was taken by a sort of ecstasy, moved and stirred by a "tremendous sense of presence." "I have been in many cathedrals since, and have never experienced anything like it," he said. "For a brief moment, I had needed and wanted God. There had been a humble willingness to have Him with me — and He came." In that moment, Bill knew that everything was all right, as it should be.

Benumbed and slightly dazed by his experience, he found his way outside to the churchyard. There, a familiar name carved on an old headstone caught his eye: Thomas T——, dead at age 26. One letter in the last name was different; still, here could be an ancestor of Bill's good school friend Ebby T. Bill read with amusement the doggerel that was Thomas's epitaph; this is his memory of how it went:

"Here lies a Hampshire Grenadier / Who caught his death / Drinking cold small beer. / A good soldier is ne'er forgot / Whether he dieth by musket / Or by pot.' '[2]

Soon afterward, Bill was sent to France, where he at last saw the devastation of war. There, too, he discovered that French wine could produce the same effects as New Bedford liquor, or the brandy he had been introduced to aboard ship. In those closing months of 1918, the war was winding down rapidly, and Bill's artillery unit was settled in a small mountain town, far from the front. The only time he and his fellow artillerymen ran into actual danger was during a practice firing session.

Their battalion had placed its guns in positions dug into a

bank. They were then supposed to practice firing over a low hilltop and into the countryside beyond. The target was a piece of canvas that had been set up about nine miles away. Bill was sent to observe the results of the practice. He and his men took up positions in a slit trench about 300 yards from the target, using a periscope to observe the operation from a distance.

The number one gun fired, and the shell came down practically on the mark. Bill was elated and congratulated the group on their skill. But when the number four gun was fired, he suddenly found the earth opening up around him, and "tons of dirt blown all over us." Crawling through the dirt, he discovered that the gun had been trained directly on him and his team. It was only a miracle that had saved them.

Bill was still in that mountain town on the day the Armistice was signed. He was kept in France until spring, and was just developing a taste for French wine when he was finally shipped home, to be separated from the service.

"Like all returning vets, I ran into a few difficulties," he later recalled. "Unlike most of them, I was heading toward a destiny that lay in directions I could not conceivably have anticipated when I stepped off that ship onto the New Jersey shore and into the waiting embrace of my lovely wife."

---

1. One explanation for the big discrepancy in Bill's memories of that time is, as he himself suggests, that he was struggling to win his mother's approval during this 1914-15 period, and deliberately lied about the fraternity bids to explain why he did not belong to one.

2. The famous epitaph actually reads: "Here sleeps in peace a Hampshire Grenadier, / Who caught his death by drinking cold small Beer. / Soldiers, be wise from his untimely fall, / And when yere hot, drink Strong or none at all. / An honest Soldier never is forgot, / Whether he die by Musket or by Pot."

Chapter Three

By the time Bill was mustered out of the Army, he had proved himself a leader, and the men of his artillery battery had given him a special token of appreciation. He had an acknowledged ability to get along with others; he had some college education, an aptitude for science and mathematics, and lots of drive. He had, too, the constant support of a loving wife who was confident of his imminent rise to great heights.

He also had a sinister new companion — alcohol. Not yet apparent as a problem, a drinking pattern was nonetheless already established. When he drank, it was often excessive and sometimes accompanied by odd behavior and blackouts.

In May 1919, Bill found himself a free man. Intensely ambitious for himself, full of great dreams for the future, he had no specific plans for the present, and like many another veteran, found it difficult to adjust. For him, it was hard to accept the status of ordinary person again, without the rank and privileges of a commissioned officer. "I was much surprised, for example, in the New York subways, when the guards failed to salute me, and when the passengers pushed me around," he said.

Because he hadn't finished college and wasn't really trained for any trade or profession, he also had trouble finding a job.

Lois's father, Dr. Clark Burnham, with whom Lois and Bill were living, was a prominent man in the Brooklyn community. He used his influence to help Bill get a job as a clerk in the insurance department of the New York Central Railroad. "In fact, I worked for my brother-in-law, Cy Jones, who was at that time the head clerk.

"Well, it was a tremendous comedown from being an officer and awfully, awfully hard to take, especially from a brother-in-law. I worked there some months and turned out to be such a very bad bookkeeper and manager that the New York Central fired me. And that produced a mighty rebellion in me that I would show that town and that I would show these friends of Lois's, in fact, I would show the whole goddamned world."

Bill's resentment toward the railroad was so intense that it actually moved him, for a short time, to turn his back on the conservative economic views he had held all his life. "At that time, the socialist plum plan for taking over the railroads was in vogue, and very briefly, despite my Vermont training and origin, I turned quite socialist — a reaction, I expect, against the New York Central."

Bill then had what he remembered as a period of "flunking and slumping" in his quest for another job. "Finally, I took a job on one of the New York Central piers, driving spikes in planks after the carpenters sawed them off and laid them down, and that got me up very early in the morning way over in Brooklyn, and I had to work up around 72nd Street, and I ran into the New York unions.

"Well, I wasn't so socialistic now. I objected very much to joining the union, and I was threatened by force, and I left the job rather than join the union. And meanwhile, the drinking had been crawling up."

It was partly to give themselves time to think and partly to get Bill away from drinking that Lois persuaded him to take a walking trip with her in Maine. From Boston, they took a boat to Portland, Maine, and walked, carrying packs and Army pup tents, from Portland to Rutland, Vermont.

A passage from the diary Lois kept on the trip shows how lighthearted and happy they were:

"Met an ultra modest red-haired man with his shirttail hanging out through a hole in the back of his pants, who, most properly, kept his eyes away from the shocking spectacle of a woman in knickers. When asked about the Saco River, he said it was three miles down the road but that he hadn't been that far this summer. . . .

"We got a fairly early start but stopped at the first brook we came to and took our morning baths. Although almost in the center of a place called Ross's Corners, we managed somehow to find a secluded spot. An auto with a horse hitched on behind passed us. . . .

"Spent the night on the shores of Lake Winnepesaukee. We spied a mink hunting among the rocks and heard a loon calling in the stillness. The northern lights were wonderful on this cold night. . . .

"We met a joyous farmer with a broad-brimmed calico hat, who sang to his team as he drove them down the hill. He explained to us his singing encouraged the horses not to stumble."

After their return to Brooklyn, Lois found work with the Red Cross, as an occupational therapist at the Brooklyn Navy Hospital. She had taken a course in occupational therapy while Bill was overseas. Unlike Bill, she never had any trouble holding a job.

Bill, too, finally found a job as an investigator in fraud and embezzlement for the United States Fidelity and Guaranty Company. He had also given up his somewhat vague ambition of becoming an engineer, and had enrolled instead in night classes at the Brooklyn Law School.

It was at his grandfather's insistence that he had abandoned engineering and taken up the study of law. Although he was not sure that he wanted to become a lawyer, he knew that a knowledge of the law would be useful, whatever he finally decided on.

While Bill was completing his plans to go to work, he had answered a blind advertisement in the New York *Times*. To his astonishment, he now received in reply an invitation from Thomas Edison himself. Bill was requested to come to Edison's laboratories in East Orange, New Jersey, for an employment test. A heaven-sent opportunity — Edison was one of Bill's heroes! Though the inventor was very old and his greatest achievements were behind him, he was still active.

When Bill arrived at the Edison facilities, he and a number of other applicants were taken into Edison's own laboratory — a long, unpretentious room — and given a written examination. Edison himself was there, seated at a cheap and battered desk in a corner.

It was a difficult test, containing 286 questions, Bill remembered: "In one question, they would want to know what was the diameter of the moon, and the next question would be what are overtones on a stringed instrument, and the next question was where do they make the most shoes, and the next question would be what kind of wood do they use for oil-barrel staves, and it just covered the gamut. The obvious idea was to see whether you'd been observant in your reading and in your observation of things in life in general.

"Well, the afternoon wore on, and people finished their papers and turned them in, and I hadn't finished. I answered all the questions I could immediately and then went over, because a lot of them were capable of estimate. Comparative populations and some scientific things could be estimated, and others you could remember if you kept working at it. So I answered a very large proportion of the questions in some fashion or other, and the old man came over and asked if I found the exam hard, and I said yes, that I thought it was very difficult.

"In the meanwhile, I'd had quite a glimpse of him. He'd

been one of my heroes as an aspiring electrical engineer. I remember how a former pupil of his, one of the Japanese nobility, had come in to pay him a visit, and then an assistant came in with a bar of platinum, which would be ruinously expensive if they were to plane it and so spoil it. And the old man burst into a volley of oaths. 'This thing is going to be planed, and you do it! You do as I tell you, see?' — showing that he was an old martinet on that side of it.''

Some weeks later, after Bill had already started working for the U.S. Fidelity and Guaranty Company, a New York *Times* reporter called to interview him — as one of the winners in the Edison test! Soon thereafter, Bill received a personal letter from Edison, inviting him to join the laboratories as a researcher in the acoustics department. In the test, Bill had demonstrated his considerable knowledge of sound and stringed instruments, a knowledge obviously related to his interests in radio and the violin.

Receiving an offer from Thomas Edison must have given Bill a tremendous boost; it might even have helped offset his shame at failing the M.I.T. entrance exams. It was well known that Edison placed a high value on persistence and attributed much of his own success to his refusal to give up. Tempting and flattering as the offer must have been, Bill did not accept it. In his recollections of the incident, he offered no reason for his refusal.

In the meantime, he had begun the job with the surety firm and was becoming interested; he was getting his first glimpse of Wall Street and the world of finance.

Although Bill no longer expected to enter engineering, he continued to pursue the interest in radio that had once impressed his East Dorset neighbors. ''I built one of the very early superheterodyne sets that were around among amateurs there on Amity Street,'' Bill recalled. ''Then I began to build sets for sale. We made a little something that way.'' His shop was in an attic in the building where he and Lois had now taken their own apartment at 142 Amity Street. ''Superheterodyne'' was the circuit for radio-frequency selection and amplification; this now common type of circuit was a vast improvement in those early years of radio. Lois remembered that Bill's sets could pick up stations as far away as Dallas, Minneapolis, and Los Angeles. (One of the sets was still in perfect working order when they moved to Bedford Hills 20 years later.)

That was not the only use to which Bill put his ingenuity. Prohibition was a new fact of life. The 18th Amendment to the Constitution, it had become law in January 1920.

It did not faze Bill any more than it deterred any other serious drinker. He bought grapes and pressed them out into big crocks. He would often drink the wine, he remembered, before it was half fermented.

While the Wilsons' life together in the early 1920's was already troubled by Bill's drinking, it was also a time of growth. Bill pursued his law studies for more than three years and completed the requirements for a diploma. He was too drunk, however, to pass a final examination. "I did make it up in the fall and then demanded my diploma, which they would never give me, because I was supposed to appear at the following commencement for it," he said. "But I never appeared, and my diploma as a graduate lawyer still rests in the Brooklyn Law School. I never went back for it. I must do that before I die."[1]

The Wilsons deeply desired children, and during the summer of 1922, Lois became pregnant. It was the first of three ectopic pregnancies that she was to suffer. In an ectopic pregnancy, the egg develops outside the uterus — in Lois's case, in a Fallopian tube.

After the second such misfortune, Bill and Lois were obliged to face the fact that they would never have children of their own. Said Lois: "Bill, even when drunk, took this overwhelming disappointment with grace and with kindness to me. But his drinking had been increasing steadily. It seemed that after all hope of having children had died, his bouts with alcohol had become even more frequent."

Years later, when they were better off financially, they applied to adopt a child. Although they waited for a long while and inquired several times, they were told on each occasion that a suitable child had not yet been found. Bill was always sure that they were not given a child because of his drinking.[2]

Though Bill's alcoholism affected the early years of his marriage, it had not progressed far enough to interfere seriously with his work. He was proving to be a capable investigator. Some of his investigations took him to Wall Street firms and brokerage houses. The great 1920's stock market boom was just beginning, and people were already making fortunes in the market. Bill found himself drawn into this exciting new world. In addition to law, he studied business and used the couple's limited savings to launch what would prove to be a short but spectacular investment program. "Living modestly, my wife and I saved $1,000," he said. "It went into certain securities, then cheap and rather unpopular. I rightly imagined that they would someday have a great rise."

Bill was primarily interested in electrical and utility stocks. "Lois and I owned two shares of General Electric, which people thought we had paid a fabulous sum for, being as they cost us $180 a share," he recalled. He was right about their growth potential: "Those same shares on split-ups became worth four or five thousand dollars a share."

Bill noticed that while many people made a great deal of money buying and selling stocks on the basis of very little information, others lost a great deal — through similar ignorance. He decided that for a wise investment, more thorough information was needed about the factories and managements that the stocks represented.

An unusual idea in the 1920's, it resulted in Bill's becoming one of the market's first securities analysts. Today, it would be unthinkable to buy shares in a company without knowing something about its management, markets, and business outlook. Brokerage firms, banks, and private companies maintain large departments to study companies and industries. Today's investors have access to computers and data storage banks. Bill may, in fact, have been one of the very first to realize that investors should look at the real values behind the stocks. As he put it, "I had the shrewd Yankee idea that you'd better look in the horse's mouth before you buy him."

His friends on Wall Street didn't think much of his idea, and refused to put up money for an extended field trip that Bill now proposed to make to investigate plants and managements. He did interest Frank Shaw, husband of Lois's best friend. Shaw was a keen-witted Maine Yankee who had started out as a speculator with some of his wife's capital. He was already worth a million dollars and, as Bill put it, "mighty well knew what I was talking about." While he refused to underwrite the project, he did ask to see whatever reports Bill wrote.

Though Bill had no guarantee that Shaw or anybody else would pay for his reports, he was so fascinated with General Electric and certain other industries that he decided to undertake a thorough investigation — with or without financial backing.

He and Lois owned a motorcycle, sidecar-equipped, that they had bought for trips to the beach. Now, they packed it with a tent, blankets, Bill's army locker full of clothes, cooking equipment, camping gear, a set of *Moody's Manuals* (financial reference books), and what little cash they possessed. In April 1925, they gave up their jobs and their apartment, and took off for Schenectady to "investigate" the General Electric Company.

Bill described their friends' reaction to the project: They "thought a lunacy commission should be appointed." In fact, Lois and Bill were "doing their own thing" — in 1925, an unheard-of notion! They loved camping; there was the lure of travel; and they were doing exactly what they wanted to do. Lois also had a hidden agenda: "I was so concerned about Bill's drinking that I wanted to get him away from New York and its bars. I felt sure that during a year in the open I would be able to straighten him out."

How did Bill feel at that time about his drinking? "I couldn't be impressed with its seriousness, except now and then when there was a humiliating episode," he recalled.

As Mr. and Mrs. Wilson roared off, they hardly had the look of people embarked on a serious business venture. Their small vehicle burst from every cranny with books, radio, gasoline stove, food, blankets, a mattress, clothes trunk, and in the sidecar, perched on top of it all, Bill himself, draped and dangling over the cowl. Lois was driving.

Their first stop was East Dorset, where they stayed in the Burnham cottage at Emerald Lake. Bill's grandfather, Fayette Griffith, had died the previous year — his grandmother, Ella, having died in 1921 — and Bill had a number of tasks in connection with settling the estate.

There, they found their business took longer than they had anticipated, and their slender hoard of cash was shrinking. By the time they arrived in Schenectady, they had only a few dollars.

Their near-penniless state did not keep Bill from donning his one good suit and marching into the main offices of General Electric, where he announced that he was a stockholder and wanted certain information about the company. "They didn't really know what to make of me — I could see that," he recalled. "I told this naive story of being a small shareholder, and they didn't know whether to talk little or talk much. And right then, it began to be evident that I had a flair for extracting information, because I did get a couple of pieces of information that were worth a little. But I couldn't get work there." He had thought a job there would enable him to make a more thorough investigation.

Bill and Lois were desperate for work. After three days of searching, they answered the advertisement of a farm couple

A motorcycle gave the young couple freedom to travel — but Lois's planned "geographic cure" didn't work out.

who needed help with the harvest. When they arrived at the Goldfoot farm in Scotia, New York, in a rainstorm, they realized that the Goldfoots were hardly the picture of prosperity. The farm couple, for their part, looked the Wilsons over, and were reluctant to hire them. "But I insisted that I could milk and knew farming, and Lois claimed that she could cook, which was a damned lie," Bill recalled. "She had a cookbook, but she thought she could cook for a farm. So we began getting up at four in the morning, and Lois, out of the cookbook, began doing the cooking, and that left the old woman and the old man and me out in the field."

At first, the grueling work almost killed Bill. But after about ten days, he got into condition and was even able to spend a few hours studying his *Moody's Manuals* after the day's work was finished.

Now, a piece of incredible luck landed on them. They discovered that the Goldfoots' farm directly adjoined the General Electric radio research laboratories! "So I got in the habit of running over and getting acquainted with the boys evenings, around the lab," Bill said, "and pretty soon I was inside the place, and boy, with what I knew about radio, I could see plenty. I got a preview of the whole radio industry five and ten years away. I saw the beginning of sound motion pictures; I saw super-heterodyne radios and console sets, and magnetic and tone reproduction, and two-way telephonic communication by shortwave." He began to send in reports that impressed his Wall Street friends. "It was just a break, and I fell right into it," he remembered.

Bill helped produce his own "breaks." He had an ability to look and listen, to gather ideas, possibilities, theories, and facts from every available source. He could digest and synthesize that information and then present it in a logical and simplified form that almost anybody could understand. As he himself explained it in a letter to Frank Shaw: "This trip has given me the time and material to indulge in what is to me the greatest pastime in the world — the construction of theories. Nothing seems to give me as great joy as evolving a theory from a set of facts, and then seeing it justified.'' If a few facts pointed to the existence of a principle or a law, Bill would test it to see whether it worked in other cases and thus had general application. He was always consolidating what worked, while carefully sidestepping theories that either were unproved or presented known dangers.

He had noticed that the farmers and others in the area used a great deal of cement, and that a considerable amount was going into concrete roads. In *Moody's Manuals*, he found several cement companies that seemed to him to merit closer investigation. One that caught his eye was Giant Portland Cement in Egypt, Pennsylvania, near Allentown. The Wilsons decided that Egypt would be their next stop.

They received their $75 for the month's work at the Goldfoots', and moved on. They had worked out well on the farm; in fact, the Goldfoots, so skeptical when the Wilsons first arrived, wrote them the following year to ask them to come back — with a raise!

In a field near Egypt, Bill and Lois were confined to their tent by a four-day rain- and windstorm. When a neighbor dropped in with a bottle, Bill started to drink. After the neighbor departed, Bill went into town to get another bottle. That was actually one of the very few bad drinking bouts of the entire trip — and so their year on the road did in a way do what Lois had hoped. It helped to retard the progression of Bill's alcoholism.

During another episode, when Bill had put in enough liquor to keep himself supplied for the weekend, Lois decided to get drunk herself, to ''hold a mirror up to him and show him what a fool a person appears when drunk.'' Of course, her plan backfired. Bill, tight himself, thought it was all wonderful fun and kept encouraging her to drink more. Finally, she was so sick she could hardly hold her head up. The next morning, as she suffered through a hangover, Bill sat calmly curing his mild discomfort by nipping away at the hair of the dog that bit him.

Bill managed to worm his way into the Giant factory, where he discovered some important facts: "I found out how much coal they were burning to make a barrel of cement," he said. "I read the meters on their power input and saw what that was doing. I saw how much stuff they were shipping. I took their financial statements, and this information and the discovery that they had just installed more efficient equipment meant worlds to production costs. I figured that they were making cement for less than a dollar a barrel, which was way down the line in costs. And still the stock was dawdling around in the Philadelphia market for very low figures, down around $15 a share."

Frank Shaw was impressed. On the basis of Bill's reports, his firm bought 5,000 shares of Giant Portland Cement for itself and 100 shares for Bill. The actual buying price was $20, which quickly climbed to $24, giving Bill a $500 profit and convincing the principals at Shaw's firm, the J. K. Rice Company, that Bill knew what he was doing. Now, Bill received the go-ahead to look into other companies and industries. He was also authorized to draw money against the rising price of his Giant shares, which eventually reached $75 a share!

On their motorcycle, Bill and Lois headed south. In Washington, D.C., they finally enjoyed the rare luxury of a hotel room. Lois went visiting. She called on Peggy Beckwith, President Lincoln's great-granddaughter, who summered at the family estate in Manchester. The two young women toured the Corcoran Art Gallery and then had luncheon at Peggy's Georgetown home — quite a turnabout from Lois's recent hobo status. Bill took himself to the U.S. Patent Office and to the Library of Congress.

Once Washington had drained their cash, they were on the road again, roaring across the Carolinas and Georgia. As they proceeded south, Bill made a number of significant investigations: the Aluminum Company of America, American Cyanamid, U.S. Cast Iron Pipe, the Southern Power Company, and the Florida real estate situation.

In Fort Myers, Florida, they visited Bill's mother, who had remarried and was living with her new husband, Dr. Charles Strobel, on a double-decker houseboat.

Dr. Strobel had been Emily's general practitioner from the East Dorset days; at that time, he had lived in Rutland. Dr. Strobel was also a cancer specialist, and for a time was connected with the Memorial Sloan-Kettering Hospital in New York City. After Emily — who was now Dr. Emily — married him in 1923, they lived for a time in Florida, where her son and daughter-in-law now visited them.

In the spring, Bill and Lois headed north again, still traveling by motorcycle and camping. Their stops included the Coronet Phosphate Company and the Tennessee Coal, Iron and Railroad Company. Bill had other plants that he wanted to investigate, but they also wanted to be back in Brooklyn by the middle of June — Lois's sister Kitty was going to be married on the 17th.

Near Dayton, Tennessee, the motorcycle part of their journey ended abruptly when Lois failed to make a turn in the road because of deep sand. Lois injured her knee, and Bill, in the sidecar, went sailing over her head and broke his collarbone. They spent the next ten days in a Dayton hotel, recovering from their injuries. Finally, they shipped the motorcycle and their equipment home, and caught the train to New York, arriving in Brooklyn just in time for Lois to limp up the aisle as Kitty's matron of honor.

It was June 1926. Bill was on the threshold of what promised to be one of the most exciting periods of his life. His financial reports to Shaw were proving enormously successful. He was given a position with the firm, an expense account, and a $20,000 line of credit for buying stocks. He described it thus:

''For the next few years fortune threw money and applause my way. I had arrived. My judgment and ideas were followed by many to the tune of paper millions. The great boom of the late twenties was seething and swelling. Drink was taking an important and exhilarating part in my life. There was loud talk in the jazz places uptown. Everyone spent in thousands and chattered in millions. Scoffers could scoff and be damned. I made a host of fair-weather friends.''

Bill had been right in believing that his on-site investigations would yield results. Lois had been wrong in believing that a year away from the New York bars would end his drinking.

---

1. He never did obtain the diploma. In later years, he would discuss this phenomenon at some length as a symptom — i.e., the alcoholic's tendency to get drunk and so destroy the well-deserved fruits of hard work and sustained effort.

2. After his death, Lois learned that this was true. They had given the names of friends as references to the adoption agency. One of these friends told the agency that they would not make reliable parents, because Bill drank so much.

Chapter Four

In the late 1920's, Bill and Lois began to enjoy a new and exciting affluence. Like many speculators of that fevered time, Bill was a margin trader. He bought shares of stock by paying only a part of the actual price. If stock rose, his profits could be enormous. But if the price fell sharply, his equity in the stock was wiped out. He might even be called on to pay additional amounts to make up the deficit — called "covering the margin." In the stock market debacle of 1929, the sudden drop in prices[1] itself drove prices even lower because of the panic selling to avoid further losses, or to obtain cash to cover margins on other holdings.

Clint F., from Greenlawn, Long Island, New York, remembered the Bill of the Wall Street years:

"I first met Bill Wilson at J. K. Rice Jr. and Co., 120 Broadway, New York City, a stockbroker firm specializing in speculative situations. My job was telephone trader during the Roaring Twenties, when Coolidge was President and Wall Street was the place to get rich quick.

"Understandably, the climate was feverish in the financial

district. This was the buildup of the nation's first mammoth bull market. Anyone who did not join in the mass exuberance to the point of unbalance was simply not with it and was a little conspicuous. Such a one was a certain tall and loose-jointed character named Bill who worked on the outside as a special investigator for one of the partners of our firm, named Frank Shaw. This Bill was a mystery to me, because with all the shouting and scrambling going on in our office, he came in and went out with the grave dignity of a circuit judge. He did not mix with the crowd much and never joined the magpie chatter around the stock ticker. I learned about a year later that his investigations uncovered some of the most profitable situations the firm got into financially. And for some reason, he never took off his hat, a soggy brown box perched straight over his eyes.'' (Clint's memory was acutely accurate; all photographs of Bill wearing a hat show it squared away.)

''A couple of years [after I met Bill], a split took place in the Rice firm. Bill's boss Frank joined another stockbroker house, Tobey and Kirk, 25 Broad Street, taking Bill with him, as well as several traders, including me. I was drinking a little at the time and made some costly mistakes, which did me no good with Frank. However, I had little contact with Bill, who was a very busy guy then, and so I stumbled along in my own losing way, and married my lifelong gal, Katy. With good business sense, Frank fired me on my wedding day.

''Up to the historic crash of 1929, everybody and his uncle seemed to be floating along to riches on the sweet euphoria of paper profits. I met Bill now and then, and although his appearance was unchanged, I knew he was going great and in on some deals with large promise. My own lack of big success depressed me, and I got a little morbid over the fact. My wife had been working in Macy's since we were married, and still I could not catch on the big train the way Bill and others did. Perhaps my own [drinking] problem was catching up to me, if there was one. The fatal earthquake came and went in the stock market with a mark 8 on the Richter scale. The mighty were swept from their seats, and we of low degree went lower."

Back in 1927, the Wilsons had no premonition of disaster. Motorcycle travel had been abandoned in favor of transportation more befitting their new, higher standard of living; they could travel by car or rail; and there was money for hotels and entertainment. Although Bill drank heavily on some of these trips, he was able to complete excellent reports.

He had begun to lie. With Lois, he was returning from a trip to Canada, where he had investigated an aluminum company development and had stayed sober the entire time. Just as they were about to cross the border back to the United States, Bill mentioned casually that he was going to stop to get cigarettes. "I realized this was nonsense, since cigarettes were more expensive in Canada," Lois said. "But liquor was cheaper and more easily available than in the U.S. in those Prohibition days."

Parked in the plaza of the bridge that was the United States-Canadian border, she waited for hours; Bill had gone off with both money and car keys. Finally, she set out to look for him. "In the very last saloon in the area, there he was, hardly able to navigate. Our money had all but vanished."

When Bill became interested in Cuban sugar, there was nothing for it but an on-site investigation. They had bought themselves a secondhand Dodge for $250, and this, outfitted for sleeping, took them in high style to Florida. It was the summer of 1927.

In Cuba, they were given a warm reception and treated as important people. A car, a chauffeur, and a motorboat were placed at their disposal. In Havana, they stayed at the Hotel Sevilla. It was apparently above their means, judging from a letter Bill wrote to Frank Shaw in which he promised that they were "going to move to another place which will be more reasonable and which from now on will answer our purpose just as well." According to Lois, they never did leave the Sevilla.

Of that trip, Lois said, "It was a frustrating time for me,

though, because of Bill's drinking. One day, to keep him from going down to the bar, I threw one of his shoes out the window, but this did no good. It landed on a nearby roof, and Bill simply called the porter to retrieve it. In no time, he was down at the bar wearing both shoes.''

In the same letter to Shaw, Bill addressed Shaw's concern about his drinking:

"Thank you for your remittance and your letter which followed. Now a few lines for your eyes alone. I have never said anything to you about the liquor question, but now that you mention it and also for the good reason that you are investing your perfectly good money in me, I am at last very happy to say that I have had a final showdown (with myself) on the matter. It has always been a very serious handicap to me, so that you can appreciate how glad I am to be finally rid of it. It got to the point where I had to decide whether to be a monkey or a man. I know it is going to be a tough job, but nevertheless the best thing I ever did for myself and everybody concerned. That is that, so let us now forget about it.''

The letter was dated September 3, 1927.

Bill made several visits to sugar plantations and sent in his reports. But those investigations were unsuccessful. To Lois, the reason seemed clear: Bill continued to drink during their entire month in Cuba.

On their way home, they stopped to see Bill's father and his second wife, Christine, in Miami Beach. Gilman had a contract to cut rock for the foundations of the Overseas Highway that would connect the Florida mainland with the Keys. On this visit, Bill also met the daughter of Gilman and Christine, his young half sister Helen, born in 1916.

Back in New York, they rented an expensive three-room apartment at 38 Livingston Street, in one of Brooklyn's good residential neighborhoods. Because it wasn't big enough to satisfy Bill's grandiose desires, they enlarged it by renting the apartment next door and knocking out the wall between. Now, they had two bedrooms, two baths, two kitchens, and a single huge living room.

The elevator man in their building was a West Indian Rosicrucian named Randolph, who did what he could to keep Bill sober — and when that failed, to keep him safe. If Bill was late getting home, Randolph would go out and look for him in the neighborhood bars. Bill was grateful; when he learned that Randolph's daughter was studying music, he gave Randolph a check to buy a piano.

By 1928, Bill was a star among his Wall Street associates. "In those days, of course, I was drinking for paranoid reasons. I was drinking to dream greater dreams of power, dreams of domination. Money to me was never a symbol of security. It was the symbol of prestige and power." He dreamed of the day when he would sit on prestigious boards of directors. "J. P. Morgan and the First National Bank were, you know, my heroes."

There was now no question about the seriousness of his drinking. As soon as the three o'clock bell sounded the closing of the stock market, he would head for a speakeasy, then drink his way uptown. "I'd be pretty much out of commission at 14th Street and completely lose my wits at 59th. Start out with $500 and then have to crawl under a subway gate to get back to Brooklyn."

There were unhappy scenes in the sumptuous Livingston Street apartment. Promise followed empty promise. On October 20, 1928, Bill wrote in the family Bible, the most sacred place he knew: "To my beloved wife that has endured so much, let this stand as evidence of my pledge to you that I have finished with drink forever." By Thanksgiving Day of that year, he had written, "My strength is renewed a thousandfold in my love for you." In January 1929, he added, "To tell you once more that I am finished with it. I love you."

None of those promises, however, carried the anguish Bill expressed in an undated letter to Lois: "I have failed again this day. That I should continue to even try to do right in the grand manner is perhaps a great foolishness. Righteousness simply does not seem to be in me. Nobody wishes it more than I. Yet no one flouts it more often.''

His drinking had begun to greatly worry his other Wall Street partners, despite his phenomenal success at ferreting out profitable situations. He embarrassed them by getting drunk on trips or by getting into arguments with company managements. Always pleasant and good-mannered when sober, Bill could become troublesome and overbearing when he drank.

He was no longer welcome among Lois's friends: ''Even though some of them drank a good deal, they couldn't stand me,'' Bill remembered. ''And, of course, I was very loud-mouthed when I drank, and I felt a terrible inferiority to some of her people, and the boy from the country had come in and made more money than they'd ever seen, and that was the theme of my talk, and people increasingly just couldn't take it. We were in the process already of being isolated, that process being mitigated only by the fact that we were making money and more money.''

As Lois said, ''By the end of 1927, he was so depressed by his own behavior that he said, 'I'm halfway to hell now and going strong.' He then signed over to me 'all rights, title, and interest' in his accounts with his stockbrokers, Baylis and Company, and Tobey and Kirk. . . . Night after night, he didn't come home until the wee small hours, and then he would be so drunk he'd either fall down just inside the front door or I'd have to help him to bed.''

Lois described the profundity of their dilemma in these words: ''Bill rarely drank socially or moderately. Once he started, he seldom stopped until he became so drunk he fell inert. He was not violent when in his cups and was deeply remorseful afterward. When he finally realized he couldn't stop, he begged me to help him, and we fought the alcohol battle together. We did not know at the time that he had a physical, mental, and spiritual illness. The traditional theory that drunkenness was only a moral weakness kept us both from thinking clearly on the subject. Yet Bill was morally strong. His sense of right and wrong was vivid, extending even to little things, and his respect for the rights of other people was extraordinary. For example, he wouldn't walk across another person's lawn, though I often would. He had plenty of willpower to do anything in which he was interested; but it wouldn't work against alcohol even when he was interested. . . .

"I suppose the pattern of his tolerance to alcohol was like that of many alcoholics. At first, liquor affected him quickly; later, he became able to drink more and more without showing it; but then, suddenly, his tolerance dramatically diminished. Even a little liquor made him intoxicated."

Early in 1929, on a trip to Manchester, he got off the train in Albany and telephoned Ebby, his school friend from Burr and Burton. He suggested that they meet downtown and take on a couple of drinks. Until this time, they had never drunk together, though they had both progressed into serious drinking. And as Ebby said, "I saw a lot of Bill. We met and were firm friends from the beginning." (Lois remembered it otherwise, however; she thought Ebby was initially much closer to her brother Rogers than he was to Bill.)

Ebby was the son of well-to-do parents, but the family business had failed in 1922. For a time, he sold insurance and worked for an investment house. He also was helped by his brother, the mayor of Albany. Ebby's drinking was gradually making him a local problem in that city.

At the time of this meeting with Bill, Ebby recalled, "I was playing around in Albany with a bunch of flyers who were barnstormers at the Albany airport. They called themselves Flyers Incorporated. Bill and I attended a party at the house of one of the pilots. Bill was headed for Vermont the next day, and I couldn't see why he would have to take that two-by-four railroad up there. Why not hire a plane? So I made a deal with a boy, one Ted Burke, to fly us up the next day." Ebby also recalled that after putting Bill in the hotel that night, "I went out and drank all night, so I would be sure to make the trip.''

Bill, whose version of the story had them both partying all night, remembered that they paid the pilot a stiff fee to take them to Vermont. He had been reluctant to take off, probably because of bad weather. A new landing field was being built at Manchester, but no planes had yet landed. ''We called Manchester to tell the folks that we would be the first arrivals,'' Bill said. ''I vaguely remember spotting the town of Bennington through the haze. The excited citizens of Manchester had got together a welcoming committee. The town band had turned out. The town delegation was headed by Mrs. Orvis, a rather stately and dignified lady, who at that time owned the famous Equinox House.

''We circled the field. But meantime, all three of us had been pulling at a bottle. Somehow, we lit on the pretty bumpy meadow. The delegation charged forward. It was up to Ebby and me to do something, but we could do absolutely nothing. We somehow slid out of the cockpit, fell on the ground, and there we lay, immobile. Such was the history-making episode of the first airplane ever to light at Manchester, Vermont.''

This exploit, hilarious as it may have appeared, actually caused Bill great remorse. He remembered wandering around East Dorset the next day, in the grip of a crying jag. He visited Mark Whalon, and he also sent off a letter of apology to Mrs. Orvis. Ebby took the evening train back to Albany.

However remorseful Bill felt about the incident, it did not make him unwelcome in Manchester; he and Lois went up there later in the year to golf at the exclusive and genteel Ekwanok Club. In that frenzied last summer of the Roaring Twenties, Bill pursued his golf game with characteristic determination to excel. In addition, ''Golf permitted drinking every day and every night,'' he said. ''It was fun to carom around the exclusive course which had inspired such awe in me as a lad. I acquired the impeccable coat of tan one sees upon the well-to-do. The local banker watched me whirl fat checks in and out of his till with amused skepticism.''

Continuing his investigation of stocks, Bill became interested in a corn products company called Penick and Ford. In a well-orchestrated maneuver, "I did the job just in reverse of everybody else. I went on the theory that I would go out and sell my friends this stock — in other words, encourage them to buy it on the open market. I got ahold of this specialist in the stock. I sold him a bill of goods — that is, after accumulating my own line. And then I figured that if I did enough advertising with this around, and solid selling, every time we got a bad market setback, I could bring in enough buying to peg the damn thing. It wasn't too big, only 400,000 shares, which by this time had gotten into the 40's (I'd started in with it at about 20 the year before). I could peg it and so protect myself, and that would enable me to run on a pretty small shoestring. In other words, I could carry lines of thousands of shares of it myself.

"And sure enough, in the spring of 1929, there was a hell of a crack in the market, and boy, I let that thing down five points, and I got thousands of shares of it into my friends' hands and meanwhile pegged the price and protected myself. So I thought, 'Well, you put your friends in on the dip instead of selling it to them on the bulges, and that gives them a wonderful break, and meanwhile they're protected. I'm not trying to trade on them and make money that way. And we've got a long, full operation, good enough for quite a while yet.' "

He even persuaded his mother to buy 900 shares, advising her, in January 1929, not to sell at less than $60 per share. He then decided that he was prepared for a possible drop in the market. It was also in 1929 that he broke with his friend and benefactor Frank Shaw. Bill Wilson was going to be a lone wolf on Wall Street, and a powerful one at that.

Few margin traders were ready for the cataclysm that hit the market that October. Even Bill had prepared only for a squall. What impended was a hurricane. When the first wave of selling sent prices plunging, his Penick and Ford shares dropped from 55 to 42, a loss of $13 per share. With the help of friends, Bill

bought heavily in an attempt to shore up the price. The stock
rallied, climbed to 52, and then made a sickening dive to 32 in a
single day, wiping out the friends who had trusted his judgment
— and Bill himself. He was broke.

"The minute my money went, the confidence in me was
suddenly zero," he recalled.

A friend named Dick Johnson offered him a job with his
firm, Greenshields and Co., a brokerage firm in Montreal. In
December, he and Lois moved to Montreal. Upon their arrival,
about Christmastime, they moved into a dingy apartment.
Within weeks, Bill was back into the market, again trading in
Penick and Ford, which in the spring of 1930 actually climbed
back to $55 a share.

It seemed that Bill was going to make a fast comeback. "I
felt like Napoleon returning from Elba," he said. "No St. He-
lena for me!" They soon found much better lodgings in Glen
Eagles, an expensive new apartment house overlooking the St.
Lawrence River. They had a wonderful time in Montreal, playing golf and dining at the Club House. By fall, Johnson had
dismissed him. His Waterloo was, as always, booze.

In the last months of 1930, Bill caught what he called "occasional glimpses of the downslope leading to the valley of the
shadow. But," he said, "I could still turn and look the other
way, even though I had been deeply shocked by the calamity of
the 1929 crash and now the dismissal by my good friend Dick
Johnson." Again, he wrote a promise to his wife in the family
Bible: "Finally and for a lifetime, thank God for your love."
The promise was dated September 3, 1930. Like those that had
preceded it, it was not kept. That was the last of the Bible promises.

While Bill stayed on in Montreal to clean up details, Lois
went back to Brooklyn, because her mother had fallen ill. "Even
at the very end with much to do, I still couldn't keep sober," Bill
said. "I remember getting very drunk, falling into an argument
with a hotel detective." He was thrown in jail, but released the

next morning by a lenient judge. Drunk by noon, he met another alcoholic, an individual of the "tinhorn confidence man" variety. This companion was still with him when he finally woke up in Vermont, at the Burnham Emerald Lake camp. It took almost every cent Bill still possessed to send the man back to Montreal.

When Lois arrived in Vermont from Brooklyn, they discussed what they should do next. "By this time, I really began to appreciate her intense devotion, courage, and still high confidence in me," Bill said. "After a season of no alcohol, we advanced again upon New York to recoup our fortunes." It was after the Montreal disaster that Bill, for the first time, tried hard to stop drinking because he really wanted to stop. He did not yet realize that he was in the grip of an obsession, that he had lost the power of choice where drink was concerned, and that all his personal efforts to control or stop his drinking would come to nothing.

Back in Brooklyn, the Wilsons were taken in by Lois's parents. While Bill must have been in some disgrace by this time, they apparently treated him with kindness and concern. "They were truly a marvelous couple," he said of the Burnhams. Of Lois's mother, he said, "Her capacity for the kind of love that demands no reward for nearly everything and everybody was quite beyond belief and understanding." Bill remembered his father-in-law as "an exceedingly handsome individual, dressed immaculately and as courtly in his speech and manner as anyone I ever knew." Underneath Dr. Burnham's politeness, Bill said, there was an extreme aggressiveness and a terrific domination that affected the whole family life, without his in the least intending it or anyone's realizing what was going on.

An indication of how totally out of control Bill's drinking had now become was his behavior at the time of his mother-in-law's death. Following an arduous course of radium treatments for bone cancer, she died on Christmas Day, 1930. Bill was drunk when she died; he had been drunk for days before; he stayed drunk for days after.

These words were written by Lois in a moment of despair:

"What is one to think or do after so many failures? Is my theory of the importance of love and faith nothing but bunk? Is it best to recognize life as it seems — a series of failures — and that my husband is a weak, spineless creature who is never going to get over his drinking?

"If I should lose my love and faith, what then? As I see it now, there is nothing but emptiness, bickering, taunts, and selfishness, each of us trying to get as much out of the other as possible in order to forget our lost ideals.

"I love my husband more than words can tell, and I know he loves me. He is a splendid, fine man — in fact, an unusual man with qualities that could make him reach the top. His personality is endearing; everybody loves him; and he is a born leader. Most kindly and bighearted, he would give away his last penny. He is honest almost to a fault. . . .

"The morning after he has been drunk, he is so penitent, self-derogatory, and sweet that it takes the wind out of my sails, and I cannot upbraid him.

"He continually asks for my help, and we have been trying together almost daily for five years to find an answer to his drinking problem, but it is worse now than ever. If we go away on a trip, he says he does not miss alcohol and goes without it a month or more at a time; but the minute we get back to the city, the very first day, in spite of all kinds of plans and protestations, he is at it again, sometimes coming home early and sometimes at five o'clock in the morning. . . .

"I hate even to think of it, but if I went away for a short time and did not come back until he had behaved himself for a week at least, and then, if things did not continue as they should, stayed away longer, would that help? Would it finally arouse his interest?

"In writing this down, I can see that . . . the problem is not about *my* life, of course, for probably the suffering is doing me good, but about his — the frightful harm this resolving and breaking down, resolving and breaking down again, must be doing to him. How can he ever accomplish anything with this frightful handicap? I worry more about the moral effect on him than I do the physical, although goodness knows the terrible stuff he drinks is enough to burn him up completely. . . .

"We understand each other as well as is possible for radically different temperaments. I admit I cannot understand the craving for liquor, for it has no appeal for me, although several times I have made myself drunk in order to try and find that appeal.

"I believe that people are good if you give them half a chance and that good is more powerful than evil. The world seems to me excruciatingly, almost painfully beautiful at times, and the goodness and kindness of people often exceed that which even I expect. Francis Bacon said that the human mind is easily fooled; that we believe what we want to believe and recognize only those facts which conform to that belief. Am I doing that identical thing? Are people bad, is love futile, and Bill doomed to worse than mediocrity? Am I a fool not to recognize it and grasp what pleasure and comfort I can?"

Bill, for his part, wrote Lois "thousands of letters. He would write to me over and over again how he never would take another drink."

Humiliated by his failures and by their dependence on his wife's father, Bill found a job as an investigator at a salary of $100 a week. A fortune to many families in those Depression days, it was a comedown for Bill. He held the job for almost a year, however, and even made a little headway in the organization. But following a barroom incident that he described as "a brawl with a taxi driver," he was fired.

With this dismissal, Bill's standing on Wall Street was totally gone. He was $60,000 in debt and out in the cold. "I began to canvass my few friends in the Street who had survived the crash, but I found their confidence in me had really oozed out years before," he said. "Now that I was penniless and obviously in deep trouble with liquor, they had nothing for me, and surely they could not be blamed for that.''

Bill now entered a phase of helpless drinking. It was compounded by the Depression, but even had times been prosperous, it's doubtful that he could have earned his living any longer. Lois found a job at Macy's, earning $19 a week plus a small commission on sales, and that became their livelihood. Bill sat around in brokerage houses during the day, trying to give the appearance of being at work.

Occasionally, he was able to develop ideas for small deals in securities, and sell them for a few hundred dollars. Lois saw little of that money. ''Most of the money by now would go to pay up the speakeasy bills in order to be sure of a line of fresh credit when I should next run out of money. I had become, too, a lone drinker, partly because I preferred it and partly because none of my Wall Street companions cared anymore for my company.''

Sometimes, he got through the day by buying a fifth of gin and nipping at it discreetly as he made the rounds of brokerage houses; he usually managed to appear sober enough. After borrowing a few dollars, then buying another bottle from the nearest bootlegger, he would ride the subway for hours, still nipping, and might appear at home at any time of night.

Such was Bill's life in 1931 and into the summer of 1932. He was beginning to show signs of mental impairment. When people tried to reason with him during a drinking bout, he would turn violent and talk gibberish that frightened them. He ''began to understand what real hangovers were like and sometimes bordered on delirium.'' He would lie in bed and drink while Lois was at work. ''The demon was now moving into full possession,'' he said.

In 1932, when blue-chip shares were selling at bargain rates, Bill decided he should form a buying syndicate to take advantage of the extremely low prices. He had the help of brother-in-law Gardner Swentzel, husband of Lois's younger sister Kitty. Swentzel, whose firm was Taylor Bates and Company, had numerous friends in the financial community.

Although Bill was no longer welcome in many offices on Wall Street, he made a superhuman effort to restrain himself during business hours. Before long, he struck up an acquaintance with two men who agreed to form the buying syndicate with him. They were Arthur Wheeler and Frank Winans; Wheeler was the only son of the president of the American Can Company.

That bleak year of 1932 appeared to be a poor time for speculative buying, but Bill had realized that it actually was a most favorable time. Many securities were selling for a half or a third of net worth. "If one could overcome his fears, have capital and patience, there could be a fortune in the recovery that was bound to come one day," he said. "America was rapidly approaching the state where a turn simply had to be made."

Bill was utterly overjoyed at this chance to make a comeback. His new partners, impressed by his ideas, assigned him a generous share but made one important stipulation in their contract: If Bill started drinking again, not only would the deal be off, but also he would lose his interest in the venture. "I signed the agreement and drew a tremendous sigh of relief," Bill remembered. Confident that he was on the road to financial recovery, he plunged into the work.

For the next "two or three months," things went well. To his amazement, he had little urge to drink; in fact, he felt a complete lack of temptation. Word soon got around, and his reputation on Wall Street began to improve. This led to another opportunity: an assignment to investigate a new photographic process at the Pathé Laboratories in Bound Brook, New Jersey.

Accompanied by several engineers, Bill arrived in Bound Brook to make the investigation. After dinner, the engineers began a game of poker and invited Bill to join them. Bill, who had never had any interest in cards, declined. From somewhere appeared a jug of applejack, called "Jersey lightning." Quickly and easily, Bill again declined.

As the evening wore on, Bill's companions would now and

then renew their offer of a drink, and Bill steadfastly refused. At one point, he even went so far as to explain that he was a person who couldn't handle liquor.

By midnight, he was bored and restive; his thoughts drifted back to his hilarious wartime adventures and his enjoyment of the excellent wines of France. The misery and defeat of recent years faded from his mind. And while he was indulging in this pleasant reverie, it came to him that he had never tasted Jersey lightning. A serious omission; no doubt he had missed a real experience. The next time the offer came his way, his one thought was: "Well, I guess one bolt of Jersey lightning couldn't hurt me much."

He was drunk for three days. Word of the debacle soon reached Wall Street. It was the end of his contract — and of his "comeback."

"Up to this time, I think my drinking had been motivated by the desire for the grandiose. But now there was a complete and abrupt shift in motivation. I still thought it was the same, but my behavior belied that. I made my way back over to Wall Street, but all my friends were so sorry, so sorry. Nothing could be done. Sometimes now, I got drunk in the morning even while trying to transact business. When I was crossed, I abused the very people upon whom I was trying to make an impression. Sometimes, I had to be led out of offices. I would repair to the nearest grogshop, throw in a few drinks, buy a bottle, and down great quantities. I would try to arrive home not clear out, always concealing a fifth of gin or possibly two. At this point, two bottles were far safer; there would be some in the morning — that is, if I could find the one that I hid.

"Like all other alcoholics, I hid liquor about as a squirrel would cherish nuts. Liquor could be found in the attic, on beams, underneath the flooring; it could be found in the flush box of toilets; it could be found buried in coal in the cellar; it could be found in the backyard. I would take pains during the times when Lois was at work to replenish my stores.

"But to return to my motivation — I now see that I was drinking for oblivion. There would be days of drinking about the house, barely able to get through supper, then the blackout, then a tearful parting with Lois in the morning, and at it again for the day. Two and three bottles of gin had become a routine.

"My morale was utterly shattered. I remember throwing a small sewing machine at poor Lois. At another time, I went around through the house kicking out door panels. Seldom had I done anything like this in all my drinking career. Now, it was routine when I was bad enough and crossed. In the more lucid times, Lois would tell me, with terror in her eyes, how truly insane I had been. What could we do about it?"

A way out of despair seemed to open when another professional opportunity appeared, in the form of his old friend Clint:

"One day at the corner of Broad and Wall Streets, I bumped into Clint F., an over-the-counter trader with whom I had a slight acquaintance. Clint told me he was working for a perfectly wonderful fellow, Joe Hirshhorn, who, despite the times, still had money and was making it hand over fist. I soon met Joe and outlined some of my ideas.

"Joe had come up in Wall Street the hard way, starting as a trader in penny stocks when people stood in Broad Street and traded in the curb market. Subsequently, his great acumen had brought him important connections, and he had an uncanny trading flair.

"He made me great promises, and I began to be faintly encouraged. Sometimes, he would tell me he had bought a line of stock and was carrying me for a few shares on credit. Now and then, he would hand me a small check. This was usually spent on fifths of gin, now the delicatessen variety."

Clint's version of the connection with Hirshhorn:

"Following the calamity in the stock market, which hurt everybody, the depression and poverty of 1931 and 1932 looked like the end. With subway fare of two nickels from my wife but no lunch coins, I ambled daily up and down Wall Street, looking for anything. Luckily, I met up with a rich and very smart broker who had survived the wreck. His name was Joe Hirshhorn, and he took me on because he liked my training in specials. But I knew that alone I would fail. I always did. Where could I get help in what was surely a great opportunity right out of the sky?

"I thought of Bill and wondered if he was still in Brooklyn Heights. He was, and no surprise to find that he had hit the roller coaster like the rest of us. Having snowed Joe under with the buildup I had given Bill's ability as an investigator in securities, there was no problem in getting Bill to come over to 50 Broad Street and get hired, which in turn would assure the safety of my own job (or jump off Brooklyn Bridge). Joe was quite satisfied with him, because I overheard him tell a broker friend what a 'schmaltz' guy he picked up — 'an Einstein, and he came in the mail.'

"Times became a little more cheerful now as the market commenced to recover, and when Bill felt a lot more affable being on the payroll, he invited me for lunch to talk about the shape of things to come. Naturally, we gravitated toward the well-known gentlemen's bar, Eberlin's, Bill saying as we went in, 'Clint, a little mild sherry will clear our vision.' He still wore that same sad brown hat and did not jar it once while we cleared our vision. The midday wore on, and a high point I recall, after a short sermon on economics, [was] his predicting what big things we were about to do for our pal Joe. 'Why, Clint, this man can become a Rothschild.' The fact that this man did just that in the years since seemed to have little relation to our kind intentions at Eberlin's saloon.

"I never did know exactly what work Bill did at our office; but he traveled extensively, I think, investigating properties in which Joe had large financial interests. For my part, in 1933 I stayed comparatively sober, making a tough living with little spare cash for booze.

"If Bill was taking a snort now and then at the beginning of this job, I didn't notice. However, there were some dangerous moments, such as the garden party our boss threw at his Great Neck estate. It was a charity affair to raise money for his new temple, and his business friends and other guests were getting their arms twisted real hard. Crates of champagne were being pushed on the crowd at an awful price, for a good purpose, of course. Although it was costly philanthropy in those hard times, Joe was a kind person at heart and wouldn't let Bill or me pay for anything. His wife sat with our wives, Lois and Kay, most of the evening. We sipped a little of the free bubbly in a dignified way, then sipped a little more, and then for real! Lois and Kay didn't look comfortable until it was time to go home.

"On a trip to the cloakroom, Bill and I discovered the storage pantry for the champagne. What a sight! Bill said something like 'Heavens to Betsy, look at this!' We each tucked away as many bottles as we could hide in our coats, and decided as an emergency to open a couple of extras. We busted the necks over the plumbing in the men's room and choked the stuff down like crazy. There was broken glass and wet sparkles all over the place and us. We tried to hurry back to join the others saying good night to our loving host, but we both got hit the same time.

"My wife grabbed my arm, but I couldn't speak or hear anymore. Lois got in front of Bill, who was slowly spinning and trying to say something to Joe. Kay said he was breathing blessings on the new temple. The fog closed in. Kay got Bill and Lois back to Brooklyn in a borrowed car. Somehow, with great effort, Bill and I got into the office the next day. We were much younger then. Joe greeted us and commented, 'Can you beat it? Some bum from the people we invited swiped some champagne and broke some bottles all over the bathroom. Imagine our own people acting like that.'

"Bill had the faculty of carrying on his work and talking to people without revealing that sometimes he was real loaded. He never staggered, although I sometimes saw him sway a bit like [in] a gust of wind.

"Before Prohibition went out, we would collect in a variety

of saloons called speakeasies, such as the Steam Club, Busto's, and a host of others now forgotten. Nearly half a century has passed, but I can still see Bill coming into Ye Old Illegal Bar on a freezing afternoon with a slow stride — he never hurried — and looking over with lofty dignity the stack of bottles back of the bar, containing those rare imported beverages right off the liner from Hoboken. One time at the Whitehall subway station, not far from Busto's, Bill took a tumble down the steps. The old brown hat stayed on; but, wrapped up in that long overcoat, he looked like a collapsed sailboat on the subway platform. I recall how his face lit up when he fished out of the heap of clothes an unbroken quart of gin.

"Another time [later, in 1934], we made a few rounds and found we were short of money. That is, Bill was short — I had none. As a result of spending all the paper currency, he had accumulated a pocketful of nickels, dimes, and quarters. This was serious, being early in the afternoon, so we took a cab to Brooklyn and stopped at Loeser's department store. There, Bill's ever-devoted wife, Lois, was holding down a job, the same as my weary wife at Macy's, while he and I were getting on our feet, so to speak.

"It was a little awkward paying off the cabby in nickels, dimes, and quarters, and after dropping several on the sidewalk, Bill dumped a shower of coins into the taxi and orated something about it being more blessed to receive than to give. Lois saw us coming down the aisle, and her face dropped a mile. After some whispered exchange, Lois went back somewhere and returned with her pocketbook. I never felt more insolvent — first Bill's last buck, now probably hers. We went to their apartment in Brooklyn Heights, closing a hard day, and plowed into a fresh bottle with emotional overtones. I sat down at their piano and pounded out the first line of something in A flat major. Never played it as well before, I thought, while Bill pulled a violin off the wall somewhere and joined me in a clatter of noise until Lois came home and quieted things down.

"However, by now the pretense of sobriety gradually crumbled. The office, especially Joe, commenced to eye Bill with concern. His final assignment was an important one in Canada. He took off with his usual self-assurance via rail to Montreal, and the next we know, Bill telegraphs that he is in jail at the Canadian border. Joe went straight through the ceiling. His secretary went up to the border to square matters with the law — something about 'very drunk and disorderly.' 'There must be some mistake,' I said. 'It can't be the same man. He might have taken a glass of beer now and then at lunch. But publicly intoxicated? Never!' I looked for a new job.

"Months later, I received a couple of rambling letters from Green River, Vermont, where Bill had now gone native like Thoreau. He was camped out in a tent on his brother-in-law's place and starting a crusade against the then New Deal administration and F. D. Roosevelt. I cannot say that there was any apple cider involved in this undertaking, but it didn't sound like good whiskey thinking."

Joe Hirshhorn remembered both Bill and Clint with great appreciation. He described Clint as "a smart boy and a nice man" and did not remember his having a drinking problem. Bill was another matter.

"He was awful; he was an alcoholic; but I liked him. He was one of the brightest stock analysts on Wall Street. There were a lot of analysts around, but they didn't know what in hell they were doing. Bill was a very thorough man. I admired him and liked him; he was brilliant; and I helped him along. You know, he used to get awfully drunk in front of [our office at] 50 Broad, and a couple of boys and myself would go down and pick him up. I had a big office, and we'd put him on the couch and let him dry out."

Said Hirshhorn, others on Wall Street were down on Bill because of his drinking — because of his making promises to lots of people and then, after a few days, getting cockeyed again. "He would fall in the street or fall in the lobby of a building. It was very embarrassing to them.''

By 1933, Hirshhorn said, he was probably one of the few people on Wall Street who would still have anything to do with Bill. But his dealings with Bill were profitable: "He gave me a report on one stock that went from $20 to about two hundred and some odd dollars," Hirshhorn said.

Their association finally came to an end that year, when Bill followed Hirshhorn to Toronto, where Hirshhorn was launching the mining ventures that would make him one of the country's richest men. After some difficulty at the border for being drunk (probably the incident described by Clint), Bill did finally arrive in Toronto, where he stayed in Hirshhorn's suite at the Royal York. But he did little work and soon had to be sent home.

The connection with Hirshhorn was Bill's last chance on Wall Street.

Bill and Lois continued to live at 182 Clinton Street, in the apartment Dr. Burnham had built for his wife on the second floor. The doctor, who had remarried in May of 1933, had moved out. Lois continued to work at Macy's, where her weekly salary in 1933 was $22.50 plus a one percent commmission on sales.

This was the darkest period of their life together. "Sometimes I stole from my wife's slender purse when the morning terror and madness were on me. Again I swayed dizzily before an open window, or the medicine cabinet where there was poison, cursing myself for a weakling. There were flights from city to country and back, as my wife and I sought escape. Then came the night when the physical and mental torture was so hellish I feared I would burst through my window, sash and all. . . . A doctor came with a heavy sedative. . . . People feared for my sanity. So did I.''

There were still times when Bill would go on the wagon or make other determined efforts to stop drinking. Once, Lois obtained a three-month leave of absence from Macy's, and they spent the summer at the Vermont farm of Dr. Leonard Strong

Jr. and his wife, who was Bill's sister Dorothy. All summer, Bill worked hard on the farm. But as soon as they returned to Brooklyn, he resumed drinking. He and Lois had long discussions about it; he was making a desperate effort to quit.

By late 1933, they both were losing hope; all efforts had failed; and they had been particularly disillusioned when he had started drinking again after the summer at the farm. Besides Lois and her father, Bill now had only two other people who still stood by him: his sister Dorothy and her husband, who, like Bill's mother, was an osteopath. Often, Dr. Strong would treat Bill for his terrible hangovers, and they would discuss Bill's problems.

It was Leonard who finally arranged for Bill's admission to Charles B. Towns Hospital on Central Park West, a facility for treating alcoholics. In 1933, it was very expensive, and Leonard paid the fee.

Towns was run by Dr. William Duncan Silkworth, the man who would have such a profound influence on Bill. "As I came out of the fog that first time, I saw him sitting by the bedside. A great, warm current of kindness and understanding seemed to flow out of him. I could deeply feel this at once, though he said scarcely a word. He was very slight of figure and then pushing 60, I should say. His compassionate blue eyes took me in at a glance. A shock of pure white hair gave him a kind of otherworldly look. At once, befuddled as I was, I could sense he knew what ailed me."

---

1. It was estimated that more than a million Americans held stock on margin during the summer of 1929. See Frederick Lewis Allen, "Only Yesterday," Harper and Brothers, 1931, pages 309-337.

Chapter Five

In the autumn of 1933, when Bill found himself in Towns Hospital for the first time, the affliction of alcoholism was generally viewed as a mystery and a terrible shame. An alcoholic could expect to receive little understanding or compassion; while some called alcoholism a sin, others viewed it as willful misconduct and gave their assent to laws that sent alcoholics to prison for "habitual drunk" convictions. The country had even suffered through a wrenching experiment with national Prohibition in an effort to curb drunkenness by banning liquor. Ironically, it was during those Prohibition years that Bill, Dr. Bob, and other A.A. pioneers did their heaviest drinking.[1]

Experts generally agree that the consumption of alcohol probably decreased during Prohibition. Deaths from cirrhosis of the liver decreased. However, because of the enormous bootlegging, smuggling, and other illegal operations that were responses to Prohibition, "the noble experiment" was counted a failure.

Towns Hospital, at 293 Central Park West, New York

City, had been a fashionable and expensive facility for treating alcoholics in the 1920's; Bill remembered it as being one of the more reputable of such places. He recalled its owner, Charles B. Towns: a tall man, perfectly proportioned, and something of a physical prodigy. "He radiated an animal vitality that hit people like a ton of bricks. He was a great believer in gymnastics, spending about two hours a day in the New York Athletic Club himself."

When Bill described Towns as "a nationally known hospital for the mental and physical rehabilitation of alcoholics," he was not exaggerating, but someone else who remembered the hospital described it simply as a place where alcoholics were "purged and puked." The purging was most probably the effect of the liberal doses of castor oil that the patients were given, together with belladonna. The belladonna treatment at Towns had been developed by Dr. Sam Lambert, a reputable New York physician, but it was the chief of staff, Dr. Silkworth, who would in time to come have the most impact on the treatment of alcoholism.

A graduate of Princeton, William Duncan Silkworth had a medical degree from the New York University-Bellevue Medical School. Silkworth became a specialist in neurology, a domain that sometimes overlaps with psychiatry. As a private practitioner, he acquired a "small competence" in the 1920's and invested it in a stock subscription for a new private hospital. This investment carried with it the promise of a fine staff post for himself. But everything — including his savings — was swept away in the 1929 collapse.

"In desperation, he made a connection with Towns Hospital. The pay was pitiful, something like $40 a week and board, I think." But, Bill said, Silkworth's arrival at Towns Hospital in 1930 was the turning point in the doctor's life. "He told me how, seeing the miserable wreckage that floated through the place, he had resolved to try to do something about it. Even to me, he admitted the great hopelessness of the situation so far as most of

those afflicted went.'' But there were certain cases that showed
hope of recovery, and Silkworth glowed as he told Bill about
them. The little doctor had forgotten all about fame and fortune.
''What could he do about alcoholism? That was the thing. All
those millions with that mysterious malady of mind, emotions,
and body.''

When Bill arrived, Dr. Silkworth had already formulated
his theory of an ''allergy.'' Later, in a 1937 article in the *Medical
Record,* ''Alcoholism as a Manifestation of Allergy,'' he likened
the alcoholic's allergic state to the plight of the hay fever patient
who gradually becomes sensitized to certain types of pollen.

Dr. Silkworth described his theory as follows: ''We believe
. . . that the action of alcohol on . . . chronic alcoholics is a manifestation of an allergy; that the phenomenon of craving is limited to
this class and never occurs in the average temperate drinker.[2]
These allergic types can never safely use alcohol in any form at
all; and once having formed the habit and found they cannot
break it, once having lost their self-confidence, their reliance
upon things human, their problems pile up on them and become
astonishingly difficult to solve.''

Bill listened, entranced, as Silkworth explained his theory.
For the first time in his life, Bill was hearing about alcoholism not
as a lack of willpower, not as a moral defect, but as a legitimate
illness. It was Dr. Silkworth's theory — unique at the time —
that alcoholism was the combination of this mysterious physical
''allergy'' and the compulsion to drink; that alcoholism could no
more be ''defeated'' by willpower than could tuberculosis. Bill's
relief was immense.

It was not only the doctor's unusual theory that impressed
Bill; it was also his obvious love for people, his special way of
caring. ''In his lifetime, the doctor was to talk to 50,000 cases of
alcoholism. But not a one was a case; they were all human be-

*Towns Hospital, New York City, was the scene of Bill's spiritual
awakening and later attempts to sober up drunks.*

ings. Each one was something very special. I instantly perceived this. He had a way of making me feel that my recovery meant everything to him, it mattered so·much. Not a great M.D., this man, but a very great human being.''

Now, Bill was sure he had finally found the answer to his drinking problem. ''I left Towns Hospital a new man, or at least so I thought. Never shall I forget the first courage and joy that surged in me as I opened the door to enter 182 Clinton Street, Brooklyn. I embraced Lois; our union was renewed; her color was so much better; her step elastic. Visiting me each night at the hospital, she had seen my courage and spirit on the mend, and she, too, had talked to the doctor. This was *it*. Of that, we were both certain.''

Because he now understood what it was about, because he now knew that he was an alcoholic and could not safely take one

Bill's final discharge slip from Towns Hospital in 1934.

drink, Bill believed that he had found his salvation. Self-knowledge dictated total abstinence, and now that he knew it — why, the problem was solved! Lois, too, believed they had whipped the problem. "She had got in flowers for the house. There were all the things that I loved to eat. She rattled on about the wonderful weekends we would soon have. How we'd go camping on the Palisades. Maybe we'd hire a rowboat at Yonkers as we once did. Cut saplings for spars; hoist on these a bath towel, as once upon a time we sailed free before the wind. She'd got together all sorts of games, silly little things. We'd play them again, and be happy children. Yes, life would begin again, and oh, how deeply we both believed it."

How long Bill stayed sober is unclear; he thought it was two to four months; Lois thought it was "a month or so." He later believed that his memory of the time was clouded by the devastating disillusionment that came when he drank again. His return to drinking was also a great disappointment to Silkworth, because he had sensed Bill's strong desire to recover, and because Bill had responded so well to treatment.

Back the Wilsons went to the country, but the second time was not nearly so good as the first. Lois, lacking the nerve to ask for a second leave of absence from Macy's, quit her job in March 1934 in order to take Bill away.

On Bill's first day of fishing in Vermont, he found a man with a bottle. The man, of course, was generous, and Bill was off again.

He had to go to Brattleboro to get his teeth fixed. Because they had no car, he took the mail coach, the only alternative form of transportation. Instead of paying the dentist, Bill bought a bottle, which he shared with the driver on the way home. This happened for a number of weeks in a row. On a day when Bill was the only passenger, the driver, to show his appreciation, drove him up the long steep driveway from the highway to the house. The frost in the ground was thawing; the coach was soon stuck in the mud; and it had to be pulled out by the neighbor's horses.

Then, Lois pulled a ligament in her knee and was laid up for three weeks. During this time, Bill waited on her hand and foot. This caused her double agony as she lay helpless on the sofa and watched Bill, tipsy, carry a lighted kerosene lamp, slanting this way and that, up the steep stairs under the roof. One misstep, and the house would have gone up in flames.

When Bill's teeth were fixed, he stopped going to Brattleboro and therefore stopped buying liquor. After that, he grew sober and became a good companion. The rest of their stay was a success. He wrote several articles on finance and economics but, typically, never did send them to a publisher.

By the time summer came and they both felt stronger, they decided to go back to the city. They also had to make some money.

Lois described the consequences of their return: "Not long after we reached Clinton Street, my husband, who had been my daily companion in Vermont, became a drunken sot who didn't dare leave the house for fear the Brooklyn hoods or the police would get him."

Bill wound up in Towns for the second time; but upon leaving, he had none of the self-confidence that had followed his first departure. He now realized that nothing could keep him from what he would later call the "insidious insanity" of taking the first drink.

Terror, self-hatred, and suicidal thoughts became his constant companions. In a state of continual torture, physical and emotional, Bill was insane with alcoholism. Death seemed to him the only escape from his agony; again and yet again, he contemplated suicide — by poison, by jumping out the window. Accounts differ as to whether it was he or Lois who dragged the mattress downstairs so that he could sleep where an upstairs window would not tempt him to jump. He would make an "im-

Dr. William D. Silkworth, "the little doctor who loved drunks," convinced Bill that alcoholism is a disease.

mense exertion to achieve sobriety. I'd work through hangover after hangover, only to last four or five days, or maybe one or two. In the night hours, I was filled with horror, for snaky things infested the dark. Sometimes by day, queer images danced on the wall. Lois would nurse me through the hangovers.''

By midsummer 1934, he was back in Towns. ''I think my brother-in-law, Leonard Strong, was of special aid on this occasion,'' Bill said. ''I was three or four days regaining any semblance of my faculties. Then depression set in.

''One hot summer night, Lois came to see me and afterward had a talk with the doctor. Downstairs, she began to ask him the questions that wives of alcoholics must have posed time out of mind: 'How bad is this? Why can't he stop? What's become of the tremendous willpower he once had? Where, oh where, doctor, are we heading?' And finally: 'What's to be done now? Where do we go from here?'

''The little man was, of course, used to questions like these. They were asked of him every day. But as he later told me, they always hurt. It was so hard to tell the stark truth. But, in his gentle way, the old man finally told her. 'I thought at first that Bill might be one of the exceptions. Because of his very great desire to quit, because of his character and intelligence, I thought he might be one of the very few. But this habit of drinking has now turned into an obsession, one much too deep to be overcome, and the physical effect of it on him has also been very severe, for he's showing signs of brain damage. This is true even though he hasn't been hospitalized very much. Actually, I'm fearful for his sanity if he goes on drinking.'

''Then,'' said Bill, ''Lois asked, 'Just what does this mean, doctor?'

''The old man slowly replied, 'It means that you will have to confine him, lock him up somewhere if he would remain sane, or even alive. He can't go on this way another year, possibly.'

''This was my sentence, though neither of them told me in so many words,'' Bill recalled. ''But I didn't need to be told. In my heart, I knew it. This was the end of the line. I became far more frightened and confused and mystified than ever. For long hours, I thought over my past life. How and why could I have come to this? Save for my drinking, Lois and I had had a wonderful life together. My whole career had teemed with excitement and interest. And yet here I was, bedeviled with an obsession that condemned me to drink against my will and a bodily sensitivity that guaranteed early insanity at best.

"This time, I left the hospital really terror-stricken. By dint of the greatest vigilance, I stayed sober some weeks. By taking extreme care to expose myself to suggestions, by going over and over again Dr. Silkworth's advice and admonitions, I kept on steering clear. Gradually, the weeks lengthened into months. Little by little, I took heart again. I even went to Wall Street and fell into a few small deals that brought home a little cash. The badly shattered confidence of a friend or two over there began to be restored. Things looked better, a lot better."

Bill was to have one last great battle with booze. It would be a running, bruising battle. It started on Armistice Day.

"The fright was getting hazier. I didn't have to exert myself so much to resist. I began to talk to people about alcoholism, and when offered drinks, I would give the information to them as a defense and also as a justification for my former condition. Confidence was growing.

"Armistice Day, 1934, rolled around. Lois had to go to the Brooklyn department store where she worked. Wall Street was closed down, and I began to wonder what I would do. I thought of golf. I hadn't played in a long time. The family purse was slender, so I suggested to Lois that I might go over to Staten Island, where there was a public course. She couldn't quite conceal her apprehension, but managed to say cheerfully, 'Oh, please do. That would be wonderful.' I soon crossed on the ferry and found myself seated on the bus beside a man with a flying-target rifle. That brought back memories of that Remington single-shot piece my grandfather had given me when I was 11 years old. We started talking about shooting.

"Suddenly, a bus behind us collided with the one we were in. There wasn't any great shock, neither too much damage. My friend and I alighted on the pavement to wait for the next one to come along. Still talking about shooting irons, we noticed something that looked like a speakeasy. He said to me, 'What about a little nip?'

"I said to him, 'Fine, let's go.' We walked into the place. He ordered a Scotch. With ease, I ordered ginger ale.

" 'Don't you drink?' he said.

" 'No,' I said.' I'm one of those people who can't manage it.' And then, I dwelt on the allergy and the obsession, among other things. I told him all about the terrible time I'd had with liquor and how I was through with it forever. Very carefully, I explained the whole illness to him.

"Soon, seated in another bus, we were presently deposited in front of a country inn quite well down the island. I was to go to the golf course nearby; he was to take another bus to the rifle range. But it was noontime, so he said, 'Let's go in and have a sandwich. Besides, I'd like to have a drink.' We sat at the bar this time. As I have said, it was Armistice Day. The place was filling up, and so were the customers. That familiar buzz which rises from drinking crowds filled the room. My friend and I continued our talk, still on the subject of shooting. Sandwiches and ginger ale for me, sandwiches and another drink for him.

"We were almost ready to leave when my mind turned back again to Armistice Day in France — all the ecstasy of those hours. I remembered how we'd all gone to town. I no longer heard what my friend was saying. Suddenly, the bartender, a big, florid Irishman, came abreast of us beaming. In each hand he held a drink. 'Have one on the house, boys,' he cried. 'It's Armistice Day.' Without an instant's hesitation, I picked up the liquor and drank it.

"My friend looked at me aghast. 'My God, is it possible that you could take a drink after what you just told me? You must be crazy.'

"And my only reply could be this: 'Yes, I am.'

"The next morning about five o'clock, Lois found me unconscious in the areaway of 182 Clinton Street. I'd fallen against the door, was bleeding heavily from a bad scalp wound. My hand still clutched the strap of the golf bag. As I regained consciousness, nothing much was said. Indeed, there wasn't anything to say. We both hit an all-time low."

After the Armistice Day fiasco, Bill settled hopelessly and without heart into a sort of bottomless bingeing. He no longer made any pretense of going out, save to replenish his supply. He could barely eat; he was 40 pounds underweight. He passed the time drinking and writing vituperative or sarcastic letters to V.I.P.'s whose policies he disapproved of. Politicians were his favorite targets, most particularly President Roosevelt.

Thus Bill on a bleak November morning in 1934 when the telephone rang. He picked up the receiver and heard the familiar voice of his good old drinking buddy Ebby T. They had last seen each other five years earlier, when together they had "opened" the Manchester airport.

Ebby was in New York. He had heard about Bill's latest difficulty. Could he come to Brooklyn to see Bill?

Two nights later, Ebby and Bill were sitting at the kitchen table at 182 Clinton Street. A pitcher of gin and pineapple juice stood between them, but Bill was drinking alone. (Bill had no great love for pineapple juice with his gin, but he thought it would be less upsetting to Lois than if she came home and found them drinking straight gin!)

Ebby looked different; there was a new way about him; Bill noticed it the moment he greeted his friend at the door. Bill, secretly glad that he would not have to share his precious gin, was also surprised. His curiosity aroused, he asked, "Ebby, what on earth has got into you? What is this all about?"

Looking directly at Bill across the table, Ebby replied, "I've got religion."

Bill later said that Ebby might as well have hit him in the

face with a wet mop. "Getting religion" was the last thing that interested Bill — though he had made an attempt to study Christian Science a few years earlier to help him strengthen his willpower.

Ebby's religion was obviously working, however. The last Bill had heard of Ebby was that he was about to be committed to the state asylum at Brattleboro. Instead, here he was in Bill's own kitchen, sober and showing a confidence he hadn't displayed in years. Bill had to know more.

What Ebby told Bill that night was a dramatic, almost incredible story.

During most of the five years since Bill and Ebby had taken their famous plane ride into the new Manchester airport, Ebby, like Bill, had been deteriorating. "Several times in Albany, I had been reprimanded by the local authorities [for] drinking too much," he said. "My brother was a prominent man in town and I wasn't doing him any good. So in the fall of 1932, I took off for Manchester and lived in the Battenkill Inn for about two years. And of course, the drinking went on up there just the same."

The inn's owner was concerned about Ebby. Just before Christmas, he sent Ebby and his own son up to one of the local lumber company's vacant cabins on the mountain — to work around the place and help improve the Green Mountain Trail. "We did some rabbit hunting with the hounds, went out and cut trails, and some of the boys would come up weekends with us," Ebby recalled. "There was no liquor up there, although on the way up, I had two pints of gin which I consumed the first night, and that was all I had."

He stayed in the mountains for six months, sober the entire time. Returning to Manchester, he continued sober for another two or three months, "when I again fell off the wagon." In the meantime, his friend the innkeeper had died of a heart attack.

Ebby moved to a tourist camp and then, at the request of one of his brothers, reopened his family home. Most of the furniture was gone, but he was able to fix up his own boyhood bedroom, and there he stayed, "doing a lot of drinking, living alone and moodily brooding, thinking of things all the time."

He had reason to brood. The family money had given out, and the empty house was a sad reminder of what had once been. Perhaps in an attempt to restore things to their former condition, he decided to paint the house. "We had a good-sized ladder there, but I was so shaky from drinking, I couldn't do it. It was all right on the first three or four rungs of the ladder, but from then on up, I couldn't do a thing."

In July of 1934, while Ebby was trying to complete his painting job, some friends came to see him. "They had heard things were bad with me," Ebby recalled. "I had already gotten in a brush with the law a couple of times, fined five dollars for each occasion. I was told if I was arrested a third time for intoxication, it might go hard on me — six months in Windsor Prison."

Two of Ebby's visitors, Shep and Cebra, had once done considerable drinking with Ebby. But this time, they "told me that they had run into the Oxford Group and had gotten some pretty sensible things out of it based on the life of Christ, Biblical times," Ebby said. "It was really more of a spiritual than it was a religious movement. I listened to what they had to say, and I was very much impressed, because it was what I had been taught as a child and what I inwardly believed but had laid aside."

It was the experience of Ebby's third visitor, Rowland H., that made the deepest impression on Ebby. Rowland was of a prominent Rhode Island family, mill owners. He later became senior director of a chemical company. "I was very much impressed by his drinking career, which consisted of prolonged sprees, where he traveled all over the country. And I was also very impressed by the fact that he was a good guy. The first day he came to see me, he helped me clean up the place. Things were a mess, and he helped me straighten it up, and he stuck by me from beginning to end."

Rowland had been so concerned about his own drinking

that he went to Switzerland to place himself under the care of Carl Jung, the psychiatrist. He was treated by Jung for about a year, but when he left Jung, he soon got drunk. He returned to Jung for further treatment, but was told that it would be useless. In Jung's opinion, the only thing that could now help free Rowland from his addiction was a "spiritual awakening." When Rowland protested that he already believed in God, Jung replied that belief was not enough; in order to have the vital religious experience that he, Jung, believed was necessary, he suggested that Rowland ally himself with a religious movement. Rowland, impressed by the simplicity of the early Christian teachings as advocated by the Oxford Group, became a member and through that alliance found the sobriety he had sought so long and so hard.

Rowland, said Ebby, had had a thorough indoctrination (in the Oxford Group teachings). "He passed as much of this on to me as he could. We would sit down and try to rid ourselves of any thoughts of the material world and see if we couldn't find out the best plan for our lives for that day and to follow whatever guidance came to us."

Rowland impressed upon him the four principles of the Oxford Group: absolute honesty, absolute purity, absolute unselfishness, absolute love. "He was particularly strong in advocating absolute honesty," Ebby said. "Honesty with yourself, honesty with your fellowman, honesty with God. And these things he followed himself, and thereby, by example, he made me believe in them again as I had as a young man."

Ebby was able to complete the house-painting job with the help of a local contractor (probably paid by Ebby's brother). When it was finished, Ebby had nothing to do. "I went right back to the bottle," he said.

"One day, it was raining hard, and I happened to look out and saw four or five pigeons that had lighted on the roof. I didn't like that — a new paint job — so I got the old double-barreled shotgun and walked out. It was very slippery on the grass; it had been raining hard. I sat down, and from that position, I started blazing away at the pigeons. The neighbors didn't like it, and they complained to somebody. So the next day, they were down looking for me, but I was sound asleep and they couldn't get in.''

Arrested the following day, Ebby was taken to court in Bennington, and ordered to appear again the following Monday. It was at this point that Rowland H. interceded and told the judge that he, Rowland, would be responsible for Ebby.

With Rowland's help, Ebby closed up the family house in Manchester. For a while, he was a guest at Rowland's home in Shaftsbury, 15 miles south of Manchester, and then came to New York City, where he stayed with Shep for a while and then went to live with one of the "brotherhood" who ran Calvary Episcopal Mission on 23rd Street. It was while he was staying there and working with the Oxford Group that he heard of Bill's desperate situation.

Bill listened intently as Ebby talked about the change that had come into his life. As Bill remembered it, Ebby especially emphasized the idea that he had been hopeless. "He told me how he had got honest about himself and his defects, how he'd been making restitution where it was owed, how he'd tried to practice a brand of giving that demanded no return for himself," Bill said. "Then, very dangerously, he touched upon the subject of prayer and God. He frankly said he expected me to balk at these notions." But Ebby went on to say that when he had attempted prayer, even experimentally, the result had been immediate: Not only had he been released from his desire to drink — something very different from being on the water wagon — he had also found peace of mind and happiness of a kind he had not known for years.

Ebby had told his story simply, without hint of evangelism. Although Bill continued to drink, Ebby's visit caused something to change inside him. "The good of what he said stuck so well that in no waking moment thereafter could I get that man and his message out of my head," he recalled. He found himself talking about Ebby's visit with Lois when she came home from work.

As the days passed, Bill continued to drink — and to engage in endless interior dialogue with himself. He admitted to himself that an unsparing inventory made sense, however difficult such honesty might be. But Ebby's talk about God contradicted everything Bill believed. Bill remembered moments of great spiritual intensity — the experience at Winchester Cathedral was one — but he could not accept what was taught by the world's organized religions.

The one fact that he could not deny — and could not escape — was that Ebby was sober, while he, Bill, was drunk.

A few days later, Ebby returned, and he brought Shep C. with him. Shep, an active Oxford Group member, delivered himself of a forthright message — as Bill put it: ''He gave me the Oxford Group's boast, aggressively and with all the punch he could pack. I didn't like this at all. When they were gone, I took to the bottle and really punished it.'' He secretly wondered how much of a drinker Shep had really been.[3]

For Bill, the turning point came one afternoon in early December. In a maudlin, self-pitying mood, he decided to make his own investigation of Ebby's mission on 23rd Street. He got off the subway far from the mission, and had to pass a number of bars on his way there. So he had to make a number of stops, and nightfall found him drinking with a Finn named Alec. ''He said he'd been a sailmaker in the old country, and a fisherman, too,'' Bill recalled. ''Somehow, that word 'fisherman' clicked. I remembered the mission. Over there, I would find 'fishers of men.' It seemed like a wonderful idea.''

Bill's destination was 246 East 23rd Street, near the southwest corner of Second Avenue. It was a rescue mission operated by Dr. Sam Shoemaker's Calvary Church, at Fourth Avenue (now called Park Avenue South) and East 21st Street, near Gramercy Park. The church also operated a more respectable hostel called Calvary House, next to the church itself, but it was the one on 23rd Street that was aimed at helping the down-and-outer. (Between 1926 and 1936, more than 200,000 men are said to have visited the mission.) The homeless men who were housed and fed there called themselves "the brotherhood" — a term that Ebby himself used.

Billy D., a brotherhood member who was assistant superintendent at the mission, remembered Bill's visit:

"On the day that Bill Wilson called at Calvary Mission, Spoons Costello was in the kitchen and more or less in charge, as I was out all afternoon. He came in two or three times that afternoon, asking for [Ebby] T——. Spoons told me about him when I arrived about suppertime, which was at 5:00 p.m. each weekday. Spoons told me a tall fellow, wearing an expensive suit of clothes, very drunk, accompanied by a down-and-out, came in and each time made too much noise for Spoons to permit him to stay. Spoons, at that time, was our cook."

As for Bill's "expensive" suit, he did have a Brooks Brothers suit that Lois's mother had found at a rummage sale. This was 1934; it was the Depression; and the place was a mission for indigents.

Billy continued:

"I asked Spoons if he had told the fellow about the meeting each evening. He said he had. When the meeting started, Bill was downstairs in the chapel, accompanied by J——, a Swede who, judging by his clothes, had been on the bum for some time.[4] John Geroldsek, one of the brothers who lived outside the mission, was on the platform and in charge of the meeting. The brotherhood took turns at conducting the meetings, selecting the Bible lesson, the hymns, and then leading off with their own testimony. Geroldsek had just finished the Bible and started to witness when Bill got up from the audience or congregation and started down the aisle toward the platform."

Bill remembered that Tex Francisco, an ex-drunk, was there when he and Alec arrived. "He not only ran the mission. He proposed to run us out of it," Bill said. "This made me very sore, when we thought of our good intentions.

"Just then, Ebby turned up, grinning like a Cheshire cat. He said, 'What about a plate of beans?' After the beans, Alec and I were both clearer. Ebby said that there would be a meeting in the mission pretty soon. Would we like to come? Sure, we'd go. That's why we were there. The three of us were soon sitting on one of the hard wooden benches that filled the place. I shivered a little as I looked at the derelict audience. I could smell sweat and alcohol. What the suffering was, I pretty well knew.

"There were hymns and prayers. Tex, the leader, exhorted us. Only Jesus could save, he said. Certain men got up and made testimonials. Numb as I was, I felt interest and excitement rising. Then came the call. Penitents started marching forward to the rail. Unaccountably impelled, I started, too, dragging Alec with me. Ebby reached for my coattails, but it was too late.

"Soon, I knelt among the sweating, stinking penitents. Maybe then and there, for the very first time, I was penitent, too. Something touched me. I guess it was more than that. I was hit. I felt a wild impulse to talk. Jumping to my feet, I began.

"Afterward, I could never remember what I said. I only know that I was in earnest and people seemed to pay attention. Afterward, Ebby, who had been scared to death, told me with relief that I had done all right and had given my life to God."

Billy D. remembered the incident somewhat differently:

"When Bill started down the aisle, I was sitting in the rear with the brotherhood men who were present. We seated the new men on the right side of the hall. By new men, I mean those that had not been cleaned up. Since Bill was accompanied by J——, his pal, he was seated with the group on the right. I asked two of the brotherhood to go down and ask him to sit down. He shrugged them off and walked to the front of the room near the platform. Geroldsek was getting mad at the interruption. [He] was a heavy-set man and by trade a house painter. I went down the aisle to the front and spoke to Bill. I asked him to sit down. He said no, he would not. He had been trying to say something in this place all day, and no one was going to stop him now. Seeing that I couldn't quiet him, I asked Geroldsek to sit down and let Wilson talk.

"I [then] told Bill we usually had the witnessing from the platform first, then opened the meeting so that anyone could witness from the floor, but seeing he was determined, we would open the meeting right away, and he could say what was on his mind.

"Bill told us he had been at Calvary Church the previous night and saw Ebby T. get up in the pulpit and give witness to the fact that with the help of God, he had been sober for a number of months. Bill said that if Ebby T. could get help here, he was sure he needed help and could get it at the mission also. When the invitation was given at the close, Bill and J——went forward and knelt down. When they got up, I suggested that J——go upstairs, but since Bill looked prosperous in contrast to our usual mission customer, it was agreed that he go to Towns, where Ebby T. and others of the [Oxford] Group could talk to him.''

But Bill was not quite ready. He drank on for another two or three days. However, going to the mission had been more than a drunken impulse, and he pondered the experience. In the charged atmosphere of the meeting room, he had been aware of deep feelings. But again he fought those feelings, brushed them away; they went against both reason and education. Yet reason also told him that his illness had made him as helpless as a cancer victim. Had he had cancer, and had recovery involved praying with other sufferers at high noon in a public square, would he not have done so? What was so different about alcoholism? It was also a cancer of sorts. Certainly, it was destroying his mind and body — and soul, if there was such a thing. Not much difference, Bill admitted silently. He finally began to see his alcoholism clearly, as a helpless and hopeless condition.

He felt a strong desire to return to the hospital and to Dr. Silkworth. Leaving a note for Lois, he set out for Towns. He had only six cents, and that left a penny after the subway fare. Along the way, he managed to obtain four bottles of beer from a grocery store where he had a little credit. When he reached the hospital, he had finished three of the bottles. Dr. Silkworth met him in the hall.

Bill was in high spirits. Waving the bottle around, he announced that he had "found something." Silkworth remembered that Bill was carrying two books on philosophy, from which he hoped to get a new inspiration. It was December 11, 1934, a month to the day since he had started drinking again.

He received the then-current Towns treatment: barbiturates to sedate him and belladonna for reducing stomach acids.

As the effects of the alcohol wore away — it had not been one of his worst binges — he fell into deep depression and rebellion. He wanted the sobriety Ebby had found, but he couldn't believe in the God Ebby had talked about. His own feelings experienced at the mission had faded with the alcohol.

In a few days, Ebby visited him. Again, they talked as they had at the kitchen table. Ebby's visit made Bill momentarily less depressed, but after Ebby left, Bill slid into a very deep melancholy. He was filled with guilt and remorse over the way he had treated Lois, Lois who had stood by him unwavering throughout. He thought about the miraculous moments they had shared: standing on the Newport cliffs the night before he sailed for England, the camping trips, the wonderful years as motorcycle bums, the triumphs and failures on Wall Street. He thought about Winchester Cathedral, and the moment he had almost believed in God.

Now, he and Lois were waiting for the end. Now, there was nothing ahead but death or madness. This was the finish, the jumping-off place. "The terrifying darkness had become complete," Bill said. "In agony of spirit, I again thought of the cancer of alcoholism which had now consumed me in mind and spirit, and soon the body." The abyss gaped before him.

In his helplessness and desperation, Bill cried out, "I'll do anything, anything at all!" He had reached a point of total, utter deflation — a state of complete, absolute surrender. With neither faith nor hope, he cried, "If there be a God, let Him show Himself!''

What happened next was electric. "Suddenly, my room blazed with an indescribably white light. I was seized with an ecstasy beyond description. Every joy I had known was pale by comparison. The light, the ecstasy — I was conscious of nothing else for a time.

"Then, seen in the mind's eye, there was a mountain. I stood upon its summit, where a great wind blew. A wind, not of air, but of spirit. In great, clean strength, it blew right through me. Then came the blazing thought 'You are a free man.' I know not at all how long I remained in this state, but finally the light and the ecstasy subsided. I again saw the wall of my room. As I became more quiet, a great peace stole over me, and this was accompanied by a sensation difficult to describe. I became acutely conscious of a Presence which seemed like a veritable sea of living spirit. I lay on the shores of a new world. 'This,' I thought, 'must be the great reality. The God of the preachers.'

"Savoring my new world, I remained in this state for a long time. I seemed to be possessed by the absolute, and the curious conviction deepened that no matter how wrong things seemed to be, there could be no question of the ultimate rightness of God's universe. For the first time, I felt that I really belonged. I knew that I was loved and could love in return. I thanked my God, who had given me a glimpse of His absolute self. Even though a pilgrim upon an uncertain highway, I need be concerned no more, for I had glimpsed the great beyond.''

Bill Wilson had just had his 39th birthday, and he still had half his life ahead of him. He always said that after that experience, he never again doubted the existence of God. He never took another drink.

---

1. National Prohibition was in effect for 14 of Bill's years of drinking. It began on January 17, 1920, and ended on December 5, 1933.

2. Since Silkworth formulated his theory, many research projects have focused on hypotheses of metabolic and possibly genetic bases for a predisposition to alcoholism. For instance, in a study at Harvard Medical School, "The scientists have found, in the blood of males suffering from severe alcoholism, a substance that appears not to be produced by nonalcoholics in their metabolic disposal of alcohol." At the University of California at San Francisco, a study involving isolated brain cells led research-'ers to suspect "an abnormality in the cell membrane function of people predisposed ·to alcoholism."

3. Shep remembered the meeting with Bill. He said that he and Ebby had attended church, so they had had a "quiet time" together, an Oxford Group practice. In the quiet time, it came to Ebby that they ought to visit Bill. The only one of the three men who had a job, Shep took Ebby, Lois, and Bill to dinner in Manhattan.

4. The same man called "Alec the Finn."

Chapter Six

Now, doubt made its inevitable appearance. The experience had been too beautiful. Bill began to fear whether he had been hallucinating. He called for Dr. Silkworth.

Silkworth sat patiently by the bed as Bill told him what had happened. "It was all so incredible that I still feared to give him the full impact of it," Bill remembered. "But the essential facts, toned down somewhat, emotionally, I did relate to him." Bill finally asked the question that was nagging at his own mind: "Doctor, is this real? Am I still perfectly sane?"

Bill was always grateful for Silkworth's answer: "Yes, my boy, you are sane, perfectly sane in my judgment. You have been the subject of some great psychic occurrence, something that I don't understand. I've read of these things in books, but I've never seen one myself before. You have had some kind of conversion experience." Whatever the experience, he said, "You are already a different individual. So, my boy, whatever you've got now, you'd better hold on to. It's so much better than what had you only a couple of hours ago."

Coming from Silkworth, now a central figure in Bill's life, this evaluation meant everything. It put the seal on Bill's experience, making it acceptable to the part of his mind that had argued long and hard against the idea of God.

Ebby, who came to see him on the third day, was not quite prepared for Bill's description of what had happened — he himself had neither seen bright lights nor stood on a mountaintop. But he brought Bill a book that offered further clarification. It was William James's "The Varieties of Religious Experience." Ebby had not read the book, but it had been recommended by Oxford Group members.

Bill said he started reading the moment Ebby left. It was difficult going. James, a Harvard professor and a founding father of American psychology, had made a detailed analysis of a wide number of religious or conversion experiences. The material had first been developed for the Gifford Lecture series at Edinburgh in 1901 and 1902. "His was the keenest sort of insight, accompanied by a most sympathetic understanding," Bill remembered. James's objective was to show that these conversion experiences had validity and value.

As Bill read on, his own powers of reasoning helped him extract some important ideas from the weighty and intricate text. He saw that all the cases described by James had certain common denominators, despite the diverse ways in which they manifested themselves. These insights became important to Bill in his thinking about the plight of the alcoholic and his need for spiritual help. (He would later say that James, though long in his grave, had been a founder of Alcoholics Anonymous.) Of the three common denominators in the case histories, the first was calamity; each person James described had met utter defeat in some vital area of his life. All human resources had failed to solve his problems. Each person had been utterly desperate.

The next common point was admission of defeat. Each of the individuals acknowledged his own defeat as utter and absolute.

The third common denominator was an appeal to a Higher

Power. This cry for help could take many forms, and it might or might not be in religious terms.

The responses were equally varied. Some had thunderbolt experiences, as did St. Paul on the road to Damascus; others had slow, gradual transformation experiences. Whatever the type of the experience, however, it brought the sufferer into a new state of consciousness, and so opened the way to release from the old problems.

As Silkworth had given Bill the information he needed to understand his own alcoholism, James gave Bill the material he needed to understand what had just happened to him — and gave it to him in a way that was acceptable to Bill. Bill Wilson, the alcoholic, now had his spiritual experience ratified by a Harvard professor, called by some *the* father of American psychology!

How did Lois respond to Bill's new condition? When she came home and found his note saying that he had gone back to Towns, she was angry. Who was going to pay the bill? What good would it do anyway? He would get drunk again the minute he left. Such were her thoughts as she rode the subway to Towns.

Her questions were answered, she said, the minute she saw him. "I knew something overwhelming had happened," she recalled. "His eyes were filled with light. His whole being expressed hope and joy. From that moment on, I shared his confidence in the future."

And, at last, they did have a future. It was a miraculous ending to a bleak year, a year that had seen Bill hospitalized four times. The Depression had not loosened its iron grip; Bill's career was in ruins; they were not even certain how long they could continue to live at Clinton Street. But Bill and Lois were deeply awed by the powerful new idea that had changed their lives in a split second.

Even while the ecstasy of his mountaintop experience lingered, Bill pondered on why he had received such a gift of grace

— why he had been released, when countless sufferers before him "just deteriorated, went mad, and finally died. The difference between these cases and my own lay in my relation to my friend Ebby, himself a onetime-hopeless alcoholic. As a fellow sufferer, he could and did identify himself with me as no other person could. As a recent dweller in the strange world of alcoholism, he could, in memory, reenter it and stand by me in the cave where I was. Everybody else had to stand on the outside looking in. But he could enter, take me by the hand, and confidently lead me out." What's more, Bill said, "He was the living proof of all he claimed. Nothing theoretical or secondhand about this."

Reflecting, Bill realized that a vast number of alcoholics could recover by accepting the same ideas that Silky and Ebby had passed along to him. He began thinking about a movement of recovered alcoholics who would help others.[1]

"At this point, my excitement became boundless. A chain reaction could be set in motion, forming an ever-growing fellowship of alcoholics, whose mission it would be to visit the caves of still other sufferers and set them free. As each dedicated himself to carrying the message to still another, and those released to still others, such a society could pyramid to tremendous proportions. Why, it could reach every single alcoholic in the world capable of being honest enough to admit his own defeat." Visionary words, those, and prophetic.

His mind worked that way; he could grasp the potential of an idea that seemed insignificant to others. On Wall Street, he had consistently shown ability to look into the future, to see growth opportunities in apparently ordinary situations. He had an entrepreneur's mind and imagination; he was stimulated by the challenge of developing what was new and different.

Those attributes were now coupled with the spiritual side of Bill's nature. Always generous, he wanted to help others receive what had been so freely given to him. One might say that the best qualities of the Griffiths — perseverance, imaginativeness, and innovativeness — now combined with the best qualities of the

Wilsons — caring, gregariousness, humanitarianism, and generosity — to form William Griffith Wilson's most magnificent
ambition.

After Bill's release from Towns on December 18, he and
Lois started attending Oxford Group meetings at Calvary
House, adjacent to Calvary Episcopal Church. The rector, Dr.
Sam Shoemaker, was a leading figure in the Oxford Group. In
time, Bill would come to regard this man as one of his closest
personal friends.

It started well for the Wilsons. At the Oxford Group meetings, they found a kind of enthusiasm and friendship that Bill
described as "manna from heaven." (He and Lois were probably experiencing what many of today's sick alcoholics and their
spouses experience when they come to A.A. for the first time —
warmth, succor, and a feeling of at last "coming in from the
cold.") They were impressed and inspired by the Oxford
Group's success in helping people change their lives. "On the
platform and off, men and women, old and young, told how their
lives had been transformed," Bill recalled.

It appeared to Bill that social, class, and racial barriers were
almost nonexistent in the Oxford Group, and even religious differences had been forgotten. "Little was heard of theology, but
we heard plenty of absolute honesty, absolute purity, absolute
unselfishness, and absolute love" — the four principles of the
Oxford Group. "Confession, restitution, and direct guidance of
God underlined every conversation. They were talking about
morality and spirituality, about God-centeredness versus self-
centeredness."

This is how Bill summarized the group's origin and early
growth:

"The Oxford Group was a nondenominational evangelical
movement, streamlined for the modern world and then at the
height of its very considerable success. It had been founded ten
or a dozen years earlier by a Lutheran minister, Dr. Frank Buchman. Among his first converts had been Dr. Sam Shoemaker

and another clergyman, Sherry Day. They would deal in simple common denominators of all religions which would be potent enough to change the lives of men and women. They had hoped to set up a chain reaction — one person carrying the good news to the next. Their aim was world conversion. Everybody, as they put it, needed changing. They had made their first effort upon the Princeton campus among students.

"Agreeing with James in the New Testament, they thought people ought to confess their sins 'one to another.'[2] Heavily emphasizing this wholesale sort of personal housecleaning, they called the process 'sharing.' Not only were things to be confessed, something was to be done about them. This usually took the form of what they called restitution, the restoration of good personal relationships by making amends for harms done.

"They were most ardent, too, in their practice of meditation and prayer, at least one hour a day, and two hours would be better. They felt that when people commenced to adhere to these high moral standards, then God could enter and direct their lives. Under these conditions, every individual could receive specific guidance, which could inspire every decision and act of living, great or small. Following meditation and prayer, they practiced what they call a quiet time, asking God [for] specific directives. Pencil in hand, they wrote down what came into their minds; one could do this alone, with his family, or in the company of a like-minded group which was called a 'team.' Such a way of life was urged upon all comers. It was a very dynamic and sometimes a very aggressive evangelism."

By the time Rowland H. turned up among these good folk, in 1931, the Oxford Group had begun to receive worldwide attention. People in every level of society were interested; the group seemed to be able to cross denominational and social lines with ease. The enthusiasm and actual power of the society were

The Rev. Samuel Shoemaker helped lead early members toward the spiritual principles embodied in the Twelve Steps.

immense. In the early days of its existence, the movement was
called the First Century Christian Fellowship. (In the late
1930's, Dr. Bob, cofounder of A.A., and the other Akron, Ohio,
members continued to refer to it that way.) It became the Oxford
Group in 1928, and was renamed Moral Rearmament
(M.R.A.) in 1938.

Although Bill placed the origin of the Oxford Group at
about 1920, the seed had actually been planted in 1908 when
Frank Buchman, a native of Allentown, Pennsylvania, under-
went a remarkable spiritual transformation. Buchman, who had
been running a home for orphan boys in Philadelphia, resigned
following a bitter dispute with his trustees. Nursing his resentments, he sailed for England. There, in his unhappiness, he
drifted to a religious conference in Keswick, where an inspiring
sermon by a Salvation Army member had a profound effect on
him. He was changed so dramatically that he sat down and wrote
letters of amends to his former trustees, a step that brought him
great relief and joy. Sharing this experience with others, he soon
began to see personal spiritual change as a way of healing the
entire world.

Buchman served as a Y.M.C.A. secretary for a time; later,
he lectured on personal evangelism on college campuses. He was
a world traveler, and he and the people who gathered around
him carried the message to foreign countries. Sam Shoemaker,
Calvary's rector, had met Buchman in China in 1918.

According to Willard Hunter, a close associate, Buchman
was a physically unattractive man who believed that God had
made him ugly for a purpose. He had a talent for attracting and
inspiring others. He had a unique ability to draw people out by
sharing his own faults with them, and he could often sense what
was troubling others.

Buchman himself was never interested specifically in helping alcoholics, although in Akron, for instance, the Oxford
Group was known from its start as a program that could work
with drunks. But as Buchman put it: ''I'm all for the drunks'

being changed, but we also have drunken nations on our hands.'' At the time the Wilsons started going to meetings, the Oxford Group was on the crest of public opinion and notice.

In those early months of 1935, Bill Wilson preached the Oxford Group message to anybody who would listen. He spent long hours at Calvary Mission and at Towns, where Dr. Silkworth, at the risk of his professional reputation, gave Bill permission to talk with some of the patients. ''Burning with confidence and enthusiasm, I pursued alcoholics morning, noon, and night,'' Bill recalled.

Nor could the lure of Wall Street divert him from his new crusade: ''Though I made a few feeble efforts to get a job, these were soon forgotten in the excitement of the chase. Lois went on working at her department store, content with my new mission in the world.'' She had taken the job at Loeser's because it was not far from Clinton Street. There, the household grew to three; Ebby moved in for the first of several times. He eventually became an almost permanent guest.

In these exciting months of new sobriety, Bill did not recognize that, along with his sincere desire to help other alcoholics and to create something new, another motive was working in him. Mingled with his humanitarian instincts and his spirituality was the same driving ambition that had created Vermont's only boomerang maker. As Bill himself described it: ''I was soon heard to say that I was going to fix up all the drunks in the world, even though the batting average on them had been virtually nil for the last 5,000 years. The Oxford Groupers had tried, had mostly failed, and were fed up. Sam Shoemaker in fact had just had a run of bad luck. He had housed a batch of drunks in an apartment near his church, and one of them, still resisting salvation, had peevishly thrown a shoe through a fine stained-glass window in Sam's church.

''No wonder my Oxford Group friends felt that I had better forget about alcoholics. But I was still mighty cocksure, and I ignored their advice. Mine was a kind of twin-engine power drive consisting of one part of genuine spirituality and one part of my old desire to be a Number One man. This posture didn't pan out well at all. At the end of six months nobody had sobered up. And believe me, I had tried them by the score. They would clear up for a little while and then flop dismally. Naturally the Oxford Groupers became very cool indeed toward my drunk-fixing.''

An experience one Sunday evening made Bill feel that he was on the threshold of a real breakthrough. He was asked to speak at a large Oxford Group meeting in Calvary House. ''I told what I knew about alcoholism, and all about my wonderful spiritual experience. Before finishing, I saw a man in the second row. He had a very red face. All attention, he never took his eyes off me.''

The moment the meeting ended, the man rushed up and grabbed Bill by the lapels. He said he was an alcoholic, too, a chemistry professor who was barely managing to hold on to his teaching post. He had come to the Oxford Group at his wife's urging, but he could not stand their ''non-sensical'' talk about God, nor did he like ''all these aggressive people'' who were trying to save his soul. And while he could not accept Bill's ''weird'' religious experience, he certainly did agree with what Bill had said about alcoholism.

Bill invited the man, Fred, to join him and a small group of alcoholics who met at Stewart's Cafeteria in the neighborhood after the meetings. ''I was overjoyed. It looked like he was a surefire convert,'' Bill said. ''If talking from a platform would produce results like this, I ought to do more of it, I thought. I decided on the spot that I liked public speaking.''

Bill had a lot to learn. Although Fred B. became a good friend, he stayed drunk on and off for 11 years before finally getting sober in the A.A. program.

During the first months of 1935, Bill encountered one such frustration after another. In later years, he was to explain the failure as being one of method: During this period, he said, he was preaching to the drunks. Also, he still believed that an alcoholic required a spectacular spiritual experience, similar to his own, in order to recover. And he was hardly humble about the crusade he was on; while he did realize that working with other alcoholics gave him a tremendous lift, he did not realize that he actually needed the sick alcoholic.

It was Dr. Silkworth who helped straighten him out; Bill was preaching, said the doctor, and his preaching was driving his prospects away. He was talking too much about Oxford Group principles and about his own spiritual experience. Why not talk instead about the illness of alcoholism? Why not tell his alcoholics about the illness that condemned them to go mad or die if they continued to drink? "Coming from another alcoholic, one alcoholic talking to another, maybe that will crack those tough egos deep down," Silkworth said. "Only then can you begin to try out your other medicine, the ethical principles you have picked up from the Oxford Group."

The first opportunity to act upon Dr. Silkworth's advice came about in a strangely circuitous manner. Bill's reputation on Wall Street had been destroyed years earlier, and most of his former business associates remained skeptical about his new sobriety. But one friend, Howard Tompkins of Beer and Company, was impressed by his recovery and, in December 1934, sent him a glowing letter of encouragement.

Through his connection with Tompkins, Bill learned about a proxy fight for control of a small machine tool company in Akron, Ohio. According to Bill's own recollections, he "insinuated" himself into this proxy fight, and actually had fantasies of becoming president of the company when his group gained control. He made a quick study of the Akron company, then, in April, went out to Ohio to persuade disgruntled share-owners to support his group's bid for control.

Bill could not have "insinuated" himself had he not had the support, confidence, and cooperation of his business associates. Although he had no money, he did have assets of considerable value to such an undertaking: for one, the ability to quickly grasp the essentials of any business or industry.

The firm was National Rubber Machinery Company, builder of rubber curing presses and other equipment used in tire manufacturing. Its machines were used throughout the rubber industry. Founded in 1909 as Akron Rubber Mold and Machine Company, it had been reorganized in 1928 and combined with three other companies in related lines. But the company had gone through difficulties during the Depression; there was dissension in management and among the shareholders. At board meetings, directors squabbled continually among themselves.

As for Bill, he had one overriding objective: to rebuild his shattered career. Success in the proxy fight could restore his standing on Wall Street. Sobriety and success could mean a new, comfortable life for the Wilsons; Lois could leave the department store forever. Coming when it did, this opportunity must have seemed heaven-sent.

But even before Bill boarded the westbound train for Akron, the rival group in the proxy fight, headed by a man named Nils Florman, had recruited considerable support among N.R.M. shareholders, and Florman was trying to convince the company's wavering managers to join him.

Beer and Company held a number of proxies in its own accounts and among acquaintances. Bill and his associates spent several weeks in Akron tracking down shareholders and persuading some of the older company members to join them. As the solicitation of proxies continued, Bill began to feel the rising excitement of prospective victory. His group already had more support among shareholders than either the management or the other faction that was fighting for control. When Bill returned, briefly, to New York, he was elated; after years of defeat and failure, the door to success was again wide open. National Rubber Machinery would be the start. He might yet build the illustrious career he had envisioned years earlier, controlling vast enterprises which he would "manage with utmost assurance." After all, he was still only 39.

The fight was almost over; Bill and his associates were confident that they had enough proxies and sufficient shares in Beer accounts to take control of the company. A quick vote, a counting of the results, and then, in a hasty organization meeting immediately afterward, Bill Wilson would become an officer in the new company management. Lois could finally leave her job at Loeser's.

But Florman's group now executed a maneuver that caught the Beer team off guard. Allying themselves with management, they pooled their resources to pull in almost 60 percent of the votes. Some of those votes, clearly, had to be shares recently assigned to Bill's group; why had some shareholders switched their proxies? It was a nasty situation.

Vowing to fight on in the courts, Bill's associates returned to New York, leaving him alone in Akron to make a last effort to salvage the venture. He had little money, but they promised to support his efforts.

They left on a Friday, and Bill faced a solitary weekend in a strange city where he had just sustained a colossal disappointment. He had time on his hands and bitterness in his heart; fate had suddenly turned against him. His self-pity and resentment began to rise. He was lonely. He did not even have his colleagues as weekend company. Saturday noon found him pacing up and down the lobby of the Mayflower Hotel in extreme agitation, wondering how to pass the weekend. He had about ten dollars in his pocket.

Now began the personal crisis that was to set in motion a series of life-changing events for Bill. There was a bar at one end of the lobby, and Bill felt himself drawn to it. Should he have a ginger ale or two, perhaps scrape up an acquaintance? What could be the harm in that?

For almost anyone else, no harm. But for Bill Wilson, the alcoholic, the idea was loaded with danger. It was just such a delusion that had led to his Armistice Day drunk. For the first time in months, Bill had the panicky feeling of being in trouble.

In New York, he had kept himself sober for more than five months through working with other drunks at Towns and at Calvary Mission. The work had been his protection; it had kept him safe. Now he had nobody. As he recalled later, "I thought, 'You need another alcoholic to talk to. You need another alcoholic just as much as he needs you!' " It was this thought that led him to the church directory at the other end of the hotel lobby.

The directory was a listing of Akron's major churches and their ministers. A typical directory of that kind might have from 30 to 50 names. Bill looked over the names and, quite at random, singled out that of a Reverend Walter F. Tunks. He had no conscious reason for picking Tunks's name; it may have been because his favorite Vermont expression was "taking a tunk," which meant "taking a walk." Or perhaps he picked out Tunks because the minister was an Episcopalian like Sam Shoemaker. Lois thought it was because Bill liked funny names. Whatever Bill's reason, he unwittingly picked the strongest Oxford Grouper among all of Akron's clergymen.

With this choice, Bill scored what he liked to call a "ten strike." He asked for help to get in touch with a drunk to talk to. And Tunks never hesitated or paused when he heard Bill's odd request — never stopped to question the wisdom of giving a total stranger the names of ten people who might help direct him to "a drunk."

Bill called all ten, without getting the name of a single drunk. But one man, Norman Sheppard, knew a woman named Henrietta Seiberling, and even knew of the efforts she had been making to help a certain friend. "I have to go to New York tonight, but you call Henrietta Seiberling," Sheppard told Bill.

Bill balked at the idea of calling Mrs. Seiberling. The name was known to him, and he was afraid of it. It was the name of the Goodyear rubber people. Bill believed that Henrietta was the wife of Frank Seiberling, the entrepreneur who had built the Goodyear company and, after losing control of that firm, later formed the tire company bearing his name. Bill had even met Frank Seiberling during the halcyon years on Wall Street. As he remembered it, "I could hardly imagine calling up his wife and telling her that I was a drunk from New York looking for another drunk to work on."

He continued to pace up and down the lobby. Something kept telling him to call Mrs. Seiberling. He went back to his room and placed the call.

Henrietta Seiberling was not Frank Seiberling's wife; she was his daughter-in-law. She did not live in the grand, 65-room Seiberling mansion on Portage Path; she lived with her three young children in the gatehouse. (Her husband, from whom she was separated, lived in the mansion with his parents.)

As Henrietta later told it, Bill introduced himself over the telephone thus: "I'm from the Oxford Group and I'm a rum hound from New York."

Her silent reaction, she said, was: "This is really manna from heaven." Aloud, she said, "You come right out here."

It may seem remarkable that a woman alone with three teenage children would be so quick to invite a strange man into her home. But there was a strong bond of trust among Oxford Group members.

Henrietta Seiberling relied on God's guidance in her life. She was certain that the telephone call was the help she and other Oxford Group members had been seeking for one of their members. Only a few weeks earlier, the man had finally admitted to the group that he was a secret drinker, and Henrietta believed that as a result of his honesty, help would come for him in some form, some way. This visitor from New York might be that very help.

When Bill arrived, she made the telephone call to the man she had in mind. The man's name was Dr. Robert Smith. He was a physician. He was an alcoholic. And he was in desperate straits. After some telephone conversation with Anne, Dr. Smith's wife, it became obvious that help would have to be delayed. It was the day before Mother's Day, and the man had just come home bearing a potted plant for his wife. Then, potted himself, he had promptly passed out. So the meeting between the two men was arranged for the next afternoon, Mother's Day, in the gatehouse of the Seiberling mansion.

In retrospect, it all seems as though it had been divinely ordained. Even the locale was symbolic. The mansion was called Stan Hywet Hall, a Welsh name that means "Rock is found here."

---

1. Until this time, help had been brought to sufferers only by professionals and experts: doctor, minister, teacher, authority. In the vanguard of a new age, Bill foresaw the efficacy and effectiveness of "group" and "peer" support and therapy. In the years to come, this concept would find application to countless other problems in addition to alcoholism.

2. "Confess your faults one to another, and pray one for another, that ye may be healed." James 5:16, King James Version.

Chapter Seven

Dr. Bob, 55 years old at the time of their meeting, was about 15 years older than Bill. He, too, was a native Vermonter — from St. Johnsbury, about 75 miles north of East Dorset. As the only child of a prominent judge, he grew up in comfortable circumstances but chafed under the strict discipline of his early years.

Bob's drinking started while he was a student at Dartmouth College. He had a large capacity for alcohol during his undergraduate years, and by the time he was in medical school, drinking had become a problem. In fact, he dropped out of the University of Michigan during his second year because of drinking. Although he made up his work and did well in his exams, he was asked to leave the university. He completed his professional studies at Rush Medical School in Chicago. He almost failed to graduate from Rush; by his senior year, his drinking became so bad that he was unable to complete final exams and was obliged to attend school for two additional quarters — and to remain absolutely dry — in order to graduate.

Bob remained dry during a hard two years' internship at

Akron City Hospital, then opened an office in a downtown Akron office building. Both his scholarship and his professional work were commendable when he was sober.

Soon after opening his office, Dr. Bob started drinking again, and was eventually in such difficulty that his father in St. Johnsbury sent another doctor out to Akron to bring him home. Several months of rest and recuperation in Vermont enabled Bob to return to Akron and his medical practice. After a "whirlwind" 17-year courtship, he and Anne Ripley married in 1915, when Bob was 36. They bought a home, and in 1918 their first child, Bob, was born. Another child, Sue, was adopted.[1]

With the passage of Prohibition, Bob started drinking yet again. His rationale was that he was now safe, because soon there would be nothing available anyhow! He continued to drink heavily through the 1920's, and both his practice and his family life deteriorated. By the early 1930's, he and his family were desperate.

During this 17-year period, Dr. Bob had worked out a grim routine that permitted him to drink and somehow still maintain his medical practice. Careful never to go near the hospital while he was drinking, he would stay sober until four o'clock in the afternoon. "It was really a horrible nightmare, this earning money, getting liquor, smuggling it home, getting drunk, morning jitters, taking large doses of sedatives to make it possible for me to earn more money, and so on ad nauseam," he wrote. "I used to promise my wife, my friends, and my children that I would drink no more — promises which seldom kept me sober through the day, though I was very sincere when I made them."

In contrast with that way of life, the Oxford Group members were attractive to Dr. Bob because of their apparent "poise, health, and happiness. They spoke with great freedom from embarrassment, which I could never do," he wrote, "and they

Though the alcoholics finally split from the Oxford Group, that movement profoundly influenced the Fellowship.

S 'DINNER JACKET REVIVAL' WAS   BEGUN AT HOTEL MAYFLOWER LAST NIGHT

—*Times-Press Photo*

Russell Firestone, left, and Dr. Frank N. D. Buchman, before the meeting, at the left. At the right a scene as the dinner jacket revival meeting got under way. Mr. Firestone is speaking. Left to right are, Reginald A. E. Holme, Oxford; Sir Walter Windham, London; Rev. Walter F. Tunks, rector of St. Paul's Episcopal church, and Mr. Firestone.

❖ ❖ ❖

Oxford Group Hits Stride In Akron Modern Revival

Buchman and Followers Begin Personal Meetings Today in New-Style Evangelism; Score Will Fill Pulpits Sunday; Hundreds Throng First Session to Hear Converts

By DON STROUSE

The Oxford group of dinner jacket revivalists started about the serious business of winning Akron to Christ today after a whirlwind opening meeting last night that drew close to 3500 people to jam two improvised meeting houses.

"Personal evangelism"—one man talking to another or a woman discussing problems with another woman was the order of the day. The clergy of the city got together with Dr. Frank N. D. Buchman, founder of the group, to talk over things that bothered them, and about 400 women gathered in Hotel Mayflower ballroom for the first women's meeting.

Another public evening meeting will be held tonight in the tea room of the A. Polsky company. The overflow crowd that is expected will be cared for at the Y. W. C. A. auditorium, corner East Bowery and South High streets.

Fill Pulpits Sunday

Arrangements were made today for members of the group to fill two-score Akron pulpits at services Sunday morning and evening and separate men's and women's meetings were arranged for 3 p. m. Sunday. The women's meeting will at the Y. W. C. A. and the at the Y. M. C.
Under

seemed very much at ease on all occasions and appeared very healthy. . . . I was self-conscious and ill at ease most of the time, my health was at the breaking point, and I was thoroughly miserable.'' He said he gave their program much time and study, but got tight every night nevertheless.

At the time of his meeting with the ''rum hound from New York,'' Dr. Bob probably knew more than Bill did about Oxford Group principles. But that knowledge by itself was hardly sufficient to keep him sober, any more than Bill had been able to stay

Henrietta Seiberling greeted Bill's historic call as ''manna from heaven,'' and at once put him in touch with Dr. Bob.

sober without the benefit of Ebby's experience.

Dr. Bob later said that he could not remember ever feeling much worse than he did on the afternoon he met Bill. He had agreed to the meeting only because he was very fond of Henrietta, and Anne had already committed them to going. But he made Anne promise that they would stay only 15 minutes. "I didn't want to talk to this mug or anybody else, and we'd really make it snappy."

Accompanied by their 17-year-old son, Bob, the Smiths arrived at the Stan Hywet gatehouse at five o'clock. Bob announced immediately that they could stay only briefly.

"Though embarrassed, he brightened a little when I said I thought he needed a drink," Bill recalled. "After dinner, which he did not eat, Henrietta discreetly put us off in her little library. There, Bob and I talked until eleven o'clock."

What caused Dr. Bob to stay for the evening instead of fleeing, as planned? To begin with, he quickly realized that this Bill Wilson knew what he was talking about. Dr. Bob had read a great deal about alcoholism and had heard the opinions of fellow professionals who had treated alcoholics. But Bill was the first person he had talked with who knew from his own experience what alcoholism was. "In other words, he talked my language," said Bob. "He knew all the answers, and certainly not because he had picked them up in his reading."

It was not only personal experience that Bill shared that day. A vital part of his message was the medical view Dr. Silkworth had explained and had urged him to present to prospective "converts." (Ironic that Bob, a physician, should learn about alcoholism as an illness from Bill, a stockbroker. However, Dr. Bob's medical training may have helped him grasp what was then a radical concept.)

While Bill Wilson and Dr. Bob Smith hit it off from their very first talk at Henrietta's home, neither had any way of anticipating the monumental ramifications that would ensue from that encounter. At the moment, all Bill knew was that Henrietta seemed determined to keep him in Akron to help Dr. Bob, but that he, Bill, could not afford to stay any longer at the May-flower. She called a neighbor, John Gammeter, and asked him to put Bill up at the Portage Country Club, a few hundred yards south of the Seiberling estate on Portage Path.[2] Bill even played golf there that summer, sharing the fairways with some of Akron's wealthiest citizens.

Gammeter was just the kind of self-made man that Bill admired, like Edison, and like Joe Hirshhorn. The son of a washer-woman, Gammeter had (as Bill noted in a June letter to Lois) started at the B. F. Goodrich Company by pushing a wheelbar-row. He had then been assigned a job hand-trimming rubber parts; in a short time, his supervisors were wondering how Gammeter could dawdle with his work and yet produce more than the other workers. They soon discovered that he had rigged up an old sewing machine to do the work. Before long, his career as an inventor was launched.

While Gammeter was "tough, big, and swore a lot," he had also been greatly affected by the spiritual change he had seen take place in Henrietta. Thus he was ready to help her friends.

Bill probably stayed at the country club for about two weeks. During that time, he saw a great deal of the Smiths. His first mention of Dr. Bob to Lois was in a May letter, written on Bob's letterhead:

"I'm writing this from the office of one of my new friends, Dr. Smith. He had my trouble and is getting to be an ardent Grouper. I have been to his house for meals, and the rest of his family is as nice as he is. I have witnessed at a number of meet-ings and have been taken to a number of people. Dr. Smith is helping me to change a Dr. M——, once the most prominent surgeon in town, who developed into a terrific rake and drunk."

Nothing came of the efforts to help the unfortunate Dr. M., and he disappears from A.A. history. The letter does show, how-ever, that Bill and Dr. Bob started immediately to work with other alcoholics.

The Oxford Group meetings Bill attended may have been held at several places in Akron, but the important one was the Wednesday evening session at the T. Henry Williams home at 676 Palisades Drive. This was within easy walking distance of the country club and of Henrietta's home.

T. Henry Williams was a teetotaler, despite his ruddy face. A native of Connecticut, he had come to Akron in 1915 and soon showed a flair for machine tool design. A humble man with simple tastes, he was nonetheless proud of being a direct descendant of Roger Williams, founder of Rhode Island and champion of religious freedom in colonial America.

Bill had actually met T. Henry in the course of the proxy battle, perhaps before either realized that the other was a member of the Oxford Group. Formerly chief engineer of National Rubber Machinery Co., target firm in the proxy fight, T. Henry had lost his job there. In the midst of the Depression, he had managed to keep his beautiful home where the Oxford Group meetings were held — but only because the mortgage holder had wearied of making so many foreclosures and was willing to accept interest-only payments!

T. Henry and his wife Clarace were deeply religious people who were committed to service to others; through the Oxford Group, they became strong nonalcoholic supporters of the early Akron work with alcoholics. T. Henry had particular sympathy for alcoholics.

His daughter Dorothy recalled riding with him on a streetcar when she was very young: "We lived up on North Hill. The saloons were all at the bottom of the hill in the slum section. And the drunks would get on the streetcar, and they'd ride partway up, and if they got disorderly, [the motorman] would stop the car and kick them off. And my father would just shake his head, and he was so distressed at this. It always upset him, and he'd say, 'What about their poor families?' Drinking particularly upset him. He never drank, but it upset him. So for years, I'm sure he had it in his mind for something he could do for these people.''

Of the Wednesday night meetings at the Williams home, Bill Wilson said, "I am afraid those early problem drinkers often gave the Williamses a bad time, ranging from jarring glimpses of life in the raw to cigarette burns on their carpets. But T. Henry and Clarace always treated us with great generosity and kindness, and none of us can ever forget the inspirational atmosphere of their home and their spiritual influence on that first frightened little group of Akron alcoholics, each wondering who might slip next."

Most of Bill's letters to Lois during that summer referred to the proxy fight, and until the end of the summer, he was optimistic about his chances. He was determined to win. As he wrote to Lois:

"It is by far the greatest opportunity to do a fine piece of work that I have ever had, and I don't see how anything can be too much to sacrifice temporarily. Think of it, darling — the opportunity to be president of this company and have some real income to pay bills with, a new life, new people, new scenes. No more Loeser's — a chance to travel, to be somebody; to have you rested at last after your long wait for me to get somewhere. All these things are at stake. Is it not worth the worry, dear heart? I have never tried to do my best before, but I have this time, and I shall not have regrets if I lose."

In another letter written at about the same time, he described the situation in the company: "There is an enormous load of internal dissension, hate, fear, envy, etc. And it is a question of adjusting personal relationships and restoring confidence. In this case in particular, confidence is the key to the whole matter. This thing has been a racket for so many years that the townspeople haven't a spark of confidence in it, and I am staying here so long as I am able to sell them on our good intentions as to them and to National Rubber. And, praise God, I believe I am doing it.

"Like this little company, the whole town is shot [through] with hate, jealousy, ambition for money and social position. A bitter and Herculean struggle for years between Firestone, Seiberling, Goodrich, etc. Many of the Groupers here believe I have been guided to come to straighten it out. Perhaps that is farfetched, but there is surely a great work for us to do here, and I hope God will use us to do it."

Bill's ability to express himself and to talk about his recovery had apparently already made him popular with the Akron Oxford Groupers.

At Anne's suggestion, Bill moved in with the Smiths. He wrote to Lois: "You see, I have helped him a lot, I think, and she is quite grateful. They are people ten or 12 years older than ourselves. He was in danger of losing his practice, though he is apparently a very competent and mighty popular fellow. You will like them immensely."

Bill now joined Bob and Anne in the Oxford Group practice of having morning guidance sessions together, with Anne reading from the Bible. "Reading . . . from her chair in the corner, she would softly conclude, 'Faith without works is dead.' " As Dr. Bob described it, they were "convinced that the answer to our problem was in the Good Book. To some of us older ones, the parts that we found absolutely essential were the Sermon on the Mount, the 13th chapter of First Corinthians, and the Book of James." The Book of James was considered so important, in fact, that some early members even suggested "The James Club" as a name for the Fellowship.

With this routine of reading and meditation, in addition to Bill's help, Dr. Bob was not drinking. Sometime in the last week in May, when he had been sober about two weeks, he announced his intention of going to the American Medical Association annual convention — it began the first week in June — in Atlantic City. He had attended regularly for 20 years. Anne, remembering previous conventions, was flatly opposed to his going. But Bill endorsed the idea; recovered alcoholics, he reasoned, had to learn to live sober in a world of drinkers.

Dr. Bob started drinking the moment he boarded the train,

and when he got to Atlantic City, bought several quarts on his way to the hotel. That was on Sunday. On Monday, he managed to stay sober until evening; but by Tuesday, he started to drink in the morning. After checking out of the hotel, he found his way to the railroad station, stopping en route to stock up for the trip home.

In the meantime, Bill and Anne were waiting in a frenzy of apprehension. Five days from the time Bob left — on the following Thursday — they got a telephone call from Dr. Bob's office nurse, saying that Dr. Bob was at her house, that he had telephoned her at about four that morning from the station, asking her to come and pick him up. She and her husband had fetched him. Dr. Bob could remember nothing from the time he boarded the train to his awakening in the home of his nurse. He had been in a blackout for at least 24 hours — perhaps longer. Bill brought him home, and they put him to bed in a corner bedroom, which had two beds. Dr. Bob never attended another A.M.A. convention.

Now, Bill occupied the other bed and took charge of the tapering-off process. There was great urgency in their efforts, because Dr. Bob was scheduled to perform an important operation three days hence. Bill and Anne wondered if they could get him sober in time. "It was a worrisome thing, because if he was too drunk, he couldn't do it," Bill remembered. "And if he was too sober, he would be too jittery. So we had to load him up with this combination of tomato juice and sauerkraut and Karo corn syrup. The idea was to supply him with vitamins from the tomatoes and sauerkraut and energy from the corn syrup. We also gave him some beer to steady his nerves."

As Bill remembered it, at four o'clock on the morning of the operation, both of them were wide awake. Dr. Bob, shaking, turned to look at Bill. He said, "I am going through with it."

"You mean you're going through with the operation?"

"I have placed both the operation and myself in God's hands," Dr. Bob replied. "I'm going to do what it takes to get sober and stay that way.''

Dr. Bob said not another word that morning. He was shaking miserably as he got into his clothes. Bill and Anne drove him to the hospital, and just before stopping the car, Bill handed him ''one goofball''[3] and a single bottle of beer, to curb the shakes. Dr. Bob got out of the car and walked into the hospital. Bill and Anne went home to wait.

After what seemed an age, the telephone rang. It was Dr. Bob — everything had gone well. But time went by, and still he didn't come home. When he finally arrived, hours later, he explained the reason for the delay.

After leaving the hospital, Dr. Bob had set out to make the rounds of creditors and others he had previously avoided. He told them what had been going on, and expressed his desire to make amends. Following up on the statement he had made to Bill early that morning, he was doing what it took to get sober and stay that way. For Dr. Bob, a professional man, one of the greatest stumbling blocks had been his prideful need to conceal his drinking — from people who probably knew about it anyhow. He had only recently admitted to fellow Oxford Groupers that he was a secret drinker. Now, he openly admitted his problem to the very people he had wanted to hide it from.

It was a difficult thing to do: ''He trembled as he went about, for this might mean ruin, particularly to a person in his line of business.''

When he came home that night, his entire outlook had changed. He was happy, and, like Bill, he was finally a free man. It was June 10, 1935 — now honored as the date when A.A. really began. The bottle of beer Bill had given him that morning was his last drink.

After months of pursuing drunks, Bill had finally helped one to recover.

---

1. Clearly, Dr. Bob's drinking had not created the obstacles to adoption that Bill's had.

2. Gammeter may have paid for Bill's lodgings, although in a letter to Lois, Bill referred to the cost ($2.50 daily) as if he were paying it himself. Whoever actually paid, it was Gammeter's membership that enabled Bill to stay there.

3. As in a November 1945 Grapevine article titled ''Those 'Goof Balls,' '' cautioning alcoholics on the use of sedatives, Bill and other early A.A.'s applied the slang term to a variety of such drugs.

Chapter Eight

Young Bob Smith, who had his 17th birthday just five days before his father's last drink, remembers Bill as a wonderful house-
guest during that summer of 1935.

Bill and Dr. Bob had long, continuous discussions.
"They'd stay up until two or three o'clock every morning, and
drink lots of coffee," young Bob said. "They were trying to develop a presentation that would make sense to the alcoholic on
the bed, and not be complicated."

Eddie R. was the man they hoped would become their third
sober member. Eddie came of a prominent Youngstown family,
and his wife was the daughter of a university professor. She had
made her "surrender" in the Oxford Group, but Eddie was still
fighting. They had lost their rented house, and he was about to
lose his job, when Anne Smith invited the entire family — they
had two young children — to come to live on Ardmore Avenue.

The Smith home was a comfortable, unpretentious two-
story house at 855 Ardmore, south and a little east of the exclusive sections near Portage Path. It had only three bedrooms; as it

became crowded, young Bob and Sue were obliged to sleep in the attic.

About Eddie, Bill wrote to Lois:

"Bob Smith and I started to work on this chap a week ago Wednesday, got him sober. . . . [Then] he rushed away to commit suicide, which he had attempted before. . . . The next day, he called up from Cleveland to bid me goodbye, having found a good dock to jump from, but having found himself unable to do it without first calling me. I advised him to drink some more and permit me to come and see him before he did anything. So we tore over to Cleveland in the middle of the night, got him here to the hospital, and commenced to give him the Towns treatment. The effect of that . . . has been magical and is creating a great stir at the City Hospital, where the doctors are all agog, being unable to do anything for these cases."

Because of Eddie's social prominence and important connections in Akron, Bill and Dr. Bob clearly hoped that his recovery would draw others in. But it didn't work out that way. Eddie had many difficulties, and at one time even threatened Bill and Anne with a knife. The Smiths did everything for Eddie except give him the deed to their house, and yet the man continued to drink. Anne's patience was almost exhausted when he and his family finally moved out.[1]

Eddie and his family were still living at the Smiths' when Lois came to Akron for her vacation. This was her first meeting with the Smiths, and with the Akron community. She said: "I loved Annie and Bob from the moment I saw them. They were so warm, so gracious, so *good*. Bob was a tall, lanky Vermonter like Bill and, like him, yearned to be of use to others. In other respects, they were very different."

In late June, Dr. Bob put in a call to Akron City Hospital. He explained to the nurse in the receiving ward that a man from New York had just found a cure for alcoholism. The nurse, who apparently had not heard about Dr. Bob's own recent recovery, asked why he didn't try the cure out on himself. When Dr. Bob explained that he had tried it, and that it involved working with other alcoholics, she responded more sympathetically. She knew just the man, she said, and he was at that very moment in the hospital with D.T.'s. He would be sufficiently sober to talk with them in a day or so.

Bill and Dr. Bob were about to meet Bill D., a stocky, handsome man with a captivating drawl, a congenial, folksy manner, and a full head of wavy hair, which would turn white in his later years. At the time of their phone call, this congenial and folksy soul had just beaten up two nurses and was strapped down in a bed at City Hospital.

Bill D. was in many ways the ideal man to become the third member of the group. A Kentucky farm boy who had come to Akron and worked in a tire plant while attending law school, he was an apparently well-adjusted family man who had inexplicably become a hopeless drunk. During the first six months of 1935, he had been hospitalized eight times for drunkenness, yet his life was otherwise respectable. He had even been a city councilman and financial director of an Akron suburb. He and his wife attended church every Sunday, and often prayed about his problem. As he told Bill and Dr. Bob when they called on him in City Hospital, "You don't have to sell me religion, either. I was at one time a deacon in the church and I still believe in God. But I guess He doesn't believe much in me."

If Bill D. thought God had given up on him, his wife Henrietta thought otherwise.[2] Dissatisfied with the progress she and Bill were making in their own church, she had recently visited another minister to pray about her husband's affliction. She became convinced that her husband would stop drinking. When Bill and Dr. Bob made their call only a short time later, she had no doubt that her prayers were being answered.

The recovery experience the two men shared with Bill D. was brief by today's standards: about seven months for Bill and only a few weeks for Dr. Bob. But they were already developing strength in their partnership; this, they passed along to the new

man. They also had hope that they had found the key to permanent sobriety, not only for the three of them, but for hundreds
who might follow.

At first amazed that a physician would offer to help him at
no charge, Bill D., after some initial resistance, responded well
to their suggestions. When he left the hospital on July 4, 1935,
he, like the two men who had called on him, was a free man. He
never drank again, and he remained an active A.A. member
until his death in 1954.

Now, there were three men who would never drink again.
They did not have a name for their Fellowship, and they were
still closely tied to the Oxford Group, a situation that would continue in Akron for another four years.

But they also shared a view of alcoholism that had not come
to them from the Oxford Group. This was the understanding of
alcoholism as an illness of mind and body that Bill had learned
from Dr. Silkworth. To them, alcoholism was not just another
human failing or sin; it was a soul-destroying malady. The alternative to sobriety was grim: death or insanity. Nothing could be
more important in the life of a recovered alcoholic than maintaining his sobriety. And both Bill Wilson and Dr. Bob Smith
believed that maintaining sobriety required carrying the message to others. (It is worth noting that all three of these now-sober
men had devoted wives who had kept the faith with them. These
early pioneers in Akron and New York worked together with
their wives, both at staying sober and at carrying the message.)

Soon, Anonymous Number Four appeared. He was Ernie
G., only 30 and "almost too young" in the eyes of his sponsors.
All three of the men called on him; Bill and Dr. Bob had lost no
time in getting Bill D. involved in the work.

Ernie stayed sober for a year, and then went on a slip that
lasted seven months (his story, "The Seven Month Slip," appeared in the first edition of the Big Book). Although he had
difficulties with drinking for the rest of his life, his early sobriety
played a part in those pioneering times. In 1941, he married Dr.

Bob's daughter Sue — reportedly against her father's wishes (they were later divorced).

During those first few months, Bill and Dr. Bob established the working alliance and partnership that would last all their lives and mark them as the co-founders of A.A. Each man brought special talents and personal traits to his role. Bill was the promoter, the "idea man" whose mind was constantly racing ahead with plans and projects. Dr. Bob represented the strength and stability of the early Fellowship; his prudent counsel often blocked rash ventures that might have retarded the development of A.A. or even ruined A.A.; and Bill would later acknowledge that debt in a tribute to his partner. "With no other person have I ever experienced quite the same relation; the finest thing I know how to say is that in all the strenuous time of our association, he and I never had an uncomfortable difference of opinion. His capacity for brotherhood and love was often beyond my ken."

Young Bob confirmed the unusual harmony: "Dad often told me that, although he and Bill saw things from different angles, they never had an argument and their two minds seemed to mesh in developing an intelligent program which they could present to alcoholics."

Another associate who knew them well compared their relationship to that of "two brothers who loved and trusted each other deeply. Bob could say anything to Bill. It might have hurt Bill's feelings a little bit, and they often disagreed; but it was never a lasting thing, and they always ended up by being able to get along in the middle somewhere, to work it out so that they were both happy about it. I never saw more complete trust than they had for each other." Their remarkable partnership would later become a topic of A.A. conversation; there were those who saw divine intervention in the bringing together of these two men.

Superficially, Bill and Bob had much in common. Both were tall Vermonters. Both were political conservatives: Bill opposed government intervention in business; Bob anticipated a dark future for doctors in an impending age of socialized medicine. Both were compassionate, kind, and generous in sharing what they had with others. Both were drawn to spiritism and to extrasensory phenomena. They had a common interest in medical matters: Dr. Bob as a professional; Bill as a layman who during his lifetime formed close ties with the world of medicine. Each had had difficulty completing his formal education, although Bill's school troubles were rooted in emotional vicissitudes, never a major problem for Dr. Bob. Each man devised nicknames for his friends; each had simple tastes; and each disliked pretense and phoniness of any sort. Both were highly intelligent.

But there were marked contrasts between the two as well. Roy Y., an oldtimer in Texas and later Florida, described it this way: "Both said they couldn't just be members of A.A. Dr. Bob, going to his meetings at King School, would sneak into the back, and nobody would know he was there. If Bill came into that same meeting, he would make sure he knocked over a chair. Bill loved the limelight."

While Bill would never have actually done anything so crude, it is certainly true that he drew the attention of others. He was never a bystander for long; people noticed him. He was impressed by and impressed people of achievement; in time, his circle of acquaintance and friendship would include distinguished people from many fields. By his own admission, he was a power-driver, a quality totally alien to his partner.

Dr. Bob had little interest in the limelight. He gave few public talks in A.A., nor, evidently, did he ever take charge of personal conversations, as Bill sometimes did. "Doc had such a great quiet way," said an admirer. "He had a sense of humor but was not able to bring it out in other people as Bill could. Doc was a great listener. I never heard him talk that much. Bill was a great talker and a great listener, too. Bill really listened, with ears opened. He knew what you were saying."

In addition to being a talker and a listener, Bill was also a writer and a planner, and neither activity interested Dr. Bob. Dr. Bob, however, furnished ideas and sound judgment that found their way into Bill's writings. Dr. Bob sometimes got Bill to change his mind, or acted as a brake on him. He also gave Bill the strongest kind of support on projects that he believed were needed. "Alcoholics Anonymous," the Big Book, was to be a prime example. Although the Akron members would endorse the venture by only one vote, Dr. Bob was strongly behind it and gave Bill warm encouragement and approval during some of his darkest moments, when the project seemed permanently stalled.

Bill was a pusher; Dr. Bob was willing to wait. Bill's style was actively to seek support for his ideas, while Dr. Bob would wait until support for a proposal developed of its own momentum. There are also some indications that Dr. Bob was the more effective sponsor. There is certainly no denying that in the first few years, A.A. grew more rapidly in Akron than it did in New York, and there were those who attributed this success to Dr. Bob's strong leadership.

Yet there was no competitiveness between the two, nor did either ever seem envious of the other. In the end, each viewed himself as an instrument of the Higher Power in the development of the Fellowship. Perhaps it was their unique partnership that was the instrument.

While Bill's work with alcoholics was moving ahead, his business career was seesawing back and forth. Following the shareholders' meeting in May, the point apparently at issue was the inspection of proxies voted by his associates and their opponents, the group headed by Nils Florman. The Swedish-born Florman was handsome and charming, and he had important connections. Both men wanted to be president of National Rubber Machinery Company, and so far, Florman was leading. The position paid about $14,000 a year (a substantial amount at the time). The company was not large — it had about 400 employees — but it had a solid place in the market, plus growth potential.

To Bill, to get on his feet financially seemed vitally important.

In his letters to Lois, Bill was highly critical of Florman and his colleagues; he would later write about this proxy fight as a "proceeding . . . shot through with much hard feeling and controversy."

In 1935, National Rubber Machinery needed leadership desperately; it had been crippled by dissension, strife, and indecision. Since 1932, the company had sustained heavy operating losses, and it now appeared to be on the road to eventual bankruptcy. But Florman and his associates were not Bill's only opponents; the largest block of the company's 113,000 shares was controlled by a management group headed by an M. D. Kuhlke, whose firm, Kuhlke Machine Co., had been one of the four family-owned businesses that merged into N.R.M. in 1928. Kuhlke was said to be an amiable and decent man who tended to agree with both sides in a dispute. He supported Florman's group at one time but would lean toward Bill's group at another. Had Bill been able to win Kuhlke's support, he could have taken control of N.R.M. Some of Bill's letters expressed his exasperation at Kuhlke's fence-sitting.

But there was little in Bill's background to indicate that he was the right person to run the company. His past must have worried Kuhlke, who therefore had little reason to favor Wilson over Florman.

The fight to get proxies inspected went on all summer, and when the race came down to the wire, Bill had managed to garner about 30,000 votes, while Florman's camp had only 20,000. But Florman received an additional 42,000 votes from mail solicitation and from Kuhlke and his friends in Akron. Florman's total of 62,000 votes gave him more than the 51 percent needed for control.

The battle was over. Bill's business venture in Akron had failed. All he had to show for his four months there was the work he had done with Dr. Bob and the two other now-sober alcoholics. In late August, he caught the train back to New York.

---

1. Eddie's story had a happy ending, however, as he turned up sober and grateful at Dr. Bob's funeral 15 years later.

2. Henrietta D. later served for 22 years as matron at the Akron City Workhouse, and helped carry the message to female alcoholics confined there.

Chapter Nine

When Bill returned to New York City on Monday, August 26, 1935, he had two immediate concerns. As pressing as was his need to find a niche for himself in business, his need to do something about alcoholism was equally urgent.

Clint F., the former drinking partner who had introduced him to Joe Hirshhorn, met Bill in a brokerage office shortly after his return. Bill told him about the proxy fight. "I was not interested in his financial affairs anymore," said Clint, "but something did interest me very much, and I listened hard. He said he had not taken a drink of booze for several months, and he certainly looked it. The old circuit-judge aloofness was missing. In fact, his expression was rather benign, as if a certain kind of personal settlement had arrived. He said that he and a doctor friend in Akron think they have found an answer to one of society's most baffling problems — the chronic drunk, the alcoholic. He said they learned to help each other in a manner that does not prohibit but rather removes the desire to drink. Something about a greater power helping."

Clint, who had been about to invite Bill for a couple of drinks, found himself hanging on Bill's every word. "It's just one day at a time," said Bill. "And no booze fighting — the fight is over." Clint wanted to hear more, but Bill was becoming impatient; he had an appointment at an uptown hospital.

"I was trying to prolong the conversation, because lately I was feeling so awfully lonely, and here was a Bill I had not known before," Clint said. "So I hung on in a feeble way. I chased after him to the elevator of the building and asked him what he did at the hospital."

Bill replied, "Well, Clint, we are on the firing line with the drunks. I'm going to see the worst cases they have and talk to them about myself. It's wonderful to see even one respond." Clint was conscious of his own drinking problem; after the elevator door closed, he recalled, he wanted to go with Bill. (It would be another 13 years before Clint "went with Bill." He came into A.A. in 1948.)

The hospital, of course, was Towns. Here, Bill found Hank P., an energetic redhead whose drinking had cost him an executive position with a major oil company. A restless promoter, Hank was the first of the drunks Bill worked with in New York who stayed sober for any period of time. (Hank is "The Unbeliever" in the first edition of the Big Book.)

At Towns, Bill also found Fitz M. (the Big Book's "Our Southern Friend"), who was a resident of Cumberstone, Maryland. The son of a minister, Fitz drank when he was assailed by a sense of inferiority, incompetence, and unworthiness, and when the needs of others in his family — their illnesses, births, and other traumas — overwhelmed him. Lois described Fitz as an "impractical, lovable dreamer." He and the Wilsons soon became devoted friends.

Bill had many of Hank's qualities, and he undoubtedly admired Hank's aggressiveness and his athleticism. Bill, however, also had an intellectual, scholarly side that gave him common ground with people like Fitz. Bill was interested in new ideas, and he, too, was a dreamer.

Both Bill and Dr. Bob were able to form close friendships with all sorts of people; the common bond was alcoholism and their own deep gratitude for their sobriety. Bill obviously recognized this when he wrote of the Fellowship: "We are people who normally would not mix. But there exists among us a fellowship, a friendliness, and an understanding which is indescribably wonderful. We are like the passengers of a great liner the moment after rescue from shipwreck when camaraderie, joyousness and democracy pervade the vessel from steerage to Captain's table. Unlike the feelings of the ship's passengers, however, our joy in escape from disaster does not subside as we go our individual ways. The feeling of having shared in a common peril is one element in the powerful cement which binds us."

This "joy in escape from disaster" gave the early Fellowship an almost euphoric atmosphere. In seeking a metaphor to describe this feeling, Bill was probably recalling his World War I experience aboard the Lancashire.

In the fall of 1935, Bill and Lois began to hold weekly meetings on Tuesday nights in their home on Clinton Street. Hank P., along with his wife Kathleen, came from Teaneck, New Jersey. Fitz M. often came up from Maryland, and according to Lois, Shep C., their friend from Vermont, also attended a few times. They were still working with Freddie B., the chemistry professor. Others mentioned by Lois as attending included Brooke B., from the Calvary Mission, Bill R. and his nonalcoholic wife Kathleen, Ernest M., Herb D. and his wife Margaret, from New Jersey, and of course, Ebby, Alec, and the others who lived at the Wilsons' home.

The practice of opening one's home, making it into a sort of halfway house, had already been started by Dr. Bob and Anne Smith, who would continue over the years to befriend homeless

182 Clinton Street, Brooklyn Heights, home and meeting place for New York alcoholics in A.A.'s formative days.

men. Now, following the lead set by their Akron friends, Bill and Lois converted their own home into a similar hostel. Bill and Lois also had a theory that alcoholics felt unloved; therefore, they, the Wilsons, would love them into sobriety. Bill and Lois occupied the second-floor apartment that had been remodeled by Dr. Burnham for his wife when she was ill; the rest of the house was made available to the "recovering" alcoholics.

Although Lois did most of the housework and cooking — in addition to going to her full-time job at Loeser's — apparently, neither she nor Bill considered it unfair. Russ R., a recipient of their hospitality for over a year, described the way it was:

"All of us were living rent-free, food-free, everything-free in Clinton Street, and Lois was doing all the work. She was working in a department store during the day and cooking for us and providing all the money the whole house had."

Russ reminisced about some of the other "guests" of that

Many alcoholics, drunk and sober, gathered in the Clinton Street living room to be loved into sobriety.

time, among them Wes W., who lived in the basement. Wes had once enjoyed the better things in life and had traveled around the world. He had a colorful anecdote about throwing up in the swimming pool of a swank hotel, and causing all the other guests to flee in disgust.

Wes never lost his taste for first-class treatment. One morning, when Lois made pancakes for the entire household, Wes came up late from the basement and discovered there were only a few pancakes left. Hurt and offended when Lois refused to make more, he rose, threw down his napkin, and stomped out of the house, vowing never to come back. Actually, he went only as far as a Childs restaurant — for more pancakes!

The last time Russ saw him, Wes was dying of cancer in Bellevue. He asked Russ to bring him a bottle of Scotch — "not any kind of Scotch; I want Johnnie Walker." Then he added, "Not just any Johnnie Walker. Make it Black Label." But when Russ returned the next day with the Johnnie Walker Black Label, Wes was gone.

One "prospect, slightly intoxicated," was sent by Dr. Silkworth. After spending the night at Clinton Street, he was terribly nauseated the following morning. Later, Lois found an empty whiskey bottle in the kitchen. A day earlier, the same bottle, a Christmas present to the Wilsons, had been full of Vermont maple syrup. In reconstructing what had happened, Lois realized that their guest must have chugalugged it before he realized what was going down his throat!

Bill C. was a "guest" of the Wilsons for nearly a year. He was a lawyer and a professional bridge player — that is, a respectable attorney by day and a gambler by night. Because of his day-and-night schedule, the Wilsons rarely saw him.

He was staying alone in the house during the summer of 1936 when the Wilsons went to visit Fitz and Co. in Maryland. Bill Wilson returned home first. The minute he opened the front door, he smelled gas. Rushing upstairs, he found Bill C.'s body; the man had committed suicide by running a tube from a gas jet into his mouth. He had apparently been lying there for some days. It was several months before Bill and Lois realized that Bill had been selling off their dress clothes, which had been hanging in a hall closet near his bedroom. Among the missing items were Bill's dress suit and his evening jacket. Lois lost several evening dresses and a velvet wrap. With his characteristic gift for over-statement, Bill said that Bill C. "sold every stitch of clothing in the house and turned on the gas in remorse."

Both Bill and Dr. Bob eventually began to question the wisdom of permitting recovering alcoholics to live in their homes for extended periods. Bill referred to the suicide as an example of literally "killing people with kindness." Russ, the man who took the Scotch to Wes and who himself did not get permanently sober until 1949, said he could not remember that any of the men sobered up while they were living at the Wilsons'.

While Lois also later admitted that their success rate was low during the 1935-36 period at Clinton Street, she pointed out that many of the alcoholics Bill worked with during that time did recover later on. In other words, Lois said, the seeds of sobriety were being planted, to take root slowly.

The Big Book, when it was published three years later, suggested caution and discretion in offering hospitality to an alcoholic: "Be certain he will be welcomed by your family, and that he is not trying to impose upon you for money, connections, or shelter. Permit that and you only harm him. You will be making it possible for him to be insincere. You may be aiding in his destruction rather than his recovery. . . . We seldom allow an alcoholic to live in our homes for long at a time. It is not good for him, and it sometimes creates serious complications in a family."

Bill and Lois had permitted some of the men to live with them for as long as a year; they apparently stopped the practice when they realized it did very little to help the men actually stay sober. During this time, Bill was often overoptimistic about the effectiveness of the work he was doing. Of Bill's naiveté during the first year or two of his sobriety, Russ said: "He would try to sober people up in an hour's talk. He would take them into a room and argue with them and expound his theories to them and come out beaming, and he would say, 'There's a man who'll never take a drink again, I bet you.'

"In those days, Bill's arguments didn't always hold together. He was such an egotist. Most all of us were egotists, but he was so tenaciously egotistical that if he wanted something, it became true. And he'd start at a conclusion. If he thought, 'This man is going to be sober,' he would assume that the man was going to be sober. He would start off on a false premise and work up logic step by step and arrive at the beginning conclusion." While Bill was a good deal smarter than most people, said Russ, he "went astray" when he wanted something very badly; he became willing to "bend things a little." The boy who had been determined to fashion a boomerang lived on; Bill continued to go after what he wanted with the same single-minded intensity. "However," Russ concluded, "if he hadn't been like that, there wouldn't have been an A.A."

Lois did not complain about the work load that had fallen to her. (She would later explain her enormous capacity for hard work by saying that her father had been a "real slave driver.") But her attitude toward Bill's new life was somewhat more ambivalent, as her description indicates:

"The next few months were a happy time for Bill. He had the companionship of his alcoholic friends, the spiritual inspiration of the Oxford Group, and the satisfaction of being useful to those he worked with.

"For my part, I would not let myself perceive that I was not as happy as I should have been after all my dreams of Bill's sobriety had come true. Although my joy and faith in his rebirth continued, I missed our companionship. We were seldom alone together now. There was no time for outdoor weekends. Bill was busy working with his alcoholics, attending to a small business he and Hank P. had started in New Jersey, and doing occasional investigating. . . . I felt left out and unneeded.

"But we did go to the Oxford Group meetings regularly. I went along with Bill for his sake, because that was what a devoted wife should do, not because I needed the meetings. I felt I already had the knowledge and discipline these kind folks were seeking. . . .

"Bill's power drives were nothing to my subtle self-assurance. . . . Even after Bill's spiritual awakening, it didn't occur to me that I needed to change. . . .

"One Sunday, Bill casually said to me, 'We'll have to hurry, or we'll be late for the Oxford Group meeting.'

"I had a shoe in my hand, and before I knew what was happening, I had thrown it at him and said, 'Damn your old meetings!' . . .

"That day, I began to look at myself analytically for the first time. Until then, I had taken myself for granted. Because I loved Bill and wanted to help him, I had felt I must be in the right. . . .

"Gradually, the true picture became clear. . . . After Bill sobered up, it was a great blow for me to realize that he did not need me in the way he had before. . . . Slowly, I recognized that because I had not been able to 'cure' Bill of his alcoholism, I resented the fact that someone else had done so, and I was jealous of his newfound friends. Little by little, I saw that my ego had been nourished during his drinking years by the important roles I had to fill: mother, nurse, breadwinner, decision maker. . . . Also, my ego was bolstered by my ability to support us both, however meagerly, and to make the family decisions that Bill was incapable of making. . . .

"I also saw that I had been self-righteous and smug, thinking I was doing for Bill all that any wife could do. I have come to believe that self-righteousness is one of the worst sins. . . . It is impregnable. No shaft of light can pierce its armor. It keeps its victims apart and aloof from others."

Lois and Bill went to Oxford Group meetings at Calvary Church from late 1934 until about 1937, and they also went to a number of Oxford Group "house parties" during those years. From 1935 on, Hank and Fitz often joined them.

Tension began to develop between the main group at Calvary Church and Bill's struggling band of alcoholics. The Oxford Group leaders resented the fact that Bill was holding separate meetings for alcoholics at Clinton Street. They criticized his work with the alcoholics as being "narrow and divisive." The alcoholics, on the other hand, felt that they needed these special meetings because many of the nonalcoholic O.G. members did not understand them.

Jack Smith, one of Sam Shoemaker's assistants, disapproved of Bill's work and finally brought the conflict out into the open. In an informal talk at a Sunday Oxford Group gathering, he made reference to special meetings "held surreptitiously behind Mrs. Jones's barn." The atmosphere of the Oxford Group then became "slightly chilly" toward the Wilsons.

Near the end of 1935, the alcoholics living at Calvary Mission were instructed not to attend the meetings at Clinton Street. "This not only hurt us but left us disappointed in the group's leadership," Lois remembered.[1]

Criticism and rejection notwithstanding, Lois and Bill did not become immediately disillusioned with the Oxford Group or with its principles, from which Bill borrowed freely.

Lois described the Oxford Group weekend "house parties" that they attended as "a cross between a convention and a retreat. People came from far and near to be with one another, to worship, to meditate, to ask God's guidance, and to gain strength from doing so together. Usually, two or three well-known persons would lead the meetings, inspiring the rest of us to do as they had done."

Bill attended his first such house party in Richmond, Virginia, in December 1935, and the following year he and Lois went to others — in Stockbridge, Massachusetts, in the Pennsylvania Poconos, and in West Point, New York. They met Frank Buchman, the Oxford Group's founder, but never became closely associated with him. When he was later asked whether he had known Buchman, Bill said he only "shook hands" with him.

In June of 1936, when the Oxford Group was at the height of its popularity as an inspirational movement, 10,000 people flocked to the Berkshires to attend the Stockbridge meeting. The ten-day affair was reported in the October issue of *Good Housekeeping*, in an article titled "The Oxford Group Challenges America."

Good Housekeeping described it thus: "The Oxford Group has no membership, no dues, no paid leaders. It has no new creed nor theological theories. It does not even have regular meetings. It is merely a fellowship of individuals who seek to follow a certain way of life. A determination, not a denomination, they say. First-century Christian principles in 20th-century application. Identified with it are Roman Catholics, Episcopalians, Methodists, Presbyterians, Baptists — members of all churches and none.

" 'Not a creed,' says its founder, 'but a revitalizing of such creed as the individual may have allowed to decay.' "

During the 1930's, the O.G. practice of "witnessing" was helping alcoholics throughout the country. The movement had proliferated all over the United States — in the South, in the Virginias, in California, all through the Midwest, and throughout Canada as well; there were alcoholics in each of these places seeking sobriety. It is possible that alcoholic members of those groups eventually came into A.A. In all probability, the Oxford Group attracted alcoholics simply because it appealed to people with problems.

The year of the great Berkshire meeting, 1936, also brought difficulties for the Oxford Group. In August, the New York *World-Telegram* published an article about Buchman, charging that he was pro-Nazi. The newspaper quoted Buchman as saying: "I thank heaven for a man like Adolf Hitler who built a front-line defense against the Anti-Christ of Communism. Think what it would mean to the world if Hitler surrendered to

God. Through such a man, God could control a nation and solve every problem. Human problems aren't economic, they're moral, and they can't be solved by immoral measures.''

While most discussions of the incident, even by Buchman's critics, have since vindicated him, the article brought the group into public controversy.

At the same time, a subtle change took place in both the message and the function of the Oxford Group. It moved from small intimate groups to large gatherings. In 1938, after Oxford University requested that the group, because of the controversy, no longer use its name, it took the name Moral Rearmament, abbreviated to M.R.A. "Increasingly, it worked with national and world assemblies. A number of the early followers withdrew from the movement, dissatisfied with the shift from individual emphasis to mass methods.''

There were several reasons for Bill's 1937 departure from the Oxford Group. He had a growing conviction that alcoholics needed to work with their own kind, a view he would continue to hold for the rest of his life. He himself had received his help from the "small intimate group" services of the Oxford Group, a concept they were about to abandon. Out in Akron, where Dr. Bob and the others stayed in the Oxford Group until 1939, the intimacy of the small group meeting continued at the T. Henry Williams home.

Because Bill's reasons were often misunderstood, he later wrote letters and articles to explain the split. One of his most extensive statements about the situation was made in a letter dated October 30, 1940, to a member in Richmond, Virginia:

"I am always glad to say privately that some of the Oxford Group presentation and emphasis upon the Christian message saved my life. Yet it is equally true that other attitudes of the O.G. nearly got me drunk again, and we long since discovered that if we were to approach alcoholics successfully, these [attitudes] would have to be abandoned. Recovery being a life-or-death matter for most alcoholics, it became a question of adopting that which would work and rejecting that which would not.

"For example:

"1. The principle of aggressive evangelism so prominent as an Oxford Group attitude had to be dropped in order to get any result with alcoholics. Experience showed that this principle, which may have been absolutely vital to the success of the Oxford Group, would seldom touch neurotics of our hue.

"2. Excessive personal publicity or prominence in the work was found to be bad. Alcoholics who talked too much on public platforms were likely to become inflated and get drunk again. Our principle of anonymity, so far as the general public is concerned, partly corrects this difficulty.

"3. The principles of honesty, purity, unselfishness, and love are as much a goal for A.A. members and are as much practiced by them as by any other group of people; yet we found that when the word 'absolute' was put in front of these attributes, they either turned people away by the hundreds or gave a temporary spiritual inflation resulting in collapse.

"4. It was discovered that all forms of coercion, both direct and indirect, had to be dropped. We found that 'checking' in the hands of amateurs too often resulted in criticism, and that resulted in resentment, which is probably the most serious problem the average alcoholic is troubled with.

"5. While most of us believe profoundly in the principle of 'guidance,' it was soon apparent that to receive it accurately, considerable spiritual preparation was necessary.

"6. We found that the principles of tolerance and love had to be much more emphasized in their actual practice than they were in the O.G., especially tolerance. We had to become much more inclusive and never, if possible, exclusive. We can never say to anyone (or insinuate) that he must agree to our formula or be excommunicated. The atheist may stand up in an A.A. meeting denying God, yet reporting how he has been helped in other ways. Experience tells us he will presently change his mind, but nobody tells him he must do so.

"7. In order to carry the principle of inclusiveness and tolerance still further, we make no religious requirement of anyone. All people having an alcohol problem who wish to get rid of it and make a happy adjustment with the circumstances of their lives, become A.A. members by simply associating with us. Nothing but sincerity is asked of anyone. In this atmosphere, the orthodox, the unorthodox, and the unbeliever mix happily and usefully together, and in nearly every case great spiritual growth ensues.

"8. Were we to make any religious demands upon people, I'm afraid many Catholics would feel they could not be interested. As matters now stand, I suppose A.A. is 25 percent Catholic, and [Catholic members] find that our suggestions do not conflict in any way with their own views or rules of religious conduct. Since there are plenty of alcoholic Catholics, why deprive them of their chance by being dogmatic, when experience shows that is entirely unnecessary?

"Finally, I am often asked why I do not publicly acknowledge my very real debt of gratitude to the Oxford Group. The answer is that, unfortunately, a vast and sometimes unreasoning prejudice exists all over this country against the O.G. and its successor M.R.A. My dilemma is that if I make such an acknowledgment, I may establish a connection between the O.G. and Alcoholics Anonymous which does not exist at the present time. I had to ask myself which was the more important: that the O.G. receive credit and that I have the pleasure of so discharging my debt of gratitude, or that alcoholics everywhere have the best possible chance to stay alive regardless of who gets credit."

Bill had friends in the Oxford Group who understood his view of the situation. One of them was John Ryder, a New York advertising executive who knew Bill in the days of the Calvary Mission. Ryder made these comments about Bill's separation from the Oxford Group:

"I was, or felt, quite close to Bill Wilson in the early days before A.A. was started. Herb Wallace, a close teammate of mine, spent much time with Bill, caused him to take a public speaking course at the Downtown Athletic Club; but I think the 'group' proper disowned Bill when he proceeded on his guidance to create a special group for A.A.'s. At that time, if you were associated with the 'group,' your guidance seemed to be of questionable worth unless okayed by Sam Shoemaker or Frankie Buchman or one of their accredited representatives.

"I recall one dear fellow sadly shaking his head as he said, 'Bill will never have any luck with that venture of his.' I asked why, and he replied, 'Because he doesn't give all the credit to the group.' Bill, by that time, had quite a few healings to his credit, and I know how hard he had tried to work with the group, and how his efforts had been received. Bill Wilson has never failed to give the group, or the members of it who helped him, much credit; in fact, he has gone out of his way in expressions of acknowledgment and gratitude.

"He, of course, couldn't say what my friend wished him to say: 'I owe it all to the Oxford Group.' He would have been a liar if he had. A man might as well say, 'I owe it all to my primary-school teacher.' "

The Oxford Group disapproved of the alcoholics' concentration on their problem to the exclusion of other group concerns. Lois even said that the "Oxford Group kind of kicked us out," that she and Bill were not considered "maximum" by the groupers. ("Maximum" was used by the Oxford Group to define the expected degree of commitment to group objectives.)

While Bill was always generous in recognizing A.A.'s debt to the Oxford Group, he would always tie the Oxford Group connection to Dr. Shoemaker.

A few business opportunities began to come Bill's way, and they were welcome; the Wilsons were still relying on what Lois earned. Early in February 1936, he received an assignment to investigate a company in Harrisburg, Pennsylvania. He also had a short-term job soliciting proxies, and a few other assignments materialized.

Most of Bill's stock market investigations then were for Clayton Quaw of the firm of Quaw and Foley. Not actually on its payroll, Bill was paid separately for each assignment, often receiving a share in the profits that resulted from his investigations. At one time, the firm almost got him placed on the board of the Fisk Tire Company in Boston. He was made a director of the Pierce Governor Company, a manufacturer of automotive parts, at Anderson, Indiana. He also had some assignments from his old friend Frank Shaw, the man who had given him his first break on Wall Street. Although Bill and Shaw parted official company in 1929, they remained lifelong friends. In a 1960 letter to Elise Shaw, Frank's wife, Bill wrote:

"It is both amazing and comforting that this experience of mine with Frank in Wall Street has had a great deal to do with the present success of A.A. It was the training I then received in large affairs and in the constant effort to foresee and to evaluate the future that has since counted for so much. Without such an invaluable experience, I would have made a great many grievous errors. By no stretch of the imagination could I have integrated the business and policy side of our A.A. affairs with its spiritual objective."

The investigatory work Bill did in 1936-37 was his last serious effort to reestablish himself in the securities field, although in the next few years he did try several other business ventures.

In September 1936, Lois's father, who owned the Clinton Street house, died. The house was taken over by the mortgage company, which permitted the Wilsons to stay on there for a small rental.

It was their acute poverty — Bill had persuaded Lois to quit her job at Loeser's in March — that almost caused Bill to accept employment as a paid alcoholism therapist. The offer came from Charlie Towns, owner of the hospital where Bill had recovered and had also found several of his most promising prospects.

One day while Bill was at Towns, Charlie called him into his office. Showing Bill statements that disclosed how much the hospital had made in earlier years (it hadn't done as well in more recent times), Charlie proposed that Bill open an office at the hospital and work as a lay therapist with a drawing account and a share in the profits.

Bill was bowled over. The offer not only made sense, it appeared to be perfectly ethical. There was even a precedent for the use of lay therapists in the treatment of alcoholism. The best-known such person had been Richard Peabody, author of "The Common Sense of Drinking." Peabody, a recovered alcoholic himself, had recently died after a short but successful career as an independent lay therapist helping alcoholics on a fee basis.

Bill thought the offer verified by heavenly guidance: As he rode the subway home, the Biblical quote "The laborer is worthy of his hire" came to him. By the time he arrived home, he was convinced that it was his divine destiny to become a paid therapist.

He was in for a big disappointment: Lois failed to share his enthusiasm. He was even more surprised by the response of the recovered alcoholics and their wives after they gathered for the Tuesday evening meeting. Although Bill's live-in alcoholics were having considerable trouble, a number of recovered alcoholics were now in the area.

The group listened with impassive faces while Bill told them of Towns's offer. Then one member volunteered: "We know how hard up you are, Bill. . . . It bothers us a lot. We've often wondered what we might do about it. But I think I speak for everyone here when I say that what you now propose bothers us. . . . Don't you realize . . . that you can never become a professional? As generous as Charlie has been to us, don't you see that we can't tie this thing up with his hospital or any other? . . . This is a matter of life and death, Bill, and nothing but the very best will do. . . . Haven't you often said right here in this meeting that sometimes the good is the enemy of the best? Well, this is a plain case of it. . . .

"Bill, you can't do this to us," he added. "Don't you see

that for you, our leader, to take money for passing on our magnificent message, while the rest of us try to do the same thing without pay, would soon discourage us all? . . . Why should we do for nothing what you'd be getting paid for? We'd all be drunk in no time.''

Bill did understand, almost immediately, that this work could be done for love only, never for money. He declined Charlie's offer. When Bill described the incident later, he portrayed himself as the impulsive, self-seeking opportunist who might have wrecked the fledgling movement had it not been for the wise and timely advice of others. Both Bill and Lois remembered the incident as an early example of the group conscience in action.

Bill may have been impulsive and self-seeking — at least, he often publicly deplored these traits in himself — but he also had a remarkable ability to accept criticism. Further, he was learning to listen and to accept advice. Some of the advice was in fact his own teaching coming back to him.

There were disappointments in that year. There was Ebby's slip. In 1936, Ebby had returned to Albany and had found himself a job with the Ford Motor Company in a small town nearby. ''I stayed with this Ford company until the last part of April 1937, went on a trip to New York, and I fell off the wagon,'' Ebby recalled. ''That was after two years and approximately seven months of sobriety and work with the Oxford Group. I returned to Albany, and the old merry-go-round started, and I was drinking heavily and continuously for a long time.''

A second disappointment was that in the new economic troubles that hit the country in the fall of 1937, Bill's work for Quaw and Foley collapsed. This was a serious matter; Lois was trying to earn a living as an independent interior decorator, but freelance decorating assignments were scarce.

Later in 1937, Bill made a trip to Detroit and Cleveland, looking for work. He didn't find a job, but he did visit Dr. Bob and Anne in Akron. It was on this visit that the two men conducted a "formal" review of their work of the past two years.

What they came to realize as a result of that review was astounding: Bill may have been stretching things when he declared that at least 20 cases had been sober a couple of years; but by counting everybody who seemed to have found sobriety in New York and Akron, they concluded that more than 40 alcoholics were staying dry as a result of the program!

"As we carefully rechecked this score, it suddenly burst upon us that a new light was shining into the dark world of the alcoholic," Bill wrote. "Despite the fact that Ebby had slipped, a benign chain reaction, one alcoholic carrying the good news to the next, had started outward from Dr. Bob and me. Conceivably it could one day circle the whole world. What a tremendous thing that realization was! At last we were sure. There would be no more flying totally blind. We actually wept for joy, and Bob and Anne and I bowed our heads in silent thanks."

Their gratitude would have surprised some: Bill, who turned 42 that year, was jobless, while Dr. Bob, at 58, was in danger of losing his house. But Bill now had nearly three years' sobriety; Bob, two and a half years.

---

1. This incident led Sam Shoemaker to apologize to Bill later, after he himself had broken with the Oxford Group in 1941. Shoemaker wrote: "If you ever write the story of A.A.'s early connection with Calvary, I think it ought to be said in all honesty that we were coached in the feeling that you were off on your own spur, trying to do something by yourself, and out of the mainstream of the work. You got your inspiration from those early days, but you didn't get much encouragement from any of us, and for my own part in that stupid desire to control the Spirit, as He manifested Himself in individual people like yourself, I am heartily sorry and ashamed."

Chapter Ten

Bill and Dr. Bob knew that their 40 cases of recovered alcoholics in Ohio and New York had proved the effectiveness of their methods, but how could they carry the message to suffering alcoholics in other places? It had taken more than two years to bring sobriety to a handful, and "the number of alcoholics in the world who wanted to get well was reckoned in millions," Bill said. "How could the great chance we had be brought to them? At the snail's pace we had been going, it was clear that most of them could never be reached.

"We could therefore no longer be a seldom-heard-of secret society. Word-of-mouth communication with the few alcoholics we could contact by our then-current methods would be not only slow but dangerous . . . because the recovery message in which we now had such high confidence might soon be garbled and twisted beyond recognition. Clearly our budding society and its message would have to be publicized."

In discussions with Dr. Bob, Bill insisted that the movement needed paid missionaries to take the message to other areas.

They also needed special hospitals, since most regular hospitals would not accept patients who were officially diagnosed as alcoholics. Finally, they needed a book that would tell the story "to the world" and would also prevent garbling or distortion of the message.

Dr. Bob liked the book idea but had doubts about the missionaries and the hospitals. He felt that paying people to carry the message could harm the spirit of the movement. In his own way, he was reiterating the response of the Clinton Street alcoholics to Bill's proposal about working at Towns Hospital as a paid therapist. But as Bill continued to press the argument, Dr. Bob finally suggested they present the proposals to the other Akron members. Despite his own doubts, he backed Bill to the hilt, "especially about the need for a book," Bill said.

The 18 Akron alcoholics who gathered at T. Henry Williams's home listened quietly while Bill, with support from Dr. Bob, presented the plan. Then, as Bill remembered, "The moment we were through, those alcoholics really did work us over!" They had many objections: Paid workers would kill their goodwill with alcoholics; hospitals would make the Fellowship appear to be a racket; even books and pamphlets could be harmful. But Bill and Dr. Bob pressed their argument. When put to a vote, the whole plan passed — missionaries, hospitals, and book — with some continuing to voice strenuous objections. The vote had been "a mighty close shave," and it was clear that the Akron members would not raise the money needed for such undertakings. That would be Bill's responsibility, and he was already thinking in millions of dollars.

Armed with this shaky mandate from Akron, Bill dashed back to New York and put the same proposal to his own group. "Our little New York group gave me more encouragement than had the Akronites," he said. "Most of them soon fell in with my grandiose notions. It was felt that raising money for such a noble enterprise should present no difficulties at all. . . . 'Certainly the rich will help us. How could they do anything else?' "

But the rich apparently had other things to do with their money. Bill was unable to raise a single dime. Even with the help of the super-promoters in the group, they found nobody interested in investing in the project. Helping a nameless bunch of drunks had become a passion for Bill and Dr. Bob, but as a fundraising idea, it fell flat. For a time, Bill was quite bitter about "the stinginess and shortsightedness" of the rich people who refused to support the cause.

Bill had critics in later years who viewed his early fundraising schemes as signs of his egotism and self-serving ambition. Bill himself constantly worried about his own motives, often describing his own plans as "grandiose." But he was inclined to be self-deprecatory, and the fact was that he was making a determined effort to broaden the work and scope of the Fellowship. The ultraconservatives who opposed his fund-raising plan may have been right, but it was not they who had accepted the enormous challenge of carrying the message to Denver, Seattle, and Houston — to say nothing of remote cities like Melbourne or Stockholm. Bill had this task very much in mind, and his concern was shared by Dr. Bob. (Their resolve anticipated by 28 years the Responsibility Declaration adopted at the International Convention in 1965: "I am responsible. When anyone, anywhere, reaches out for help, I want the hand of A.A. always to be there. And for that: I am responsible.")

One day in the autumn of 1937, disappointed and dispirited, Bill visited his brother-in-law Dr. Leonard Strong Jr., who could always be depended on as adviser and confidant. The doctor listened quietly while Bill poured out his frustration. Then, perhaps more to console Bill than for any other reason, Leonard volunteered that he had once known someone connected with the Rockefeller philanthropies. He was not sure that this man, Willard Richardson, was still alive, or would remember him.

But he, Leonard, was willing to telephone him on Bill's behalf. Perhaps Bill might find some help there; hadn't John D. Rockefeller Jr. been an ardent champion of Prohibition?

Willard Richardson was not only alive; he remembered Leonard Strong and was delighted to hear from him. Moreover, he graciously consented to see Bill — the very next day.

Leonard, always proper and formal, prepared a letter of introduction, dated October 26, 1937, for Bill to take with him: "Dear Mr. Richardson, This will serve to introduce my brother-in-law, Mr. William Wilson, of whom I spoke in our telephone conversation yesterday.

"His work with alcoholics appears very effective and I think

Bill's brother-in-law, adviser, and confidant, Leonard V. Strong, later became a nonalcoholic A.A. trustee.

Willard Richardson provided Bill and others with a first contact with John D. Rockefeller Jr. — and his millions.

merits your interest and possibly that of the Rockefeller Foundation.

"Your courtesy in seeing him is greatly appreciated by me, and I regret my inability to be present."

Bill met Richardson — "an elderly gentleman who had twinkling eyes set in one of the finest faces I have ever seen" — in his office on the 56th floor of the RCA Building. Richardson was warmly cordial. He showed deep interest as Bill told his own story and that of the struggling Fellowship.

A few days later, Leonard received the following word

(dated November 10) from Richardson: "I have now had conferences with four men whose judgment as to the interesting
story of Mr. Wilson I think is good. I assure you that even my
repeating of the story was impressive to them, and they thought
the matter very important. They were all inclined to agree with
me that, if possible, any organization of this project and anything that tended to professionalize or institutionalize it would be
a serious matter and quite undesirable. Some of them thought
quite as highly of Mr. Wilson's experience as a religious one as
they did of it as a liquor one."

The letter then went on to suggest an early luncheon meeting for Bill, Leonard, and Richardson.

Out of this meeting came Richardson's offer of a meeting in
John D. Rockefeller's private boardroom. As Bill remembered,
"He would bring with him Mr. Albert Scott, chairman of the
trustees for Riverside Church, Mr. Frank Amos, an advertising
man and close friend, and Mr. A. LeRoy Chipman, an associate
who looked after some of Mr. Rockefeller's personal affairs."
Bill would be accompanied by Leonard, Dr. Silkworth, some of
the New York alcoholics, and Dr. Bob with certain Akron members. This meeting could be the moment of truth. If Bill and Dr.
Bob could sell their plan to these men, John D. Rockefeller Jr.
would probably give it financial backing.

Getting so close to Rockefeller money was a staggering notion, and as Bill remembered it, "We were riding high on pink
cloud number 17." He rushed home to telephone the good news
to Dr. Bob, who, with Paul S., arrived in New York for the
meeting. Bill also gathered together a group of reliable New
York alcoholics.

The meeting, which took place after a dinner, got off to an
awkward start until somebody suggested that each alcoholic in
the room tell his own story. After listening to a number of such
accounts, Albert Scott declared, "Why, this is first-century
Christianity!" Then he asked, "What can we do to help?"

Bill went over the entire list: hospital chains, paid workers, literature. Dr. Bob, Dr. Silkworth, and the others in Bill's contingent seconded his presentation.

But now Mr. Scott, in his turn, asked an important question: "Won't money spoil this thing?" Later on, when the proposal finally reached John D. Rockefeller Jr., he expressed the same misgivings.

The meeting ended, however, on what Bill considered to be a favorable note: Frank Amos offered to make an investigation of the tiny Fellowship to explore the possibility of establishing a hospital for alcoholics in Akron, and to see Dr. Bob and consider his needs.

Thus, in February 1938, Amos spent several days in Akron, and as Bill described it, "ran a fine-tooth comb through the situation there." The 57-year-old Amos, an Ohio native himself — his family owned the newspaper in Cambridge, 70 miles south of Akron — was very much at home among the professional people

A. LeRoy Chipman (left) and Frank Amos were among the Rockefeller associates who supported a budding Alcoholics Anonymous.

he interviewed in Akron. He was quickly put in touch with people who knew about the Akron alcoholics and expressed high praise for Dr. Bob and his work in the area.

The Amos report showed just how much Dr. Bob and his fellow members had accomplished in the not-quite-three years since that first meeting with Bill. It stated that there were now 50 men and two women who had been ''reformed,'' and it emphasized Dr. Bob's all-important role as leader. ''Apparently, with most cases, it takes a former alcoholic to turn the trick with an alcoholic — and a fine physician of excellent standing, himself formerly an alcoholic and possessed of natural leadership qualities, has proven ideal.''

One plan then proposed by Amos was the establishment of a small alcoholic hospital, 30 to 50 beds, to be run by Dr. Bob. Another proposal was to continue using the City Hospital, but to provide a smaller facility to use as a ''recuperating home.'' In any case, Dr. Bob would need some kind of financial remuneration for a minimum of two years, in order to get the work under way.

Amos recommended a total sum of $50,000 for the early work. Though far short of the millions Bill had envisioned, it was nonetheless a princely sum in early 1938. Albert Scott, however, reiterated his fear that ''too much money could spoil the work.''

John D. Rockefeller Jr. agreed. He also agreed that both Bill and Dr. Bob deserved some financial help, particularly since the mortgage had to be paid off on the Smiths' house. He consented to place $5,000 for their use in the treasury of Riverside Church, with Richardson and his associates to allocate the funds. He also expressed the opinion that the movement should soon become self-supporting. ''If you and the others do not happen to agree, if you really think that the movement needs money, of course you can help them to raise it,'' he is said to have told

A.A.'s concept of self-support came from John D. Rockefeller Jr. — a gift far more valuable than money.

Richardson. "But please don't ever ask me for any more."

Rockefeller's decision was a crushing disappointment for Bill. Yet, he admitted, Rockefeller did help see them through: Some of the money went to pay off Dr. Bob's mortgage, and the rest was used as a weekly draw of $30 for each of them. (Later, Bill always gave Rockefeller credit for helping A.A. steer clear of the trap of professionalism, although it is unclear whose idea this had originally been. Richardson had already voiced this opinion in his letter of November 10. Thus, while Rockefeller may have arrived at the same conclusion independently, he was nonetheless voicing a conviction already strong among his associates.)[1]

But something important other than money did come out of the meetings. Richardson, Amos, and Chipman had become sold on the budding movement and offered their own services. They continued to meet with Bill, Dr. Strong, and the New York alcoholics, to discuss how the movement could be given a structure.

These meetings produced a plan for a tax-free charitable trust or foundation. With Frank Amos's help, a gifted young attorney named John Wood was recruited to join the group and do the legal work in establishing the new foundation.

Many details had to be worked out. (One of the stumbling blocks, ironically, was everyone's inability to provide a "legal" definition of an alcoholic!) It was finally agreed that the trust would be called the Alcoholic Foundation. Its board of trustees was formally implemented on August 11, 1938, with five members, three of whom were nonalcoholics: Richardson, Amos, and John Wood. The alcoholic members were Dr. Bob and Bill R., of the New York area. The trust agreement stipulated that an alcoholic trustee would have to resign immediately if he got drunk. (This actually happened in the case of the New York member, and he was replaced forthwith.)

Bill Wilson served on an eight-member advisory committee created at the same time to advise the board. (The advisory committee, unlike the board, had a majority of alcoholics.) In January 1939, the board was increased from five to seven members, the nonalcoholics still holding a majority. While the foundation had little money and virtually no authority over the groups, it gave the movement a legally formed, New York-based center. It also served as a fund-raising unit for the book project.

The Alcoholic Foundation, with its trustees and its slender financial resources, was small potatoes next to Bill's dream of alcoholic hospitals and paid missionaries.[2] But the effort to raise money had at least resulted in the beginnings of a structure for the movement.

Bill and Dr. Bob had already begun to think seriously about what kind of book would best publicize the program. It would be a book about their own personal experience; it would tell what they had done to keep themselves sober; and it would help others in the process.

----

1. Henrietta Seiberling always maintained that it was she and others who convinced Amos that money would ''spoil this thing,'' and that he in turn reported it to Rockefeller, who agreed.

2. Years later, Bob P., at the A.A. General Service Office, remarked on how far-sighted Bill actually was. ''The alcoholism field has grown so much, and there is such an inflow of money into the field, and all of these facilities have sprung up as he dreamed, except that they are not under A.A. auspices. Yet the A.A. program is an essential part of the therapy in most of them, and A.A. eventually gets many who go through.''

Chapter Eleven

Of all the plans Bill and Dr. Bob had discussed in 1937, the proposal to publish a book about the program was the most realistic. Even to many of those who opposed hospitals and paid missionaries, the book made sense (although the plan had been passed by only a bare majority). By setting forth a clear statement of the recovery program, a book could prevent distortion of the message. It could be sent or carried to alcoholics in distant cities; it could help publicize the movement among nonalcoholics. It might even make money — which could be used to establish an office to handle inquiries, publicity, etc.

Both Bill and Dr. Bob worried constantly about money. Losing the connection with Quaw and Foley was a shocking disappointment to the Wilsons. Bill had been assured that he was doing well for the firm, and that his investigations had been thorough and accurate. The fact that Quaw and Foley went out of business probably did not make it seem any less harsh that he could not gain a permanent foothold in the field he knew best.

But as with the National Rubber Machinery affair more

than two years earlier, Bill's apparent loss proved, in the long run, to be a blessing. He now began to direct all his attention to activities that would help expand the tiny band of recovered alcoholics.

In 1937, Dr. Silkworth often called Bill to say he had a prospect. Fitz M. was the first; Hank P., the second. Hank was full of ideas, and Bill now became associated with Hank on one of his many entrepreneurial ventures. This was a plan to organize gasoline dealers in northern New Jersey to form a cooperative buying organization. It had a name — Honor Dealers; an address — 17 William Street, Newark; and a secretary — Ruth Hock.

Ruth Hock had no idea what she was getting into on the Monday morning that she walked into the Honor Dealers office to apply for a job she had seen advertised. After a breezy interview with Hank, she was pleasantly surprised to be hired to start work immediately at $25 per week, $3 more than she had previously earned. "My immediate impression of Hank was that he had a vibrant personality," Ruth recalled, "that he was capable of strong likes and dislikes, that he seemed to be possessed of inexhaustible energy — and that he liked to make decisions." She was right; Hank was as impatient as Bill was patient.

Presently, Bill came in, and Ruth's first impression was of quiet warmth. She saw a person of slow, deliberate decisions and, she suspected, not much real interest in the service station business.

Later in the day, when Bill had a visitor, Ruth found herself overhearing fragments of an odd conversation: "drunken misery" . . . "miserable wife" . . . "drunk is a disease." When she heard Bill and Hank roaring with laughter shortly afterward, she thought them rather hardhearted. But the pay was good, and she liked the men, so she decided to stay.

A few days later, she was astonished to discover Bill, Hank, and a stranger kneeling at a desk in the private office and praying! (In both Akron and New York, early members followed the Oxford Group practice of kneeling together in prayer. This was apparently discontinued following the final break with the Oxford Group in 1939.) Such behavior hardly seemed compatible with the earlier laughter and buoyant mood of the office. But as the days wore on, Ruth said, "I was pretty soon touched by everybody who came in."

Ruth was a native of Newark and had grown up in a thrifty German family. She attended German-speaking church and lived in an ethnic section of the city. Bill and Hank began calling her "Dutch," and also sometimes "the Duchess," as she presided over the office. Ruth recalled that there was a nickname for everybody; nobody in that office was called by his given name. Only 24, she had already gone through a bad marriage and had a young son to support. But, she said, "All of you made me feel as though I were a very worthwhile person in my own right and very important to you, which in turn made me want to always give my best to all of you. To me, that is part of the secret of the success of A.A. — the generous giving of oneself to the needs of the other." Like many nonalcoholics who became associated with the Fellowship, Ruth found help for her own problems through its principles.

Ruth Hock proved to be a godsend to the little group. She was a tireless and loyal worker. She would remain with them for five years. Bill and Hank might have gotten somewhere in the service station business, Ruth believed, if they had given as much energy, thought, and enthusiasm to it as they did to helping drunks. She soon realized that the Honor Dealers business was really only a means to an end — "that end being to help a bunch of nameless drunks." She found herself becoming "more and more interested in each new face that came along with the alcoholic problem and caring very much whether they made the grade or not."

Before long, Bill and Hank began to have difficulty paying both Ruth's salary and the rent on the office. Ruth went without pay for a while, but the landlord — who had not been caught up in the contagion of their work — eventually forced them out, and they moved to a smaller office, also in Newark, that was more within their means. Until 1939, Bill's major headquarters was in Newark.

Bill began work on the book in March or April of 1938. Ruth, who typed the manuscript, remembered that he would arrive at the office with yellow scratch sheets of notes outlining each chapter. "My understanding," she recollected, "was that those notes were the result of long thought, after hours of discussion pro and con with everybody who might be interested. That is the way I remember first seeing an outline of the Twelve Steps."

Bill would stand behind Ruth and dictate the material while she typed. He would dictate a section and then look back over the typed pages while his thoughts were still working in that vein. The work went slowly, said Ruth, because Bill was ready to drop it any time anybody came into the office wanting to talk!

Working in his own rather unorthodox way, Bill soon completed his personal story and the chapter called "There Is a Solution." These, which would become the first and second chapters, were Multilithed immediately to be used in the money-raising campaign in the summer of 1938. Bill and the new trustees still believed that contributions from the wealthy would be forthcoming as soon as the significance of the new movement was fully understood.

Now, an exciting thing happened. Through Frank Amos, Bill was put in touch with Eugene Exman, the religious editor of Harper & Brothers. Exman read the two chapters, sounded Bill out on his ability to complete the book, and then offered to publish it, with a $1,500 advance against royalties.

Bill was back in the clouds. Not many first authors receive such quick acceptance. Yet he later said he had instant second thoughts about the offer. The Fellowship would not own its book. What if it became a smashing best-seller? They would be unable to handle the thousands of inquiries from desperate alcoholics and their families.

The trustees were delighted, however, and urged Bill to accept the Harper offer.

It was Hank who now stepped in. Hank, whom Bill described as "one of the most terrific power-drivers" he had ever met, convinced him they should bypass the trustees and sell shares in their own company to publish the book themselves. It bothered Bill to go against the trustees, but he liked the idea of publishing their own book. When he went back to see Exman at Harper, "To my utter amazement, he agreed, quite contrary to his own interest, that a society like ours ought to control and publish its own literature. Moreover, he felt that very possibly we could do this with success," Bill later recalled. Finally, even the trustees' disapproval could not keep Bill and Hank from charging ahead on their new venture.

Hank was able to talk most of the New York members into supporting the self-publishing plan. Dr. Bob also agreed to go along with it, but he was so dubious that he did not at first tell the other Akronites. Bill and Hank then approached Edward Blackwell, president of Cornwall Press in Cornwall, New York. He explained that the printing cost of an average-size book was only about ten percent of its retail price. That excited them still further; they could afford to pay as much as a dollar per book for distribution and still make huge profits.

Hank worked up a prospectus for a new company that would sell 600 shares of stock at $25 par value. One-third of the shares would be sold to the members for cash; the other two-thirds would be divided between Hank and Bill for their work. The customary author's royalty would be assigned to the Alcoholic Foundation, a gesture meant to mollify the trustees. Hank supported his plan with charts showing estimated profits on sales of 100,000, 500,000, and even 1,000,000 books, Bill recalled.[1] Bill, though not so optimistic, did hope that income from the book would enable him and a few others to become full-time workers for the Fellowship and to set up a general headquarters.

Hank's next action was to form a company that he called

Works Publishing, Inc. How that title was chosen is a matter of some dispute; some said it was named for the Akronites' (particularly Anne Smith's) favorite quotation from James, "Faith without works is dead"; others said it was named for a favorite slogan of the membership, "It works!" Hank bought a pad of stock certificates at a stationery store, typed the name of the new company at the top of each certificate, and signed his name, with the title "President," at the bottom. "When I protested these irregularities," Bill recalled, "Hank said there was no time to waste; why be concerned with small details?"

Bill may have later regretted this early haste, as ownership of the Works Publishing shares eventually became a sharply controversial issue. In retrospect, accounts differ as to who was responsible for what. Hank's son said that it was Hank who got the book project rolling, and that his father and Bill both expected to make a million dollars from the project. Ruth disagreed; she remembered that the two men were about equally responsible. "At that time, it wouldn't have been written without Bill, and it wouldn't have been published without Hank," she said. Nor did she believe that either man "expected to make a fortune." The motive, always, was to help the Fellowship; their original idea was to begin giving the books away as soon as possible.

Whatever their intentions, what happened next was totally unexpected by both Bill and Hank: None of the New York alcoholics would buy any of the 600 Works Publishing shares!

Bill and Hank approached the *Reader's Digest*: Would that publication consider doing a story about the Fellowship and the book? With the same luck that had been riding with them at Harper, they obtained from a *Digest* editor what they heard as a promise of a story when the book was completed in the spring.

It didn't work out that way, however. When they returned the following year with the newly published book, the *Digest* editor had all but forgotten them. But in the meantime, on the strength of the *Digest* promise, other members and friends of the Fellowship were persuaded to invest. Bill and Hank soon sold

200 shares for $5,000, and Charlie Towns lent them $2,500. That was enough to support the work during the writing process, although it would not cover printing costs.

Bill continued to work up basic ideas on yellow scratch paper and then dictate rough drafts of the chapters to Ruth. He had no real outline, but followed only a list of possible chapter headings. He would then send copies of the chapters out to Akron to Dr. Bob for checking and criticism, and would himself review the same material with the New York members.

While Bill received "nothing but the warmest support" from Akron, he got what he called "a real mauling" from the New York members. Possibly, the Akron members were strongly attuned to Bill's spiritual ideas, while the New York group contained members who were either agnostic or skeptical. Another possible reason was Dr. Bob's enormous influence and stature; his support of the book virtually guaranteed that most of the Akron members would also support it.

After the third and fourth chapters — "More About Alcoholism" and "We Agnostics" — were completed, Bill came to a place that had been a barrier in his own mind and had given him considerable worry. He had to set down the actual program for the alcoholic to follow, and he wanted to make it as powerful as possible.

He had a great fear that the message might be misunderstood by alcoholics in distant places. It was one thing to pass on the message face-to-face, when one could personally observe the other's reactions and be present to respond to objections, questions, or confusion. In print, there was no second chance. What was printed on the page might well be the only information the suffering alcoholic would have access to. It had to be powerful — and thorough. As Bill put it, "There must not be a single loophole through which the rationalizing alcoholic could wiggle out." Bill was about to write the famous fifth chapter, "How It Works."

The basic material for the chapter was the word-of-mouth

program that Bill had been talking ever since his own recovery. It was heavy with Oxford Group principles, and had in addition some of the ideas Bill had gleaned from William James and from Dr. Silkworth. Moreover, Bill had worked with Dr. Bob and other alcoholics in testing and sifting the workability and effectiveness of the early program. While he would be the nominal author of the fifth chapter, he was in fact serving as spokesman for all the others.

According to Bill, their word-of-mouth program had thus far been a pretty consistent procedure, containing six steps[2] to achieve and maintain their sobriety. There is no evidence that the Oxford Group had such a specific program; yet the Oxford Group ideas prevail in these original six steps, as listed by Bill:

"1. We admitted that we were licked, that we were powerless over alcohol.

"2. We made a moral inventory of our defects or sins.

"3. We confessed or shared our shortcomings with another person in confidence.

"4. We made restitution to all those we had harmed by our drinking.

"5. We tried to help other alcoholics, with no thought of reward in money or prestige.

"6. We prayed to whatever God we thought there was for power to practice these precepts."

Although those steps had helped in the recovery of New York and Akron alcoholics, Bill felt that the program still was not definitive. "Maybe our six chunks of truth should be broken up into smaller pieces," he said. "Thus we could better get the distant reader over the barrel, and at the same time we might be able to broaden and deepen the spiritual implications of our whole presentation."

Bill wrote the Twelve Steps, he said, while lying in bed at 182 Clinton Street with pencil in hand and pad of yellow scratch paper on his knee. He wrote them in bed, said Lois, not because he was really sick, but he wasn't feeling well, and if he could lie down, he did: "He got into bed, that being the best place to think."

As he started to write, he asked for guidance. And he relaxed. The words began tumbling out with astonishing speed. He completed the first draft in about half an hour, then kept on writing until he felt he should stop and review what he had written. Numbering the new steps, he found that they added up to twelve — a symbolic number; he thought of the Twelve Apostles, and soon became convinced that the Society should have twelve steps.

The very first draft of the Twelve Steps, as Bill wrote them that night, has been lost. This is an approximate reconstruction of the way he first set them down:

"1. We admitted we were powerless over alcohol — that our lives had become unmanageable.

"2. Came to believe that God could restore us to sanity.

"3. Made a decision to turn our wills and our lives over to the care and direction of God.

"4. Made a searching and fearless moral inventory of ourselves.

"5. Admitted to God, to ourselves, and to another human being the exact nature of our wrongs.

"6. Were entirely willing that God remove all these defects of character.

"7. Humbly on our knees asked Him to remove these shortcomings — holding nothing back.

"8. Made a complete list of all persons we had harmed, and became willing to make amends to them all.

"9. Made direct amends to such people wherever possible, except when to do so would injure them or others.

"10. Continued to take personal inventory and when we were wrong promptly admitted it.

"11. Sought through prayer and meditation to improve our contact with God, praying only for knowledge of His will for us and the power to carry that out.

"12. Having had a spiritual experience as the result of this course of action, we tried to carry this message to others, especially alcoholics, and to practice these principles in all our affairs."

Bill's first three steps were culled from his reading of James, the teachings of Sam Shoemaker, and those of the Oxford Group. The first step had to do with calamity and disaster; the second was an admission of defeat — that one could not go on living on the strength of one's own resources; and the third was an appeal to a Higher Power for help.

As Bill remembered it, he had two late callers that evening: his close friend Horace C.[3] and with him a "newcomer, dry barely three months." The two men had some objections: to the frequent use of the word "God" and to asking on one's knees to have one's shortcomings removed.

Ruth Hock said that Bill appeared in the office one day with the steps practically complete. But when he showed the manuscript to local members, there were heated discussions and many other suggestions. Jimmy B. opposed the strong references to God, in both the steps and the rest of the early chapters; Hank wanted to soft-pedal them; but Fitz insisted that the book should express Christian doctrines and use Biblical terms and expressions. Ruth remembered: "Fitz was for going all the way with 'God'; you [Bill] were in the middle; Hank was for very little; and I — trying to reflect the reaction of the nonalcoholic — was for very little. The result of this was the phrase 'God as we understood Him,' which I don't think ever had much of a negative reaction anywhere."

Bill regarded these changes as "concessions to those of little or no faith" and called them "the great contribution of our atheists and agnostics. They had widened our gateway so that all who suffer might pass through, regardless of their belief or *lack of belief*."

In writing the steps, Bill also produced the hard-hitting promise of the introductory paragraphs, beginning, "Rarely have we seen a person fail who has thoroughly followed our path ['directions' in the earlier manuscript]. Those who do not recover are people who cannot or will not completely give themselves to this simple program, usually men and women who are constitutionally incapable of being honest with themselves.'' (According to an apocryphal story, Bill was asked in later years whether there was any change he wished he could make in the Big Book, and he replied that he would change ''rarely'' to ''never.'' Bill himself said he never considered that change.)

Bill wrote at least ten of the opening chapters of the book; there is some reason to believe that ''To Employers'' may have been written by Hank. But there is no doubt about the authorship of ''To Wives.'' Of that chapter, Lois said, ''Bill wrote it, and I was mad.'' She added, ''I wasn't so much mad as hurt. I still don't know why Bill wrote it. I've never really gotten into it — why he insisted upon writing it. I said to him, 'Well, do you want me to write it?' And he said no, he thought it should be in the same style as the rest of the book.''

Each week, Bill would read what he had written to those who gathered at his home on Tuesday evenings. While he was working his way through the explanatory chapters, New York and Akron members were submitting their personal stories. Jim S., an Akron journalist, interviewed members in that area and then helped write their stories. The New York members wrote their own, with editing by Bill and Hank — sometimes over the objections of the authors. In addition to Bill's and Dr. Bob's stories, the book eventually contained 16 stories from Akron and 12 from New York.

By the end of January 1939, the manuscript was ready for preliminary distribution; 400 copies were Multilithed and circulated to members, friends, and other allies for comments and evaluation.

Perhaps one of the most important contributions was ''The Doctor's Opinion,'' by Dr. Silkworth, which appears at the very beginning of the book. The idea to include a chapter by a medical person had come from Dr. Esther L. Richards of Johns Hopkins Hospital in Baltimore. Of the prospectus Bill had sent her, she said, "I give it no higher compliment than to say that I read through the first two chapters without stopping, so gripping was the presentation of the material." Then, she suggested getting "a Number One physician who has a wide knowledge of the alcoholic's medical and social problems to write an introduction." Bill evidently acted on the suggestion at once, because a letter dated only nine days later contains the message from Dr. Silkworth that appears in the first edition. Silkworth had already written two articles about alcoholism for the *Medical Record* (a third would appear in 1939). He made a powerful case for alcoholism as an illness of mind and body, using the term "moral psychology" to characterize the work of the New York Fellowship.

Bill was worried about the reaction of organized religion. Dr. Harry Emerson Fosdick, the highly respected minister of the Riverside Church, warmly approved an advance copy and promised to review the book when it was published. Fosdick's endorsement virtually guaranteed interest in Protestant circles. Bill was more apprehensive about the response of the Roman Catholics. What if that church was to decide that A.A. was a heretical cult?

Luck was on their side. A new member, Morgan R., himself a Catholic, happened to know somebody on the Catholic Committee on Publications in the New York Archdiocese. He hurried over with the book and soon received a wonderful book report: The committee members had high praise for the book and its message. They suggested some minor changes, which Bill quickly accepted. The most significant of these was at the end of Bill's own story. Where he declared that the recovered alcoholics have found heaven right here on earth, the committee gently suggested that he change "heaven" to "Utopia." As they said, "After all, we Catholics are promising folks something much better later on!" Although the committee members gave no official approval of the book, their unofficial endorsement allowed Bill to breathe easier.

Bill always said that more than 100 titles were considered for the book. The title that appeared on the Multilithed copies was "Alcoholics Anonymous." There is some dispute about who first thought up this title; most thought it was Joe W., a *New Yorker* writer who remained sober only "on and off." That was Bill's recollection, and he believed that the name first appeared in their discussions in October 1938. The first documented use of the name in the A.A. archives is in a letter from Bill to Willard Richardson dated July 15, 1938. It is an invitation to Messrs. Richardson, Chipman, and Scott of the Rockefeller Foundation to come to any of the Clinton Street meetings. "Certainly in the cases of you gentlemen," Bill wrote, "we shall gladly waive the heavy drinking that has qualified us for Alcoholics Anonymous. We think you are one of us, and there are no honorary members." There, the name is used in such a way as to indicate that Richardson was already familiar with it.

According to a letter dated July 18, 1938, from Dr. Richards of Johns Hopkins, Bill, at that time, was using "Alcoholics Anonymous" both as the working title of the book and as the name of the Fellowship.

Among other book titles suggested were "One Hundred Men," "The Empty Glass," "The Dry Way," "The Dry Life," "Dry Frontiers," and "The Way Out." In a jab at his own egotism, Bill said that he had even proposed calling it "The B. W. Movement"!

The name "One Hundred Men" fell by the wayside because of the objections of Florence R., at that time the only female member. (Her story in the first edition was "A Feminine Victory." She later returned to drinking and died an apparent suicide in Washington, D.C.) The title page, however, did describe the book as "The Story of How More Than One Hundred Men Have Recovered From Alcoholism." By the second printing, this had been changed to "Thousands of Men and Women."

"One Hundred Men" was still the working title in a letter from Frank Amos to the Rockefeller associates dated January 6, 1939. But "Alcoholics Anonymous" headlined the letter, indicating that this had by now become an informal way, at least in New York, of identifying the movement. Also, a pamphlet prepared as a fund-raising presentation early in 1939 was titled "Alcoholics Anonymous."

The choices quickly boiled down to "The Way Out," favored by a majority in Akron, and "Alcoholics Anonymous," preferred by most in New York. When a vote was taken in the two groups, "The Way Out" prevailed by a bare majority.[4]

Although Bill favored "Alcoholics Anonymous," he knew that he could not arbitrarily settle upon his own preference — he was already learning to work with the group conscience. So he asked Fitz, who lived near Washington, D.C., to check titles in the Library of Congress. How many books were called "The Way Out"? How many were called "Alcoholics Anonymous"?

Fitz is supposed to have replied by telegram to the effect that the Library of Congress had 25 books entitled "The Way Out," 12 entitled "The Way," and none called "Alcoholics Anonymous." That settled the matter; nobody wanted to struggle with the burden of being simply another "way out."

The title of the book quickly became the name of the Fellowship, although debate continues about where and how the name was first used by a group. Oldtimer Clarence S. stated that the Cleveland group he founded in May 1939 was actually the first *group* to use the name "Alcoholics Anonymous." Whatever the individual groups called themselves (usually just "meetings"), the name certainly was used earlier than that to describe the Fellowship as a whole. In the book "Alcoholics Anonymous," which came off the press in April 1939 but was set in type much earlier, two passages from the foreword read:

"We, of Alcoholics Anonymous, are more than one hundred men and women who have recovered from a seemingly hopeless state of mind and body. To show other alcoholics *pre-*

cisely how we have recovered is the main purpose of this book. . . .

"When writing or speaking publicly about alcoholism, we urge each of our Fellowship to omit his personal name, designating himself instead as 'A Member of Alcoholics Anonymous.' "

By April 1939, Alcoholics Anonymous was a fellowship with its own basic text and program.

Final editing of the book was done by Tom Uzzell, member of the faculty at New York University. Uzzell cut the book by at least a third (some say half — from 800 to 400 pages) and sharpened it in the process. He was very firm in declaring that "Alcoholics Anonymous" was the right title; it described the Fellowship, and it was catchy. Dr. Howard, a psychiatrist in Montclair, New Jersey, made a vitally important contribution. He suggested that there were too many "you musts." Bill said the psychiatrist's "idea was to remove all forms of coercion, to put our Fellowship on a 'we ought' basis instead of a 'you must' basis."

Jimmy B. had a colorful description of this interchange: "Dr. Howard read [the manuscript] and brought it back the next day," he recalled. "He said Bill was making a damn big mistake. 'This is the Oxford Group,' he said. 'You have to change the whole damn thing.'

"We asked, 'Why? What is the matter with it? It is perfect.'

"He said, 'You have to take out the must. You have to take out the God — the complete God.' Did Bill go into a tizzy then! He almost blew his top. Here was his baby being torn apart by a screwball psychiatrist."

With all the chapters completed and edited, Hank and Bill went back to Edward Blackwell at Cornwall Press and said they were ready for printing to begin. But there was one problem — they were almost broke. They still believed, however, that the *Reader's Digest* article would make the book a runaway success.

Blackwell helped them in two ways. First, he agreed to print the book and accept $500 — all they could afford — as a down payment. Then, he suggested an initial printing of 5,000 copies instead of the unrealistically high numbers Bill and Hank were thinking of. Bill believed that Blackwell had caught the spirit and wanted to help them — even at the risk of financial loss for himself and his firm. (Bill never failed to express gratitude to Blackwell in later years. A.A. continued to have the Big Book printed at Cornwall Press for a long time after it became a steady seller, so the venture also became profitable for the company.)

The manuscript that they delivered to the printing plant in Cornwall, New York, had been revised and changed so much that it was almost unreadable. The plant manager was so appalled that he nearly sent it back to be retyped. But as Bill remembered, supersalesman Hank persuaded him to accept the copy, and soon printer's galleys were issuing forth for corrections and approval.

There was one last question to be discussed and argued before the presses began rolling: What would be the list price? They finally decided on $3.50, rather high for 1939. To compensate for the price, they chose the thickest paper in Blackwell's plant. "The original volume proved to be so bulky that it became known as the 'Big Book,' " Bill recalled. "Of course the idea was to convince the alcoholic purchaser that he was indeed getting his money's worth!" The first printing was a half inch thicker than the current edition — although the latter has 14 more personal stories, plus other additional copy.

Ruth Hock remembered a different reason for the book's size: She thought it was produced with the new or prospective member in mind. "The idea, as I understood it, was that everybody who read this book, to start, was going to be shaky and nervous, and they didn't want fine print or fine pages. They thought an alcoholic would handle [thick pages] better."

By March 1939, pages were coming off the presses. The pages were bound in a thick, dark red cloth cover with a simple "Alcoholics Anonymous" in cursive lettering embossed in gold. For all the stumbling blocks in its preparation, "Alcoholics Anonymous" turned out to be both attractive and appealing, worthy of its role as the basic "textbook" of this new Fellowship. It had been completed in a single year, and it presented A.A.'s experience with alcoholism, plus the Twelve Steps program, in simple, direct language. The personal stories were dramatic and persuasive. Significantly, almost everything the book had to say about alcoholics' problems and their recovery is still applicable today.

The foreword of that first printing, published in April, stated: "We are not an organization in the conventional sense of the word. There are no fees nor dues whatsoever. The only requirement for membership is an honest desire to stop drinking. We are not allied with any particular faith, sect or denomination, nor do we oppose anyone. We simply wish to be helpful to those who are afflicted."

With a few changes and additions, that statement of purpose would be repeated as a preamble to thousands of A.A. meetings every day in the years to come.

---

1. By March 1991, 10,000,000 copies of the Big Book had been printed and distributed.

2. In later years, some A.A. members referred to this procedure as the six steps of the Oxford Group. Reverend T. Willard Hunter, who spent 18 years in full-time staff positions for the Oxford Group and M.R.A., said, "I never once saw or heard anything like the Six Tenets. It would be impossible to find them in any Oxford Group - M.R.A. literature. I think they must have been written by someone else under some sort of misapprehension."

3. In "Alcoholics Anonymous Comes of Age," which was published in 1957, Bill referred to Horace C. as "Howard A." Horace had resigned as a trustee following a dispute, and Bill did not wish to offend him by using his name.

4. The results of the voting support the belief that the term already was in use among New York members, who had broken ties with the Oxford Group. The term was less familiar to members in Akron, where the break was still several months away (to occur in November and December 1939).

Chapter Twelve

The 5,000 copies of the Big Book lay idle in Edward Blackwell's warehouse. For months after their publication, it seemed that they were a waste of the paper they were printed on.

Bill and Hank were convinced the book would catch on if it could be gotten into the right hands — the hands of suffering alcoholics. But for the moment, they couldn't sell it. They weren't sure they could even give it away. Seeking coverage, they had tried all the national magazines without a single nibble; no editor had yet spotted A.A.'s great potential. To get the book moving, they needed some kind of national publicity.

Then Morgan R., their recently sober member who had guided the book through the Catholic Committee on Publications, had a splendid idea. Before landing on hard times, Morgan had been a successful advertising man. "I know Gabriel Heatter very well, and I'm sure he would give us a hand," declared Morgan.

Heatter had an immensely popular radio program called "We the People." He specialized in human-interest interviews, followed by heartrending commentary issued by him in a soothing, fatherly voice. In 1939, an interview on "We the People" had publicity value equivalent to that of present-day late-night talk shows.

It was a long shot, but it paid off. Heatter accepted the proposal and scheduled Morgan for an interview. He would outline Morgan's drinking career and recovery, and include material from the book. It would be only three minutes, but it would be national exposure. Bill and Hank were sure that Gabriel Heatter would provide the big breakthrough they had been waiting for. The program was scheduled for a week hence, on April 25, at 9:00 p.m.

There was one hitch: What if Morgan got drunk? He had only recently been released from the Greystone institution. To guard against this possibility, Hank persuaded the reluctant Irishman to submit to continuous surveillance for the week that remained until the night of the broadcast. To this end, they secured the use of a double room in Manhattan's Downtown Athletic Club, and there someone stayed with Morgan at all times. They did it in relays, never for a moment letting him out of their sight.

Hank's promotional plan to accompany the broadcast was to send postcards to all doctors east of the Mississippi, announcing the Heatter broadcast and urging them to buy a copy of "Alcoholics Anonymous." The replies would be sent to P.O. Box 658, Church Street Annex, mailing address for the Alcoholic Foundation. To raise the $500 they needed for the mailing, they issued promissory notes against Works Publishing — a bold action in view of the company's bankrupt condition. After mailing 20,000 postcards, the men were confident of an avalanche of replies in response to Heatter's broadcast.

Breathlessly, they waited for the moment that would make A.A. a household word. Again, they were talking of book sales in carloads. "An hour before broadcast time, our whole membership and their families gathered about their radios to wait for the great moment,'' Bill remembered.

''Sighs of relief went up in every New York member's home when Morgan's voice was heard. He had hit the deadline without getting drunk. It was a heart-stirring three minutes. Gabriel Heatter saw to that, and he was well assisted by Morgan, who was no slouch as a radio man.''

This is the entire text of the ''We the People'' broadcast:

HEATTER: ''The man beside me now has had one of the most gripping and dramatic experiences I've ever heard. I'm not going to tell you his name. And when you hear what he has to say, I think you'll understand why. But after checking the facts, the Listener's Committee of 'We the People' decided to grant him time because they feel that if one person is helped by hearing his story, then 'We the People' will have done a real service. All right, sir.''

ANONYMOUS: ''Six months ago, I got out of an insane asylum. I'd been sent there because I was drinking myself to death. But the doctors said they could do nothing for me. And only four years ago, I was making $20,000 a year. I was married to a swell girl and had a young son. But I worked hard, and like lots of my friends, I used to drink to relax. Only they knew when to stop. I didn't. And pretty soon I drank myself out of my job. I promised my wife I'd straighten out. But I couldn't. Finally, she took the baby and left me.

''The next year was like a nightmare. I was penniless. I went out on the street — panhandled money for liquor. Every time I sobered up, I swore not to touch another drop. But if I went a few hours without a drink, I'd begin to cry like a baby and tremble all over. One day after I left the asylum, I met a friend of mine. He took me to the home of one of his friends. A bunch of men were sitting around, smoking cigars, telling jokes, having a great time. But I noticed they weren't drinking. When Tom told me they'd all been in the same boat as I was, I couldn't believe him. But he said, 'See that fellow? He's a doctor. Drank himself out of his practice. Then he straightened out. Now he's head of a big hospital.' Another big strapping fellow was a grocery clerk. Another, the vice-president of a big corporation. They got together five years ago. Called themselves Alcoholics Anonymous. And they'd worked out a method of recovery. One of their most important secrets was helping the other fellow. Once they began to follow it, the method proved successful and helped others get on their feet — they found they could stay away from liquor.

"Gradually, those men helped me back to life. I stopped drinking. Found courage to face life once again. Today, I've got a job, and I'm going to climb back to success.

"Recently, we wrote a book called 'Alcoholics Anonymous.' It tells precisely how we all came back from a living death. Working on that book made me realize how much other people had suffered — how they'd gone through the same thing I did. That's why I wanted to come on this program. I wanted to tell people who are going through that torment — if they sincerely want to, they can come back. Take their place in society once again!'' (APPLAUSE) (MUSIC)

Bill and the others sat back then, and speculated on how they would handle the flood of inquiries they knew were already in the mail. Bill remembered the great self-restraint they exercised to stay away from the post office for three whole days. When they finally went to check the box, they took empty suitcases to carry the reply cards.

A bare handful of cards awaited them. ''Sick clear through, we looked through the 12 replies,'' Bill said. ''Some ribbed us unmercifully. Others, evidently inscribed by medics in their cups, were totally illegible. The two remaining cards were orders for the book 'Alcoholics Anonymous.' ''

April 1939 continued to unfold as a disastrous month in a most difficult year. There were a few bright moments, but these would not be recognized as such until much later. One was the arrival of Marty M., the first woman to achieve lasting sobriety in Alcoholics Anonymous. A.A. had been forcibly brought to her attention while she was a patient in the Blythewood Sanitarium in Greenwich, Connecticut. Psychiatrist Harry Tiebout, medical director at Blythewood, was already interested in the movement. He had been sent an advance Multilith copy of the Big Book for review. He gave it to Marty, an attractive woman of 34 who was as difficult as she was appealing. At first, she refused to read it; she finally consented, scanning it with skepticism and disdain. ''I couldn't stand all those capital G's,'' she said. ''I didn't believe in God. I didn't want to read a book that was all about God.'' A.A. people had hypnotized themselves, she informed Tiebout defiantly; they were fanatics. Because Tiebout kept pressuring her, she would read just enough of the book to give herself fuel to provoke an argument with him.

This intellectual squabbling continued over a period of months until the day Marty found herself in a crisis, a crisis of personal resentment and fury. In her rage, she said, she literally saw everything in red — including the pages of the book lying open on her bed. ''But,'' she remembered, ''in the middle of the page there was a line that wasn't red. It was jet black. And it stood out as if it was cut out of wood. And it read, 'We cannot live with anger.'[1] And that did it. I was on my knees beside that bed. I had been there quite a while, because the bedspread had a big wet spot on it from my tears. I felt something in that room, and the main feeling I had was that I'm free. I'm free!''

Shortly after that incident, Marty attended her very first A.A. meeting:

''We [Horace ''Popsie'' M. took her] got on a subway to go over to Brooklyn after dinner. We arrived at this brownstone house. I was sent upstairs to leave my coat. And I wouldn't come down. I had taken a look, and there was this room that swept all the way through with the partitions. There was a front living room, and a back dining room — you know the first floor of an old brownstone. And I looked in there, and I had never seen so many people in my life. There were probably 30 or 40 people. Everybody brought their families if they had them.

''I might never have come down if somebody hadn't come

upstairs. Lois came up. And she put her arms around me, and she said, 'You know, we have been waiting for you for such a long time. Everybody wants you downstairs. You come down.' And I never felt such love as I had felt from that woman. And I went like a little lamb with her downstairs.

"It became evident to me that first night that [Bill] was a leader. The group I was with and a few others went upstairs to their upstairs living room, and Bill sat, and we asked him questions. I had read the book about 20 times by then. I knew whole chunks of it by heart, and I had a thousand questions. I remember Bill looking at me and laughing, and he said, 'You know, this is a Tuesday night. And you know, Marty, you can't do it all by Thursday.' The second thing I loved was: He said to me, 'There is one thing we have to be very careful of and avoid' (I think Dr. Tiebout may have talked to him . . . who I was and so on) — 'resentments. How do you handle your resentments?'

"And I said, 'Resentments? I've never had a resentment in my life.'

"He said, 'Don't tell me that. You can't possibly be your age . . .' I was only 34. They all laughed.

"I was very put out, very upset, and very hurt. I said, 'I don't know why you are laughing. I don't think it's funny at all.'

"And Bill said, 'What do you do, how do you feel when somebody does something that you find is unjust, or they do something hurtful to you? Or they do something that is very wrong from your point of view, that directly applies to you?'

"And I said, 'Oh, I'm hurt.'

"And they said, 'And you don't know that you have a resentment? What do you think that is?'

"I said, 'Well, when people hurt me like that, I avoid them. I just withdraw into myself.'

"And Bill said, 'Well, you realize who you were hurting, don't you?'

"And I said, 'No, I don't know what you mean.'

"He said, 'You were only hurting yourself.' In other

words, I had my first lesson with Bill as a teacher that night. He was a great teacher.''

Lois, too, remembered that night: ''She [Marty] was afraid of what she would find at the meeting, so she preferred to stay upstairs with me. I finally persuaded her the A.A.'s wanted and needed her. We went down together.''

Back in Greenwich, Marty reported her Brooklyn trip to her close friend, another alcoholic at Blythewood: ''Grennie, we are no longer alone,'' she said — a now-famous A.A. statement, for it summarizes the relief felt by every isolated alcoholic who finally finds the Fellowship.

Marty's first meeting was one of the last to be held at 182 Clinton. Since Dr. Burnham's death in 1936, Lois and Bill had been paying the mortgage company a small rental to stay on in the house. But in 1939, as the Depression eased, more money became available, and property values rose, the mortgage company was able to sell the building. On Wednesday, April 26, 1939, the day following the ''We the People'' broadcast, Lois and Bill were forced out of the house that had been the Burnham family home for half a century.

Lois said, ''It was necessary not only to pack up our own possessions, but also to get rid of those accumulated by my parents from 1888 on. The Salvation Army and Goodwill Industries got carloads.'' Their own furniture, including Lois's fine grand piano bought in their affluent days, went into storage. One can only wonder what must have gone through their minds as they watched each piece being lifted into the moving van.

One can only wonder — and imagine — what must have gone through their hearts as they relinquished their last vestige of security and ''normality.'' They had no home and no income. Lois's diary entry for that day is terse: ''Left 182 for good. Went to P——s'' (Hank and his wife).

For the next two years, they would have no permanent home of their own; they would live as vagabonds, first with one A.A. family, then with another.

When later someone asked Bill how he and Lois had gotten through the next two years, Bill explained, in a masterpiece of understatement, "We were invited out to dinner a lot." Estimates vary, but Lois's best guess at the number of their "homes" during the next two years comes to about 50 — not counting weekend "visits."

Arduous as it must have been, this sort of peripatetic "living around" came more easily to the Wilsons, perhaps, than it might have to another couple. Ever since the early days of their marriage and their life on the road as "Wall Street hoboes," they had always moved around. Except for the dark years of Bill's worst drinking, their life-style had always involved many friends and a great deal of visiting back and forth, both as hosts and as guests. The Wilsons had the sort of energy and liveliness that would have emotionally and physically exhausted a less gregarious couple. To judge from the entries in Lois's diaries, she and Bill were almost indefatigable. Privacy was an experience that they often yearned for but seldom received.

A typical week's worth of moving around, as taken from entries in Lois's diary, will illustrate this:

Saturday, February 10: "Spent the night with Dot. Bill and I drove out with Leonard around 4 p.m."

Sunday, February 11: "Dot drove Bill and me to ferry at Tarrytown. Not running, so drove to Yonkers, and Bill and I took ferry to Alpine. The Rockland bus took Bill to N.Y., but through comedy of errors, I waited three hours for Mag. Finally came here to Monsey. Jimmy B —— came back with Bill. He has job in Philadelphia, so needs his car. So that's the end of the car for us."

Tuesday, February 13: "Took bus to town. Met Edith M ——. Had tea. After meeting, Bill and I spent night at Chris'."

Friday, February 16: "Drove back with Cy and Barb to Ardsley to spend night. Bill is to go to Greenwich meeting."

Sunday, February 18: "Took a noon train to N.Y., and to my surprise, Bill met me at Grand Central. He had misunderstood where I would be and thought I was at Ora T——'s. We went on to the South Orange meeting. Spending the night with the M——s.''

Monday, February 19: ''Bill and Gordon went to the book office. Herbert drove me and my bag later to Newark, where I took the tube to N.Y. to look for a furnished room. I decided to leave my bag at Morgan R——'s apartment, where he had asked Bill and me to come for a while. When I reached here, it was so luxurious and quiet, with a piano and a maid, and Morgan seemed to want us to stay, so we decided to stay here until the first of March anyway.''

Lois termed it ''living around.'' With one notable exception, she seems to have endured their two years of gypsy existence with her usual forbearance, good cheer, and extraordinary ability to find the positive.

Typically, her initial reaction to their first temporary dwelling — a summer bungalow at Green Pond in northern New Jersey — was to admire its beauty:

''It was delightful to be in the country, especially when spring was transforming the world. Delicate new leaves slowly embroidered the stark silhouettes of the trees, each variety making a different lace pattern against the sky. . . .

''We had no car, so we had to walk about four miles to Newfoundland [New Jersey] for provisions and to take the train to New York. Bill had many things to attend to about his book and the Alcoholic Foundation, so he went to New York frequently. . . .

''Many A.A.'s visited us at Green Pond. When we were alone on the days when Bill didn't have to go to New York, we did many fun things: rowing on the lake, hiking, even trying out our old bath-towel-sail idea. . . .

''Roaming through the area, we found many lovely wildflowers, such as arbutus and pink lady slippers. After a good hike, we would often duck in the pond and then sunbathe on a large, flat rock.''

Whatever their circumstances, no matter how shaky their

future looked, Bill and Lois always retained their capacity for enjoying themselves, each other, and nature. They did not let anxieties about past or future interfere with that enjoyment. As a couple, they were gifted with that elusive ability to "live in the now." (It is hardly surprising, then, that this is one of the most potent and useful suggestions of the A.A. program.)

The one exception to Lois's good cheer — or at least the one exception that survives in the histories of this period — took place on a day in February 1940, as the Wilsons were (appropriately) walking through Grand Central Station. Lois suddenly found herself sitting down in the middle of a flight of stairs and weeping. Would they never have a home of their own? Would they never stop moving around?

It was at that point that they began looking in earnest. Wherever they went, they would look for possible homes. But, as Lois said, "The hunting was mostly a gesture, for we did not yet have the wherewithal for such a move."

When they lived at Clinton Street, A.A. meetings had been held there. A.A. followed Bill and Lois wherever they went. Green Pond, their first temporary home, became their point of departure for New Jersey meetings, in Montclair and South Orange.

Of meetings in those days, Lois remembered:

"At least a dozen A.A. groups had evolved in the New York metropolitan area, and those of us who were mobile went to as many meetings as possible, no matter how far away. In 1939, soon after we left Clinton Street, Hank and Kathleen started holding Sunday meetings at their new home in Montclair, New Jersey, and Bert T. let us continue our Tuesday meetings [formerly held at Clinton Street] at his elegant Fifth Avenue tailor shop. While Marty and Grenny were patients at Blythewood Sanitarium in Greenwich, Connecticut, the two of them, together with Bill, persuaded Mrs. Wylie, the owner, to let them hold meetings there. Then, a friend of Leonard and Helga H. lent us an apartment for a few months at 72nd Street and Riverside Drive in Manhattan. . . .

"Harold and Emily S. constantly opened their Flatbush home to the group. Bert T. suggested that his tailoring loft on the West Side was more practical for A.A. gatherings than his Fifth Avenue shop, so when the 72nd Street apartment was no longer available, we switched to his loft."

Of course, Lois and Bill had no car. They either walked to the bus at Newfoundland, four miles away, or relied on friends to transport them from place to place, meeting to meeting. There was a courageous spirit in the air, but no money. Lois's diary entry for Sunday, May 14, 1939, two weeks after their arrival at Green Pond, indicates their states of heart and purse:

"Bill decided we better go in to get some things about the foundation settled and to see Leonard [Dr. Strong] about my hip, which hasn't been so good. Chrys, Tom K——, and his wife dropped in, and then Bert T. and Henry K—— came to take us to the meeting at the P——s', where, when we arrived, they had already decided to subscribe enough money for us to live on a year."

Bill and Lois, whose only income had been $30 weekly from the Rockefeller Foundation, now had the "Bill and Lois Home Improvement Fund" voted them at Hank and Kathleen's home. Lois remembered that it gave them an extra $20 monthly — which just about covered the storage bill for their furniture.

Her diary entry for the next day, May 15, is lighthearted, indicating the relief and gratitude she may have been feeling, although not showing. That would have meant revealing past worry and anxiety, and that was not her style. She rarely expressed anything less than complete confidence in Bill.

Monday, May 15: "Went to town early and saw Leonard. New York seemed in a gala mood. The trees in full leaf in front of Radio City somehow had an exotic air. A lot of strangers in town for the fair. You can often spot them."

Their pleasurable sojourn at Green Pond was brief. A month later, they were obliged to leave the peaceful bungalow to make way for the summer tenants. That month, June 1939, saw the beginning of the Wilsons' two-year routine of "living around." The tables were turned: At Clinton Street, they had operated a home for homeless recovering (they hoped) alcoholics; now, recovering alcoholics opened their homes to Bill and Lois. The tradition of generosity and hospitality within the Fellowship was already well established in the New York area, as it had been in Akron.

At Bog Hollow, in Monsey, New York, Bill and Lois stayed with Bob and Mag V., in a rambling old farmhouse. They had a huge room on the second floor of the "Siberian" wing of the house. It was so cold, it was called Upper Siberia; the room below it, Lower Siberia. Several miles east of Monsey is Rockland State Hospital, and there in the hospital, Bob V. started meetings for alcoholic inmates. Dr. Russell E. Blaisdell, then head of the hospital, was so pleased that "a few months later he actually let busloads of committed alcoholics go to the A.A. meetings which by then had been established in South Orange, New Jersey, and in New York City. For an asylum superintendent, this was certainly going way out on a limb." Graduates of Rockland State were often housed in Upper and Lower Siberia after the Wilsons left.

A.A. continued to grow — a book sold, a member added, a message passed. But there was no money, no prospect of money, no real evidence that things were changing. Indeed, all during the summer of 1939, "things" got steadily worse. The situation in Europe was darkening daily; Hitler's aggression was spreading; war looked imminent. At home, unemployment remained widespread, and for the tiny band of sober alcoholics, there was continued financial destitution. Their loyalty to one another, to their newfound sobriety, and to their leader, Bill W., seemed to increase as their circumstances declined. And everywhere, through acts of commitment, they buoyed themselves and one another, and kept their courage and confidence high.

Their courage and confidence were also bolstered daily by

the meetings themselves. Ruth Hock described them: They were "structured to the extent that there was always one speaker and Bill — maybe half an hour each — and then a long coffee session, a real get-together. We were often there till 12 o'clock, started at eight." She also said, "At that time, we did not go into Step work. Didn't have 90-days requirements. No birthdays — no recognition was made if you were sober a week or a year. If you felt you would like to speak in a year or in a month or in two weeks, they let you get up and speak, and they didn't throw you out if you got there drunk, either. They felt it was encouraging, hoping some word would stick."

Each time Bill spoke, he had a different approach. There was no preformulated message, and his talks apparently varied in length as much as subject matter.

At one meeting, he spoke of Helen W., an early female member whose recent suicide was causing anxiety and deep foreboding throughout the New York membership. At that meeting, Bill urged the members not to let their faith be destroyed by the tragedy.

Those early meetings saw the introduction of some customs so traditional today that their presence — not to mention their origins — is rarely questioned. One of these was the humor — sometimes black, always deeply empathic. This atmosphere of laughter was a direct legacy of Bill's personality. His own talks were always shot through with humor, much of it self-deprecating. Said Ruth: "He could always bring on laughter out of pathos. There would be deep belly laughter."

Another was the way in which members introduced themselves: "My name is Bill W. I'm an alcoholic." Never one to pass up an imaginative or appropriate idea, Bill probably picked up this custom from the early Oxford Group days, when Frank Buchman (who later abandoned such modesty) referred to himself as Frank B. At the O.G. meetings Bill and Lois attended during the middle 1930's, members sat in a circle for the "sharing" sessions, and they would say, "My name is so-and-so" to identify themselves.

Some "A.A. saws" were also used as long ago as the late 1930's: "First Things First," "Easy Does It," "Live and Let Live." Because these appear in the first edition of the Big Book (at the end of the chapter on "The Family Afterward"), it's probable that the use of the slogans originated with Bill and that he brought them with him from Vermont — old saws with new teeth.

In that year of 1939, another personal disappointment was the eviction of Honor Dealers from its offices at 17 William Street in Newark. Since 1937, the office had been the de facto headquarters of A.A., where much of the Big Book had been written. Even the letterhead said "Works Publishing, 17 William Street." As a business, Honor Dealers had never had much of a chance; Bill, Hank, and Ruth had spent most of their time and all of their energy on the struggling drunks. Now, the three of them were obliged to move to still smaller quarters — a tiny office space in the same building.

The new situation was not much different from the old. "Somehow we made a small down payment on the rent, wondering how many months it would be before the sheriff showed up once more," Bill remembered. As Ruth described it: "Even then, I was front man to explain to the superintendent why the rent wasn't paid on time."

By late 1939, Bill was becoming convinced that he had to divorce himself from A.A. activities, which were taking so much of his time. This was a problem that had plagued him from the beginning of his sobriety and would continue to trouble him for a number of years, until he was able to work out a satisfactory compromise between his principles and what, given his special situation, was practical. He and Lois had to live somehow. Now that he was sober, he wanted desperately to assume his proper role — as he saw it, that of breadwinner.

In a letter dated November 14, 1939, near the fifth anniversary of Bill's sobriety, the New York members and their spouses sent him a letter of support and encouragement: ''We all know that, like the rest of us, you are confronted with the necessity of making a living and that there are certain obligations in that respect which you have to face. We feel that we owe a debt to you which can be measured only in terms of life itself, and therefore, perhaps, it is hardly appropriate that we should ask that you continue to make the sacrifices which you have in the past for the benefit of ourselves and others yet unknown. Yet we ask you, if you can find it possible to do so, to continue for a time with the work of Alcoholics Anonymous. We feel that the loss of your guidance at this most critical period in the development of the movement would be nothing less than a major catastrophe. On our own part, we pledge ourselves to do whatever we can in every way to help you carry the load.''

The letter was signed by more than 50 people, including Jimmy B., Bert T., Morgan R., Tom B., and Leonard V. Harrison, a nonalcoholic who served as a trustee. Morale booster that it must have been, it did not dissuade Bill from seeking employment.

During all this time, when Bill and Lois had nothing of their own, he was deeply worried about Dr. Bob's financial situation! In 1939, he sent a letter to the Guggenheim Foundation, inquiring about a grant — not for himself, but for his friend. In describing the great service performed by Dr. Bob, he wrote, ''For more than four years, without charge to sufferers, without fanfare and almost without funds, Dr. Smith has carried on work among alcoholics . . . Because of his great amount of voluntary alcoholic work, the doctor has been unable to rebuild his surgical practice.

''If he continues work at the present pace, he may lose the remainder of his practice and probably his home. Obviously, he should continue, but how? . . . He knows nothing of this approach on his behalf.''

Bill was apparently unaware, as he wrote, of how accurately (except for minor details) this eloquent plea on his friend's behalf in fact described himself.

Nothing ever came of the application (the Guggenheim Foundation supports the arts); the letter remains nonetheless as a testament to Bill's constant concern for the welfare of others, often to the detriment of his own.

In 1940, Bill tried to become a wire rope salesman, a position he obtained with the help of Horace C. Lois described his efforts: "All summer, Bill heroically tried selling wire rope, although he had no interest in the product and few entrées into maritime and other industries where it was used." Bill finally gave up the position when it became clear he was unsuited to it.

If it is true that Bill was a genius at endeavors in which his emotions were invested, it may be equally true that he was less than competent at undertakings that did not interest him. (This indeed applied to Bill as a conversationalist. If the subject interested him, he was an ardent and attentive talker — and listener. If not, "He would stretch, say 'Ho-hum,' slap his knees, get up, and amble away," recalled a longtime coworker at the A.A. General Service Office in New York.)

Bill was acutely conscious of the dilemma involved in his own money problem. In a 1940 letter, he wrote: "From the beginning, we have wrestled with the question of the paid alcoholic worker. He seemed an absolute necessity and probably was that until recently. How to make people like myself appear to be voluntary workers yet receive their sustenance was the conundrum. Though I rather expected to make A.A. my lifework in just that sense, I have always felt a certain inconsistency about such an arrangement. The idea looked good, but there was always a feeling that the best was not yet."

In early 1941, Bill was still actively looking for a job. Yet he was still thinking in terms of nonprofessional, volunteer workers for the Fellowship — including himself, who was putting in more than full-time hours.

This was a vexing issue. Two principles seemed to be in direct opposition to each other. On the one hand was the need to keep A.A. nonprofessional, nonpaying, work-done-for-the-love-of-it — the rock-bottom founding principle of the Fellowship and the reason that it worked in the first place. On the other hand was the co-founders' need for an income while they worked for the Fellowship, which desperately needed their full-time attention. The satisfactory reconciliation of these two seemingly irreconcilable forces would not be made until some years later, in the very careful wording of the A.A. Eighth Tradition.

Sales of the Big Book, a first step in that direction, were marking time in the summer of 1939. Even a few good reviews had shown no results.

The New York *Times* review of June 25 had said, in part: "Lest this title should arouse the risibles in any reader, let me state that the general thesis of 'Alcoholics Anonymous' is more soundly based psychologically than any other treatment of the subject I have ever come upon."

Dr. Harry Emerson Fosdick's review, which had appeared in religious publications, had read, in part: "This extraordinary book deserves the careful attention of anyone interested in the problem of alcoholism. Whether as victims, friends of victims, physicians, clergymen, psychiatrists, or social workers, and there are many such, this book will give them, as no other treatise known to this reviewer will, an inside view of the problem which the alcoholic faces. Gothic cathedral windows are not the sole things which can be truly seen only from within. Alcoholism is another. All outside views are clouded and unsure. Only one who has been an alcoholic and has escaped the thralldom can interpret the experience."

Charlie Towns, staunch supporter and confident creditor, had, in Bill's words, been "raising heaven and earth to get publicity for us and had succeeded." He had told the A.A. story to Morris Markey, a writer, who took it to Fulton Oursler, at that time editor of *Liberty* Magazine, a popular national weekly. (Oursler later became well known as an author of best-selling religious books, most famous of which was "The GreatestStory Ever Told.") Oursler accepted an A.A. piece by Markey entitled "Alcoholics and God" (the title caused Bill some apprehension).

The piece was scheduled to appear in the September 30, 1939, issue. That meant, Bill calculated, it would be October before they could expect any book orders on the strength of the piece. Meantime, they simply had to have money to pay their creditors, to pay their rent in Newark, and to pay Ruth Hock, who had been working for months for now-worthless Works Publishing stock certificates.

Bert T. (of the Fifth Avenue tailoring establishment where early meetings were held) now transacted a piece of business that was characteristic of the spirit of the group; it was the sort of gesture that kept them going in the face of seemingly insurmountable odds. Bert undertook the task of borrowing $1,000 to keep A.A. afloat. The only acceptable collateral he had to offer was his own elegant tailoring business, and he put it at risk. A.A. now had the $1,000 it needed to keep it afloat for yet another moment.

The *Liberty* article inspired the sale of several hundred Big Books at the full retail price of $3.50, and set the tiny Newark office to work answering 800 urgent pleas for help from desperate people around the country.

Publicity at the local level also proved effective. In the autumn of 1939, Clarence S. (who had started a group in Cleveland in May of that year) persuaded a writer named Elrick B. Davis to do a series of newspaper articles about A.A. Published in the Cleveland *Plain Dealer*, they were run in a prominent space and were supported with pro-A.A. editorials. As Bill described the series: "In effect the *Plain Dealer* was saying, 'Alcoholics Anonymous is good, and it works. Come and get it.' " Hundreds did; by the following year, the city had 20 to 30 groups and several hundred members. Said Bill, "Their results were . . . so good, and A.A.'s membership elsewhere . . . so small, that many a Clevelander really thought A.A. had started there in the first place."

The problems that surfaced in connection with the spread of

the Fellowship were legion. Many of them arose simply from the newness of the situation. A 1939 letter from Bill to Earl T., a Chicago member, indicates just a few of the difficulties that confronted the A.A. pioneers:

"It is a great thing to be able to sit down and write to you just as though you were an old friend, and it gives me a mighty cheerful feeling to hear about your doings in Chicago.

"It is usually a big job, in fact a hell of a job, to get a group functioning in a new locality, but once you have eight or ten really on the ball, things go faster and much easier.

"Our experience shows that we cannot in the beginning walk into public hospitals or snatch lushers off the street willy-nilly and have much but a big headache.

"It is very easy in this way to attract a big following of pan-handlers and mentally defective people. Surely, they are all as important in God's sight as any of the rest of us. They have just had a tougher break, and we are finding that later on, when a group gets size and power, quite a number of such individuals can be assimilated, and those who can't, or won't, fall away quickly; but if you get too many of them at the beginning, you are likely to find that your home becomes a drinking club, a hospital, a bank, or a nursery.

"We all want results, and surely that requires we first get hold of the people who can and want to stop right now, giving such persons maximum attention and the minimum to those contra-minded. So we try very hard to learn what we can of a case before tackling him. Does the candidate want to stop badly and is he mentally sound aside from his alcoholism? Of course, there is no rule about these matters; people who look strong sometimes turn out badly; and weak sisters occasionally make the grade with a bang.

"Above all, don't get discouraged if the going is slow at first — that seems to be part of our education along this line. The summer I worked in Akron with Doc Smith, we tore about frantically and only bagged two who made the grade, Ernie G ———

and Bill D ——.

"Here in New York, it was the same story. I went along six months talking to a lot of them before any permanent results were obtained, and at that time, I was laboring under the delusion I was divinely appointed to save all the rummies in the world!

"People who write in saying they are getting results from the book are likely to be good prospects, and we shall continue to refer those in your area we hear from to you.

"By educating doctors, hospitals, ministers along this line, you will surely pick up some strong prospects after a bit.

"Please let us know what we can do to help out there."

In addition to the logistic problems — organizing and finding housing for a new group — there was the problem of just who was a promising candidate for Alcoholics Anonymous. It would be many years before the Tradition of "attraction rather than promotion" would be formulated; in those days, active promotion was very much the order of the day, and the A.A. pioneers naturally wanted to put their attention and energies into helping those drunks who they believed had the best chance for recovery. (The operative word at that time was "drunks" as opposed to the later, more genteel "alcoholics.")

Bill and Hank then believed that a drunk had to be at absolute rock bottom physically, spiritually, and financially in order to "get" the program. Ruth Hock recalled Bill asking a prospect, "Do you still have your job?" Or Hank would say, "Still married? Have your wife and children living at home?" And then they would say, "Well, we don't think we can do a thing for you — we can't help you." But as Bill's letter to Earl T. clearly indicates, while the newcomer had to be "practically a gutter drunk," he could not be so low as to have given up hope completely; he had to want to stop drinking. Bill and Hank were looking for prospects who still had a spark of life and, most important, hope burning somewhere inside them.

Another lesson is reflected in Bill's letter: They learned

early on to stop making predictions about who would or would not stay sober. As Ruth put it, ''The most impossible-looking cases so often made the grade, while our most promising so often fell by the wayside.''

She reminisced about one such case: ''Do you [Bill] remember the two young hopefuls we practically made bets on? I think they were Mac and Shepherd. They were specially interesting because they were younger than most. Shepherd was a high betting favorite, while 'poor Mac was hopeless.' To our surprise, Shepherd had trouble almost immediately, while Mac seemed to make steady progress in sobriety. The whole situation blew up in our faces when one day Mr. Chipman [the Rockefeller associate] promised to visit us, so that you could show him what wonderful progress A.A. was making in every way. And to top off the performance, you invited Mac to appear to prove that even very

Ruth Hock didn't know what she was getting into when she went to work for Bill and Hank P.

young men could achieve sobriety.

"The stage was all set, and you met Mr. Chipman for lunch. Meanwhile, Mac appeared at the office completely polluted for the first time in about six months. He was so far gone that he collapsed in a coma in the big chair in your private office. I couldn't budge him, so all I could think to do was shut the door and try to head you off. When you appeared with Mr. Chipman, though, you were talking a blue streak complete with gestures, and I couldn't get a word in edgewise. So you swept open the door to your office to reveal Mac in all his drunken glory. After the proverbial moment of stunned silence, you broke into roars of laughter. And a minute later, bless his heart, Mr. Chipman joined you."

Sometime during that difficult year, 1939, Hank began to drink again. Nobody quite knows when he started, but Lois's diary for June 13 and 14 indicates that Hank was fighting with his wife and was determined to divorce her.

Her diary for September 5: "Kathleen [Hank's wife] phoned to say she thought Hank was drunk." September 6: "Hank drunk, phoned Bill in the afternoon." The September 7 entry notes that he was still drunk.

Hank was not only Bill's partner; he was the first New York alcoholic Bill had been able to sober up. Nobody really knows why he began to drink again, but it must have been terribly upsetting for Bill. As time went by, it became clear that the slip was somehow connected with his feelings about Bill and the Fellowship.

Hank was an impatient man. He always thought of big things, in terms of *now* — "You have to do it *now*." Ruth described Hank as a man who had been successful all his life, had worked for big companies, and had made huge sums of money until he hit the skids. She said he was trying to pressure Bill into a pace that wasn't Bill's way, so he became dissatisfied and critical of many of the things Bill did and believed.

Part of Hank's unhappiness, Ruth added, involved her:

"Hank and I were interested in each other. I had at one time seriously considered marrying him." When Ruth finally decided not to, Hank blamed Bill, charging that she was more committed to A.A. and Bill than she was to him. "Hank's thinking became more and more erratic," said Lois. "Soon, he was drunk and blaming Bill for Ruth's refusal." After this first slip, Hank was never able to really get back to the A.A. program, or to regain lasting sobriety.

There was another source of friction: Bill had decided that a general service office was needed in Manhattan — there were no members to speak of in Newark; Hank wanted to stay in New Jersey, so that he could continue to attend to what was left of Honor Dealers.

In late 1939, Hank wrote Bill the following memo:

"Please believe me when I say this letter is not written in the least argumentative mood. I only wish to develop some thoughts which I have had.

"I have been thinking about combining the book office with the foundation office. I wonder if, as long as it is economically possible, we should not keep the two separate.

"What are my reasons for keeping the book office out here? Why a foundation office?

"Did Jesus Christ have an office? Was there a central clearing-house? Is this work going on soundly? Are drunks being cured? Would money that would be spent on an office be better spent for traveling expenses for people spreading the good news? Will there be a Grand Pooh-bah of A.A.? Would an office tend to take away the endearing amateurism of this work and tend to professionalize it? Gee, Bill, this all used to be so wonderful that I wonder if that old touch isn't being lost. Are you the simple country boy that used to be so enthused and happy in seeing someone get out of the hole? Didn't I tend to become a little tin god in telling everyone how to lick all this instead of just telling my story? Hasn't the strength of Christianity always been in the home? Will this work gain by organization?

"I honestly believe a tide is rising on the book. You and I are going to profit from it if it rises high enough. If and when the time came, I think we would find it the subject of less criticism if it had taken nothing from the foundation or the work itself. Let the book company be the giver, not the receiver.

"Then again, if this book rises to five hundred to a thousand a month, good sales promotion may be done upon it. Again, your sales promotion department would be hampered by the very fact of many people pushing their ideas. True, all sales promotion ideas should be checked through the foundation trustees, but they should be born from one source.

"Another point — essentially, Works Publishing Company, if successful, must be a business organization. Does this mix with humanitarian and charitable work? The rules of business and the rules of work like that are diametrically opposite, particularly when every person in the work has the interest you wish them to have. In other words, how can you successfully operate what might be a large business organization when everyone naturally feels a proprietary interest in it? Along this line, I have had a couple of conversations with early Scientists. They say that Eddy[2] assiduously kept the business and the work separate.

"Anyhow, my best. I so hope that a few months will see a resumption of our former closeness."

Bill's reply suggests that Hank had already resumed drinking at the time:

"Your question of combining the book and the foundation is an old one, with which I supposed you had come to agree — that if funds were available, the whole outfit should be centered in New York. As there are no funds, there is no issue about it so far as I am concerned, though I have to constantly resist pressure from the whole gang to make the move now. Though you may still be right when you say that the book business and the foundation activities should be separate, I am afraid you would not find anyone who would agree. Throughout the crowd, the contrary opinion is 100 percent unanimous. If I were to stand out against it alone in order to agree with you, I am afraid I would be doing what you seem to fear, i.e., playing God. The gang's money has gone into the venture; they have contributed material for half of the book; and the book and the work are unavoidably tied together. I would like to agree with you if I could, but I don't see how I can.

"When the book was written, I know I found it sometimes hard to accept suggestions and ideas from you when they really should have been accepted. And then it comes to the business end of our deal. I think you have always had the same difficulty in considering my advice.

"Another point — the gang would like you to come back with us very much. It would be helpful to you, to them, and most helpful to me. Even with respect to the book, it is difficult to sell your suggestions and ideas to people who sometimes feel that you are no longer one of them. And please, please do not feel that when I disagree, I am in any way unfriendly. That is an idea I would give a great deal to explode. Very much yours,"

Their falling-out was painful and in many ways bewildering, because Hank had been one of Bill's staunchest supporters and allies. It was Hank who earlier in the year had helped organize the fund aimed at giving the Wilsons a regular monthly income. Whether the drinking caused the split or the split caused the drinking will never be known now; but after Hank resumed drinking, many resentments against Bill surfaced and found their way into the relationship.

---

1. The line is: "If we were to live, we had to be free of anger."

2. Christian Science founder Mary Baker Eddy, whose life Bill had studied.

Chapter Thirteen

In 1940, John D. Rockefeller Jr. gave a dinner for A.A. Although Rockefeller had stayed in the background, he had continued to follow A.A.'s progress with real interest.

Willard Richardson, by now "Uncle Dick" to Bill, announced the proposed dinner at a trustee meeting. Bill was elated; he again started to think in millions. He assumed, not without reason, that Mr. Rockefeller had changed his mind and had decided to give A.A. money. The invitation list, he said, was "a veritable constellation of New York's prominent and wealthy. Anybody could see that their total financial worth might easily be a billion dollars."

The dinner was held on February 8, at Manhattan's exclusive Union Club. Of the 400 prominent and influential people invited, 75 accepted. As the guests gathered before dinner, many were wearing puzzled expressions, attributable, Bill decided, to the fact that most of them could not decide exactly what Alcoholics Anonymous was. With characteristic foresight, Bill had placed one A.A. at each table. As he had expected, "There were many queries, and some of our answers amazed the notables. At one table sat our hero, Morgan, as impeccably dressed as a collar-ad boy. One gray-haired banker inquired, 'Mr. R., what institution are you with?'

''Morgan grinned and replied, 'Well, sir, I am not with any institution at the moment. Nine months ago, however, I was a patient in Greystone Asylum.' ''

Dr. Bob had come from Akron, bringing with him Paul S. and Clarence S. Dr. Russell Blaisdell of Rockland State Hospital was there, as was Dr. Silkworth. Dr. Harry Emerson Fosdick spoke for A.A. on behalf of religion, and Dr. Foster Kennedy represented the medical profession. Bill and Dr. Bob both told their personal stories. Because John D. Rockefeller had been taken suddenly ill, his son Nelson, then only 31, chaired the proceedings. The menu, Bill remembered, was squab on toast.

As the evening wore on, it was obvious that the assemblage was deeply impressed with what they were hearing. Bill's hopes — and expectations — soared:

''As we watched the faces of the guests, it was evident that we had captured their sympathetic interest. Great influence and great wealth were soon to be at our disposal. Weariness and worry were to be things of the past. . . .

''Breathlessly we waited for the climax — the matter of money. Nelson Rockefeller obliged us. . . . 'Gentlemen, you can all see that this is a work of goodwill. Its power lies in the fact that one member carries the good message to the next, without any thought of financial income or reward. Therefore, it is our belief that Alcoholics Anonymous should be self-supporting so far as money is concerned. It needs only our goodwill.' Whereupon the guests clapped lustily, and after cordial handshakes and good-byes all around, the whole billion dollars' worth of them walked out the door.''

Once again, A.A. had received no millions. Once again, Bill's expansive hopes were dashed.

The Fellowship did receive some money as a result of the

dinner, and it came in the following manner: Mr. Rockefeller bought 400 copies of the Big Book. To each of the invited guests, he sent a copy, together with transcripts of the talks made at the dinner, plus a personal letter in which he reiterated his conviction that A.A., to be successful, would ultimately have to be self-supporting. But he hinted that a little temporary help might be in order, until the movement was more solidly established, and he personally was hereby donating $1,000 to that cause. (Because Mr. Rockefeller had bought his 400 copies of the Big Book for $1 each — $2.50 discount off the original price — the $1,000 was in fact the equivalent of the discount he had received!)

Having thus set the tone and the precedent for contributions, Rockefeller then consented to the Alcoholic Foundation's request for permission to make an independent solicitation of the dinner guests. These solicitations (which would be repeated annually for the next four years) brought in an additional $2,000. The money was used, in part, to give Bill and Dr. Bob a weekly stipend of $30 each.

Millions or no, Rockefeller knew exactly what he was doing. Bill was soon to learn that the Rockefeller name added luster to all with which it was connected. The multimillionaire had permitted no press coverage of the actual dinner. "Understandable," said Bill. "Had any of us alcoholics turned up stewed, the whole affair would have collapsed ignominiously." But when it was over and had clearly been a success, A.A. was put in touch with the Rockefeller public relations firm, and together they drafted a statement to the press. "The ensuing publicity was favorable and widespread." Despite some sensationalism and tabloid journalism ("John D. Rockefeller Dines Tosspots," read one headline), more inquiries and more book orders started to arrive at the foundation office.

The dinner also gave impetus to the trustees, who now began to provide more direction for the business and public affairs of the Fellowship. The board had been enlarged; it comprised three alcoholic and four nonalcoholic trustees. In order to protect the foundation in the unlikely event that all the alcoholic trustees should be simultaneously "struck drunk," the nonalcoholic members were given a voting majority on the board. Bill approved of this arrangement; in fact, it was probably he who proposed it in the first place — ironic in light of the fact that this very ratio, when he proposed to change it some years later, was to be the source of prolonged and sometimes bitter wrangling among both trustees and the general membership.

On March 16, 1940, a month after the Rockefeller dinner, Works Publishing moved its offices from Newark to 30 Vesey Street in lower Manhattan. Its precarious finances had been improved only slightly by the Rockefeller dinner, so it was a gamble. This move gave A.A., for the first time, a headquarters of its own.

In the move, much was thrown out — including, probably, the original drafts of the Steps and the rest of the Big Book's fifth chapter, which was written there. The total office force (Hank was gone — he had not attended the Rockefeller dinner) consisted of Bill, Ruth, and Ruth's new assistant, Lorraine Greim, also a nonalcoholic, who had started work at the Newark office a month before the move into Manhattan. (To compensate Lorraine for the move — she had believed she would be working in New Jersey — they raised her salary from $12 to $15 per week.)

Now that the Big Book was beginning to sell, some of the subscribers began to demand a share of the profits. There were 49 subscribers. Bill and Hank each held a third of the stock, and Ruth had also received shares, in lieu of pay. Early in 1940, Bill and the trustees decided that the book should belong to A.A., not to the individuals who had subscribed for shares. By issuing some preferred shares, and obtaining a loan from the Rockefellers, they were able to call in all outstanding shares at par value of $25 per share. Most of the shareholders were delighted to come out even; some even donated all or part of the money to the Alcoholic Foundation.

But Hank resisted all their pleas to turn over his one-third ownership (200 shares) in Works Publishing to the foundation. "One day, completely broke and very shaky, he turned up at the Vesey Street office," said Bill. "He pointed out that most of our office furniture still belonged to him, particularly the huge desk and the overstuffed chair."

That gave Bill an idea. He proposed that the foundation buy the furniture for $200 if Hank would then turn in his Works Publishing stock. After some prodding, Hank finally consented, and signed the necessary papers.

But he resented Bill's persuading him to turn over his shares. To make matters worse, it was not long after this incident that Bill was granted a royalty on the book, similar to one that had already been voted for Dr. Bob. While this royalty was at first very modest, it eventually became substantial and provided both Bill and Lois a lifetime income.

Hank's son said that Hank always felt he had been treated badly. He thought Bill had made a deal with the foundation that excluded Hank from any future share in the book's profits. What clouds the entire issue is the fact that Hank's drinking had put a wall between Hank and many of the members who eventually supported royalty payments for Bill.[1]

In the spring of 1940 came a turn of events that was puzzling to all, and a source of great distress to some. In May, in A.A.'s first anonymity break at the national level, Rollie H., catcher (he had just caught a no-hit game pitched by Bob Feller) for the Cleveland Indians, revealed that he had been sober in A.A. for a year.[2] The story, when it broke, was carried on the sports pages of newspapers across the country. Because his drunkenness was a matter of public record (he was called Rollicking Rollie) and had all but ruined his career, his sobriety was very big news.

When the story appeared, complete with names and photographs, it provided A.A.'s first challenge on a national level to its still evolving, slowly emerging principle of anonymity. It presented Bill with a deep dilemma: What response should he make?

The dilemma was particularly profound because the ensuing publicity did in fact attract many, many people to the Fellowship and also gave it much-needed exposure. To have a national figure such as Rollie H. in the ranks of A.A. and to have him praise it publicly was a tremendous boost. But it was nonetheless in direct contradiction to the Fellowship's principles.

What follows here is Bill's version of what happened:

"Years ago a noted ballplayer sobered up through A.A. Because his comeback was so spectacular, he got a tremendous personal ovation in the press, and Alcoholics Anonymous got much of the credit. His full name and pictures, as a member of A.A., were seen by millions of fans. It did us plenty of good, temporarily, because alcoholics flocked in. We loved this. I was specially excited because it gave me ideas.

"Soon I was on the road, happily handing out personal interviews and pictures. To my delight, I found I could hit the front pages, just as he could. Besides, he couldn't hold his publicity pace, but I could hold mine. I only needed to keep traveling and talking. The local A.A. groups and newspapers did the rest. I was astonished when recently I looked at those old newspaper stories. For two or three years I guess I was A.A.'s number one anonymity breaker. . . .

"At the time, this looked like the thing to do. Feeling justified, I ate it up. What a bang it gave me when I read those two-column spreads about 'Bill the Broker,' full name and picture, the guy who was saving drunks by the thousands!"

Other sources, however, indicate that Bill did little traveling at that time. Lois's diary for 1940 shows that with the exception of one April trip to Washington and Baltimore, he stayed within the New York - New Jersey area.

The explanation for the discrepancy in these histories may in fact lie with Bill himself. If this is so, it reveals an endearing — and important — facet of Bill's character.

When Bill told this story on himself, he was speaking figuratively, in metaphor, rather than relating events as they actually happened. He did not at this time become "A.A.'s number one anonymity breaker"; indeed, the anonymity breaks he did make came two years later, not directly following the Rollie H. publicity in May of 1940. But Bill was never likely to pass up the opportunity to deliver a parable where he thought it could do some good, never afraid to use himself as a negative example (something he would not do to anyone else) when he thought he could make a point or highlight a principle, and never reluctant to stretch a fact for the sake of emphasis. Most probably, he combined those two incidents — Rollie H.'s anonymity break and his own later — to illustrate how baser human emotions such as competitiveness and envy can be disguised as motives of altruism and desire for the highest good. He may have been tempted to do what he professed to have done; Rollie's anonymity break may have aroused Bill's old competitive and envious feelings. But the truth is that he did not act on those feelings.

An entire book could be written about the period 1939-41, when A.A. was in its character-forming years. One significant event in 1940 was the Fellowship's acquisition of a center for meetings, the first of its very own — the 24th Street Clubhouse.

New York members had been growing restive and unhappy with all the moves from place to place for their meetings. In February of 1940, Bert T. (of the tailoring establishment) and Horace C. (at whose Green Pond bungalow Bill and Lois often stayed) discovered and guaranteed the rent on an extraordinary little building at 334½ West 24th Street.

From Lois's diary of June 11, 1940: "It used to be a stable, so is set back from the street and entered through a covered passage with a doorway on the street. It used to be the Illustrators Club, so is very attractive. One large room, with fireplace and paneled in knotty pine, and kitchen are downstairs. Upstairs there is a large room with skylights and two small bedrooms and two toilets. The rent is $75 a month and with gas and light and extras will probably come to $100."

Another view emphasizes the atmosphere of life at the 24th

Street Clubhouse: "It was Clinton Street 1935, only more so. There were always visitors, people driving in from Westchester or Connecticut, winos shuffling in from the Salvation Army down the street, or out-of-towners far from the safety of their group, who needed the security of this crazy, solid oasis in the city. These were men from every rung of [the] social ladder, who never conceivably would have drunk together, never would have gone to the same bars, yet here they were in one room, helping each other keep sober. Whatever hour Bill wandered in, there was the feel of a meeting. In a sense they were all members of an exclusive club, and only they understood what dues they had had to pay to get there."

On November 4, 1940, Bill and Lois moved into one of the two upstairs bedrooms at the clubhouse. They would call this room home for the next five months. Lois, with her usual combination of domesticity, inventiveness, and ability to make "lemonade out of lemons," increased the apparent size of the small room by knocking out unnecessary shelving and painting the walls white with red trim. A dressing table was fashioned out of an orange crate.

Wherever Lois and Bill moved, she would improve their surroundings in some imaginative way. She was also talented at improvising with clothes — making them over, restyling them, dyeing and stitching a garment to make it more attractive or a better fit. In those years of the Wilsons' extreme neediness, people often gave them clothes, which she would rework until they suited and fit. Some typical entries in her diary from that period:

"Made a hat to go with my tan dress, using the pheasant feathers Ken gave me. . . . Mended and put a pocket in a pair of trousers for Tom. . . . Tried to fix the fur collar of one of the black coats given me. . . . Finished embroidering the stockings for Muriel. Sewed for Barb after supper. . . . Made a hat to go with my dark blue dress — wore it. . . . Did some shopping at Macy's, then came home and made a skirt for Ruth J—— to take to Florida if she goes next weekend. . . . I made over a silk coat and

then tried to dye it. . . . Had to dye my coat again. . . . Francis C —— gave Bill a suit.''

For Bill, these were tantalizing days; his hopes would be raised, only to be dashed. They still had no home of their own; he had no job; the Big Book wasn't selling; A.A. wasn't getting the wide publicity it desperately needed; the Rockefellers hadn't come through; Hank was drinking. Bill was frustrated, impatient, restless, dissatisfied, and depressed. Some even described him as being on a dry drunk — in other words, he had all the symptoms of being drunk except the alcohol.

What happened next was unexpected and unforeseen; if Bill had been asked what would have made him feel better, he would hardly have thought to name the gift that came to him, apparently at random.

On a cold and rainy night late in 1940, deep in the winter of Bill's discontent, ''I was in our little club in New York, the first one ever to open its doors. I was lying upstairs alone, except for old Tom M ——, who made the coffee downstairs. Lois was away someplace. I was suffering from an imaginary ulcer attack — I used to have a lot of those. I felt very sorry for myself. It was a rather bitter night, sleeting outside, and old Tom, a very brusque Irishman, came up and said, 'Bill, I hate to bother you, but there is some bum from St. Louis here.'

''Well, it was ten at night, and I said, 'Oh, no, not another one! Well, bring him up.' So I heard a painful progress up the stairs, and I said to myself, 'This one is really in bad shape.' He finally stood in the door of my little bedroom, a terribly crippled figure, coat drawn up around him, leaning on a cane. And he sat down and turned back his collar, and then I saw that he was a clergyman.

''He said, 'I'm Father Dowling from St. Louis. I belong to the Jesuits out there, and we've been looking at this book 'Alco-

Father Edward Dowling wandered in out of the rain one night and into a 20-year ''spiritual sponsorship.''

holics Anonymous.' ''

Thus began a conversation that lasted for 20 years. Father Dowling, crippled Jesuit priest from St. Louis and editor of *The Queen's Work*, a Catholic publication, said he was fascinated by the parallels he had discovered between the Twelve Steps of Alcoholics Anonymous and the Exercises of St. Ignatius, the spiritual discipline of his Jesuit order. When Bill confessed that he knew nothing of the Exercises of St. Ignatius, Father Dowling was delighted, and Bill warmed to him.

''We talked about a lot of things, and my spirits kept on rising, and presently I began to realize that this man radiated a grace that filled the room with a sense of presence.'' (Bill had used the same term, ''sense of presence,'' to describe the atmosphere of Winchester Cathedral.)

That evening, Father Ed began sharing with Bill an understanding of the spiritual life that then and ever after seemed to speak to Bill's condition. Bill, author of the Fifth Step, would later characterize that evening as the night he took his Fifth Step, and also as a ''second conversion experience.'' He unburdened himself of his commissions and omissions, all of which had lain heavily on his mind, and of which he had found, until then, no way to speak. This extraordinary communication, this openness of sharing, was to be vital for Bill. Father Dowling's ''spiritual sponsorship'' would endure, grow, and be nourished during a correspondence and a deep friendship that would last for the next two decades. The subjects of this interchange, although interspersed with ''business'' matters of the Fellowship — Father Ed was one of its staunchest supporters, responsible for founding A.A. in St. Louis — were almost always the questions Bill continued to ask throughout his life, about faith and no faith, about the church and its role in human affairs.

That night, Bill ''told of his high hopes and plans, and spoke also about his anger, despair, and mounting frustrations. The Jesuit listened and quoted Matthew: 'Blessed are they who do hunger and thirst.' God's chosen, he pointed out, were always distinguished by their yearnings, their restlessness, their thirst.

"In pain, Bill asked if there was never to be any satisfaction. The priest almost snapped back: 'Never. Never any.' He continued in a gentler tone, describing as 'divine dissatisfaction' that which would keep Wilson going, always reaching out for unattainable goals, for only by so reaching would he attain what — hidden from him — were God's goals. This acceptance that his dissatisfaction, that his very 'thirst' could be divine was one of Dowling's great gifts to Bill Wilson and through him to Alcoholics Anonymous."

---

1. Hank, who died in Pennington, New Jersey, in 1954, had little to do with A.A. for several years. He did get back on the program for a short time later on, and remarried Kathleen after a couple of bad marriages. Lois ascribed his death to drinking, and it was reportedly his disagreement with Bill that kept him from returning to the Fellowship.

2. According to "Dr. Bob and the Good Oldtimers": "When the Akron A.A.'s left the Oxford Group, Rollie stayed with T. Henry [Williams] for a time. So, when the story of his alcoholism broke in 1940, credit for his recovery was given to the Oxford Group. At that time, however, Rollie broke his silence and said no, the credit for his sobriety belonged to Alcoholics Anonymous."

Chapter Fourteen

When, in the issue dated March 1, 1941, the *Saturday Evening Post* published an article about Alcoholics Anonymous, the struggling Society was finally charted on the map of national consciousness through the telling power of America's Number One family magazine.[1] It was, as Marty M. said, "the most exciting thing that had ever happened, because we wanted publicity so badly. We wanted somebody to know about us."

Judge Curtis Bok, owner and publisher of the *Saturday Evening Post*, had heard about A.A. through two Philadelphia friends, Drs. A. Wiese Hammer and C. Dudley Saul, who were singing its praises.

A.A. had reached Philadelphia in much the same way it had reached Akron and was now reaching other parts of the country. Men traveling on business, once again employed after having gotten sober, would find themselves alone in strange hotel rooms in strange cities. As Bill had done, they would seek out other alcoholics — to help them get sober and to help themselves stay sober.[2] Early in 1940, Jimmy B., the salesman who had earlier insisted on toning down the "God" references in the Big Book, had gone to Philadelphia to take a job. Bill had supplied him with the names of some Philadelphia prospects, including George S., who had sobered up after reading "Alcoholics and God" in *Liberty*.

"I quickly found I would need a few fellow alcoholics around me if I was to stay sober," said Jimmy. "Thus I found myself in the middle of a brand-new group."[3]

During the winter of 1940-41, Judge Bok, interested in learning the truth behind all the rave rumors he had heard, called in the reporter Jack Alexander because of the latter's reputation for being hard-nosed. Alexander had just completed a major exposé of the New Jersey rackets; he prided himself on his cynicism. Would Alexander care to do a story for the *Post*? asked Bok. At first, the reporter was hesitant, but when he learned that this Alcoholics Anonymous "had connections with both religion *and* Rockefeller," his appetite was whetted.

Of the four A.A. members who called on him at his apartment, Alexander said: "They were good-looking and well-dressed, and as we sat around drinking Coca-Cola (which was all they would take), they spun yarns about their horrendous drinking misadventures. The stories sounded spurious, and after the visitors had left, I had a strong suspicion that my leg was being pulled. They had behaved like a bunch of actors sent out by some Broadway casting agency."

Of Bill himself, whom he met the next day at Vesey Street, Alexander said, "a very disarming guy and an expert at indoctrinating the stranger into the psychology, psychiatry, physiology, pharmacology, and folklore of alcoholism." But Bill's openness may have had the initial effect, as can sometimes happen, of sharpening Alexander's already sharp skepticism. Bill spoke frankly of his own drunken past and just as candidly of his grandiosity and of errors in judgment he had more recently made. His candor struck the reporter as being "either incredibly naive or a bit stupid."

Bill himself had a quite different perception of the same events: "After Jack checked in with us at Headquarters, we took him in tow for nearly a whole month. In order to write his powerful article, he had to have our fullest attention and carefully organized help. We gave him our records, opened the books, introduced him to nonalcoholic trustees, fixed up interviews with A.A.'s of every description, and finally showed him the A.A. sights from New York and Philadelphia all the way to Chicago, via Akron and Cleveland."

Alexander had been right in his initial perception: Bill was candid. But there was nothing naive or stupid about his candor; it was deliberate, and it achieved its purpose. As Bill's honesty was to work with literally thousands of alcoholics in years to come, so it now worked with Jack Alexander. As Bill later described it: "The kind of help we gave Jack Alexander — our organized service of public information — is the vital ingredient in our public relations that most A.A.'s have never seen." It was not long before Alexander was "converted"; his cynicism evaporated; and his endorsement of the Fellowship was so wholehearted that he was to remain a close friend for years to come. (He became a trustee in 1951 and remained on the board until 1956, although, because of poor health, he attended few meetings.)

But there were some knotty problems with respect to the article. One of these was how to describe A.A.'s relationship to the Oxford Group. By the time the article was written, A.A. had become independent and separate from the Oxford Group in both New York and Ohio, and Frank Buchman's remarks about Hitler had given rise to accusations that the O.G. was pro-Nazi. With war in Europe against the Nazis and feelings on all fronts running very high, Bill understandably wanted to avoid being associated with anything controversial, particularly when the Fellowship so badly needed favorable publicity. In addition, he wanted A.A. to appeal to all religions and societies. Bill wrote to Alexander: "I would give anything if you could avoid mentioning the matter [A.A.'s connection with the Oxford Group] at all, but if it must be noted, I'm quite anxious to avoid words carrying criticism or sting. After all, we owe our lives to the group."

The article finally finished, it was approved by the editors and scheduled for the March 1, 1941, issue. At the last moment, the *Post* handed the A.A.'s a real dilemma. Although the editors were perfectly willing to use pseudonyms in the text, they wanted real photographs to illustrate the article. "Pictures they *had* to have, and some of them had to be on the sensational side," Bill recalled. "We objected that this might keep people away. Finally the *Post* said, 'No pictures, no article.' The choice was ours, and it was a hard one."

On this point, there was strong protest from "conservative and fearful members," but Bill decided to give the *Post* the pictures it wanted. "It was a crucial decision which happily turned out to be the right one — that is, for the time being," Bill said.

"Alcoholics Anonymous" (with the subhead "Freed Slaves of Drink, Now They Free Others") was the lead story in the issue, which appeared on the newsstands on February 24. Out in Toledo, Ohio, a new member named Garth M. was given a two-dollar roll of nickels by the group and sent on a tour of magazine outlets until he had bought 40 copies.

Approximately 7,500 words long, the article was illustrated with four photographs of members (unidentified, of course) in typical alcoholic and A.A.-related circumstances. One photograph, taken before the fireplace at the 24th Street Clubhouse (the slogan "But for the Grace of God" hung prominently over the mantel), showed Bill sitting front row, center, surrounded by Horace C., Helen P., Tom M., Tom B., Ruth Hock, Dick S., Ray W., Lois, Gordon M., and Bob F. Many of them had their backs to the camera. The photograph was captioned "A typical clubhouse discussion group."

The article itself opened with a description of the A.A. sobering-up technique. In what is probably the most important paragraph of the entire piece, the author explained exactly what it was that made A.A. work. First, the A.A.'s outtalked the man on the bed with their own horrendous experiences. ''These and other bits of drinking lore usually manage to convince the alcoholic that he is talking to blood brothers. A bridge of confidence is thereby erected, spanning a gap which has baffled the physician, the minister, the priest, or the hapless relatives. Over this connection, the troubleshooters convey, bit by bit, the details of a program for living which has worked for them and which, they feel, can work for any other alcoholic. They concede as out of their orbit only those who are psychotic or who are already suffering from the physical impairment known as wet brain.''

After a thorough survey of A.A. at that time — its acceptance by many professionals, its development, its program, and its membership — the author gave a brief history of the movement, telling Bill's story (calling him ''Griffith'') and Dr. Bob's (''Armstrong''). He ended the article with four other personal stories, including that of Marty M. (''Sarah Martin''). Most important of all, he included the mailing address of the Alcoholic Foundation.

The article, although not long, was intelligent, compulsively readable, and entirely comprehensive. It accomplished exactly what Bill had first hoped the Gabriel Heatter broadcast would do, and had then hoped the Rockefeller dinner would do: It put A.A. irrevocably on the map of national consciousness.[4]

This is how Bill described public response to the article:

''By mail and telegram a deluge of pleas for help and orders for the book 'Alcoholics Anonymous,' first in hundreds and then in thousands, hit Box 658. . . . Pawing at random through the incoming mass of heartbreaking appeals, we found ourselves crying. What on earth could we do with them? We were really swamped.[5]

''We saw that we must have help. So we rounded up every A.A. woman and every A.A. wife who could use a typewriter. The upper floor of the 24th Street club was converted into an emergency headquarters. For days Ruth and the volunteers tried to answer the ever-increasing tide of mail. They were almost tempted into using form letters. But experience had shown that this would not do at all. A warm personal communication *must* be sent to every prospect and his family.''

While the previous publicity had not accomplished the spectacular growth that Bill had hoped for, it had been of benefit in a specific way, on which the Fellowship could now capitalize. The earlier trickle of mail had established outposts for A.A., small groups and lone members in widespread areas of the country. With inquiries now pouring in from everywhere, those responding to the *Post* story could be given contacts in their own areas. Two years earlier, those contacts would not have been available.

Bill, with characteristic foresight (he was *always* looking down the road) not only had hoped this would happen, he had made advance preparations for the actuality. Entries in Lois's diaries indicate as much:

"Fri., Jan. 31, 1941: Worked out a program for procedure after the *Post* article [comes] out.

"Tues., Feb. 4, 1941: We all returned early to club for meeting about handling volunteers and new prospects after *Post* article comes out. I'm to be liaison between office and club and handle volunteers.

"Tues., Feb. 25, 1941: Typed 'Plan of Action' after *Post* article.''

Meeting attendance increased immediately and dramatically scarcely more than a week after the article appeared. "Even as early as March 4,'' wrote Lois, ''150 were present at the club meeting, and by March 31, the South Orange group had more than doubled its membership. It was the same everywhere. Groups outgrew their meeting places and had to be divided. Older members worked frantically with newcomers. These newcomers, in turn, after a month or so of sobriety, were sent on Twelfth Step calls to help still newercomers. It is estimated that 6,000 A.A.'s owe the start of their sobriety to the *Post* article, and nobody knows how many more thousands were sparked by them.'' Al M., who joined the program in Los Angeles during those exciting days, described how it worked. Everybody, he said, went on Twelfth Step calls. There was no phone, so the local A.A.'s had an ad running in the paper. ''Then they would bring the letters up and open them. Whether you were on the west side or the east side, you made a call every night.'' Al said that he himself went on a Twelfth Step call the second week he was in the program.

In New York, life at the Vesey Street office took on a changed atmosphere, a new activity. The office was actually one large room; Bill's part was partitioned off so that visitors could have some privacy with him. Ruth's and Lorraine's desks, each with a portable typewriter, were in the main section of the room. A large table stood against one wall, next to a filing cabinet. In another cabinet were stored about 100 copies of the Big Book.

Under the table were rolls of wrapping paper and packing materials. It was Lorraine's job to wrap and mail copies of the book. Most of the orders were for six books. ''If we got an order for a dozen books, we thought we had a big business going,'' she said. Sometimes, Bill would help her carry the books across the street to the post office.

Lorraine (dubbed ''Sweetie Pie'' by Bill) also opened the mail. Correspondents often inquired on behalf of ''a friend,'' she remembered, and A.A. always replied in kind; they would give the writer, for the benefit of the ''friend,'' the location of the nearest member or group. All mail was sent out in unmarked envelopes.

Bill did not like to dictate; indeed, he did not like to answer letters. Ruth said, ''He preferred to talk, and he was so much better at it — warmly, on a one-to-one basis. And he spent hours doing that. He would always say, 'Aw, you know what to write, Dutch. Go ahead and answer them.' So I took care of the mail — living it day after day gave me an idea of how to say what.

''When I originally started writing the letters, I'd sign them 'R. Hock,' because we had the idea that if it [was known that I was] a girl, and fairly young and not A.A., a lot of people would say, 'Well, that's for the birds.' ''

While Ruth's memory of answering the mail at Vesey Street is surely correct, it is also true that Bill himself did write many letters; his signature appears often on early correspondence. Via this correspondence, he was already creating the backbone for what would later come to life as the A.A. Traditions. His letters from that time reflect, too, the working of his mind as it shaped the attitudes and philosophy that have become integral ingredients of the program, without ever being expressed as precisely as in the Steps or the Traditions. He wrote letters as some people keep diaries or journals — he worked out his ideas in the thousands of letters he wrote during his lifetime. (Providentially, he was surrounded by people who recognized the importance of his work, and had the wit to keep copies of what he wrote.)

The following passage, from a letter to Jennie B., founding mother of Boston A.A., is a good example of the way Bill's evolving attitudes and philosophy were voiced through his communications:

''What you say about your discouragement in working with alcoholics surely brings the past before me. I guess I told you the story of 182 Clinton Street, Brooklyn, where we took in alcoholics for two years without any result whatever. In those days, Lois and I used to blame ourselves, thinking that somehow we failed. Only the other night, she and I looked over a list of the people we worked with in those days, both at 182 Clinton Street and elsewhere. The number of them who have since dried up was truly astonishing. This made us realize that in God's economy, nothing is wasted. At the time of our failure, we learned a little lesson in humility which was probably needed, painful though it was.

''We now see so clearly that the immediate results are not so important. Some people start out working with others and have immediate success. They are likely to get cocky. Those of us who are not so successful at first get depressed. As a matter of fact, the successful worker differs from the unsuccessful one only in being lucky about his prospects. He simply hits cases who are ready and able to stop at once. Given the same prospects, the seemingly unsuccessful person would have produced almost the same results. In other words, you have to work on a lot of cases before the law of averages commences to assert itself.

"So cheerio, Jennie — it ain't your fault."

Without naming the Serenity Prayer, Bill is here calling upon its first element, acceptance. The prayer had found its way into the Vesey Street office shortly before that letter was written.

It was discovered in the "In Memoriam" column of an early June 1941 edition of the New York *Herald-Tribune*. The exact wording was: "Mother — God grant me the serenity to accept the things I cannot change, courage to change the things I can, and wisdom to know the difference. Goodbye." Said Ruth: "Jack C. appeared at the office one morning, and he showed me the obituary notice with the Serenity Prayer.[6] I was as much impressed with it as he was and asked him to leave it with me, so that I could copy and use it in our letters to the groups and loners. Horace C. had the idea of printing it on cards and paid for the first printing."

Another example of the way Bill's philosophy was worked out through his letters appears in a letter he wrote to Evelyn H. The subject is slips:

"There have been a number of slips this summer, among A.A.'s who have been dry two or three years. Naturally, these episodes have brought a lot of worry to the families involved, who find the old nightmare revived. Yet I do not know of any case but that has, in a sense, benefited. These occurrences simply serve notice on all of us that no one is ever really cured of alcoholism. We only have a reprieve day by day, contingent on

Alcoholics Anonymous "came of age" at the 20th Anniversary International Convention in St. Louis in 1955.

our spiritual well-being. But nothing is more sure than that our release can be perpetual if we make it so. In the case of these older members who have slips, the effect is to remind them of these eternal verities of the alcoholic sickness. The slip invariably kicks them upstairs instead of down. I'm positive you will find it that way with Bern. He has only been getting a little instruction the hard way.''

That letter is typical of Bill's deep generosity of spirit, love for others, and abiding consideration of their feelings. It also demonstrates his ability to perceive and use disaster and calamity, even tragedy, as an opportunity for growth and learning. Of the Fellowship itself, he often said, ''A.A. is nothing more than capitalized grief.''

He would, during the writing of the Big Book and the ''Twelve and Twelve,'' try out his ideas and his prose on others, polishing and refining and revising according to the reactions of his listeners. When he was working out a new aspect of the Fellowship, such as the Traditions or the General Service Conference, he would become nothing less than monomaniacal, talking (some described it as monologuing) endlessly about the project. It was not only uppermost in his mind, it was the only thing on his mind. Devising ways to make A.A. more effective, workable, and attractive, he whittled, honed, pushed, pulled, and molded — a process that lasted, *in toto*, for 15 years, from 1941, when the survival of A.A. seemed finally assured, until 1955, when, at the St. Louis Convention, he declared A.A. officially ''of age.''

He was enormously popular; within the Fellowship, affection for him spread as A.A. grew. Of those early years, Ruth said: ''I don't remember a meeting when Bill was in town that he didn't have to speak, at least briefly. Bill loved it, and had a terrific rapport with everybody. Even when he had to repeat something, it didn't matter. People still wanted to hear him speak.''

Such adulation, however, had its price. It was almost inevitable that there would also be detractors, and Bill had them. Said

Bob H., an early A.A. and later general manager of the General Service Office, ''I think it boiled down to the fact that they were just plain envious. He was the one that was getting all the kudos, so to speak, and they weren't.''

That it was envy is, of course, only one man's opinion. Contrariness can also be a characteristic of the ''alcoholic personality,'' and no one knew this better or acknowledged it more openly than Bill. After all, was not he himself the quintessential alcoholic? Whatever the reason, it is true that some early A.A.'s, including a number of Bill's confidants and friends, dropped away. Hank got drunk and forged myriad resentments against Bill, or else did the two in reverse order. Horace C., who had lent the Wilsons his Green Pond Camp and had named his daughter for Lois, did the same. In those days, naturally, no member had as much as ten years' sobriety in A.A.; the lack of long-term experience in living the program may have accounted for some of the trouble.

Bitterest of all, perhaps, was the falling-out that Clarence S., founder of Cleveland A.A., had with Bill. Shortly after Hank had been persuaded to relinquish his share in Works Publishing stock in exchange for a $200 payment for the office furniture — furniture that he claimed belonged to him — Hank went to Ohio, ostensibly to ''take his case'' to the membership there. The book ''Bill W.'' describes what happened in Cleveland:

''. . . The rumors about the New York office and the grand rackets Bill was promoting, which Hank P. had ignited during his visits, had never been totally doused. Now they all flared up again, to incredible heights. At Vesey Street they began to hear reports of several Cleveland groups wanting to secede and break off all connection with Bill's brand of A.A. . . .

''Bill had constantly to remind himself that these did not always spring from malcontents, nor were they all the politically motivated schemes of a few individuals who wanted to take over and run their own show. There was a strong and serious group who were genuinely distressed by what they regarded as an attempt to commercialize A.A."

The rumors had Bill getting rich — with the help of the Rockefellers — by taking all the Big Book profits for himself.

Bill's own description of what happened: "A few A.A.'s set up a dinner in the city where these rumors had the largest currency. Dr. Bob and I were invited to speak. The dinner was not any too well attended and the usual good cheer seemed mysteriously lacking. When the festivities were over, the chairmen of all the groups in town conducted Dr. Bob and me to a hotel parlor. There they produced an attorney and a certified public accountant. They had been hearing awful stories about the foundation. They had heard that the book 'Alcoholics Anonymous' was making vast sums of money, that Dr. Bob and I shared profits of $64,000 the year before. They believed that I, the Wall Street promoter, had my truck backed right up to Mr. John D. Rockefeller's strongbox and had persuaded him to fill it with coin for me and my friends. The interrogating committee let us know that a member from their city had met one of our trustees in New York who was said to have confirmed these appalling reports.

"This incredible but more than halfhearted fantasy hit Dr. Bob and me quite hard. Fortunately, I happened to have with me a certified audit of all of our affairs from the beginning.[7] This showed that Dr. Bob, though he had been assigned a royalty, had never received any because his money had been needed for the A.A. office work. He was still on a $30-a-week stipend from the Rockefeller dinner. Like Dr. Bob I received $30 a week from the dinner guests, and since the *Post* article I had begun drawing $25 a week from the publishing company, which had seemed justified from the book sales. My total income was $55 a week. The foundation itself still had practically no cash balance; the group contributions coming into it were promptly spent on the office in order to carry on there.

"The investigating committee's accountant read our modest financial statement aloud and testified to its correctness. The committee was crestfallen and we received an apology.''

Out of this incident came, in part, the philosophy that would later take form as the Eighth Tradition. From this incident also evolved Bill's policy of total candor and openness so far as A.A.'s financial matters and his own personal finances were concerned.

Bill, as was his practice, turned this bitter experience into an opportunity for personal growth. But that the incident hurt him deeply is indisputable. He wrote to a friend:

''Once upon a time, I left a certain Middle West town we both know well with a great feeling of emptiness, futility, and heartache. But mine was one I had no business to have. It was a kind of experience I never expected to meet in life — an impossible situation which I knew I must survive alone. In retrospect, I see it was my first great test of spiritual principles in this old world of ours, God's proving ground. Found wanting as I was in so many ways, I'm glad to say that I found His hand outstretched when I became willing enough to put mine into it.''

This was not the first controversy with which Clarence had been involved; one A.A. historian has described Clarence as an ''abrasive'' personality. Nonetheless, Bill refused then, as later, to hold a grudge against him; on the contrary, he ended a 1943 letter to Clarence: ''I want you to know how grateful I am for your work in Cleveland. It has meant much to so many. No difference of opinion can ever change my feeling about that.'' And more than 20 years later, when they met at the 1965 International Convention in Toronto, they actually spent some hours together, reminiscing.

-----

1. It retained its prominence until the 1950's. In great financial difficulty during the 1960's, it suspended publication for a time. It was later revived but never regained its former reputation — or circulation.

2. In 1940, Fitz M., long a loner in the Washington, D.C., area, was joined by Hardin C. and Bill A.

Boston A.A. was founded by Paddy K., whom Marty M. had taken to Blythewood. One of Paddy's first two successes, Jennie B., daughter of a Back Bay family, was Boston's first woman A.A.

3. Jimmy was also responsible, later, for the start of A.A. in Baltimore. The second Baltimore meeting, held in June 1940, was attended by six people; by autumn of that year, the city had a regular Wednesday night group. Jimmy's Big Book story is "The Vicious Cycle."

4. In recognition of the *Post* story's effect on A.A. history, A.A. World Services, Inc., has reprinted it regularly in pamphlet form (at first under its original title and now as "The Jack Alexander Article").

5. Ruth Hock said: "Of all Bill's stories, that's quite exaggerated — mountains of mail. In a way it was, because comparatively speaking, it was fantastic. And of course, it didn't last too awfully long. It never really stopped, but I suppose [there were] as many as 50 letters a day for a while, and that was a great deal." By 1984, the General Service Office was receiving about 500 pieces of mail a day — letters, orders for literature, and other sorts of communications.

6. The origins of the Serenity Prayer are obscure. It may date back to Boethius, a philosopher who lived about 500 A.D., and was martyred by the Christians. Before his death, he was in prison for a long time, and he wrote, among other things, "Consolation of Philosophy."
   It is usually credited to Reinhold Niebuhr, a 20th-century theologian, who in turn credited an 18th-century theologian, Friedrich Oetinger.

7. Bill had probably been warned ahead of time about what was to take place.

Chapter Fifteen

Although Bill and Lois were still living in the 24th Street Club-house, they had been diligent about looking for a permanent home, as they had promised themselves and each other when, a year earlier, Lois had burst into tears of homesickness for the home she didn't have.

In 1941, they finally found a home. During the first week-end of the new year, they stayed with friends in Chappaqua, New York, north of the city. Lois's diary entry for Saturday, January 4, reads in part:

"We all drove to Bedford Hills to see Mrs. Griffith's house there, which Bill and I have had in mind ever since she told us about it. It has a fascinating location on top of a hill with a view. We broke in, and there is a huge living room, 32 x 25 perhaps, with a big stone fireplace.

"Sun., Jan. 5: Drove up again and broke into the house. It was still fascinating, but we could see greater drawbacks this time. If Bill gets this Chinese job,[1] we might be able to get the house."

The Bedford Hills house was the home they had been longing for. As they learned the circumstances of its building and its sale, it seemed almost to have their name written on it. It had been built by a woman named Griffith (no relation to Bill's maternal forebears) — "a woman whose husband had died of alcoholism and whose best friend has been retrieved by the Jersey group." She had built it for a friend, but it wasn't the small weekend cottage the friend wanted.

It had an interesting layout. The centerpiece of the first floor was a huge living room with a stone fireplace and French doors opening onto a veranda facing, in an easterly direction, a vista of the hills and woods. Opening off the living room were bedrooms on three corners, and on the fourth, a kitchen. The master bedroom and a long room lined with bookshelves were upstairs.

The Wilsons did not imagine that they could afford such a wonderful, interesting house in the heart of Westchester County, but they had underestimated Mrs. Griffith and her friend Joan, who worked out a plan. They wanted the Wilsons to have the house, and were willing to sell it for $6,500; no money down and payments of $40 a month. Since Bill and Lois were already paying $20 monthly for storage, it was not an impossibility to raise the extra $20.

On April 11, 1941, for the first time in the 23 years of their marriage, Bill and Lois spent the night in their own home. (It did not acquire a permanent name until 1944, when they visited Nantucket, saw a house named Stepping Stones, and decided that was an ideal choice for their still-new home.) After years of having to work, having to move, having to improvise, Lois finally had a lasting and satisfying outlet for her strong domestic impulses, in growing plants, decorating rooms, making furniture and curtains, painting, sawing, and redecorating.

There was an enormous amount of work to be done on the house: ceilings to be painted, floors to be scraped and stained. Lois accepted this new challenge with a will:

The house at Bedford Hills, New York — a home at last for the Wilsons after 23 years of marriage.

"The wall around the six French doors onto the porch looked bare and unfinished, so I painted swags of draperies across the top and down the side wall — really quite effective. As the windows of the house framed pictures of the lovely outdoors, I didn't want to obstruct the view with curtains. A few remnants and seconds that I picked up at sales were sufficient to make valances and decorative shades, which emphasized the windows. By laboriously prying out all the tacks from an old Victorian chair, I learned how to reupholster it. For many other pieces of furniture, I made slipcovers. In the kitchen, I carefully laid squares of linoleum in an interesting pattern."

Bill was much less domestic, much less interested in working around the house and grounds — indeed, his lack of domesticity would later become something of a legend in the Fellowship. It wasn't that he was lazy; witness the nonstop way he worked for the Fellowship. But he did not love domestic chores, nor did he particularly like physical work. As Lois put it: "Bill would spend hours sitting. Just sitting. And I'm a person of action. I've got to be doing something. And there'd be things to do — the garden spaded, a lock on the door that needed to be fixed, or something else that would need to be done. But Bill would sit. He aggravated me beyond anything by just sitting. But, of course, while Bill was sitting, he was thinking.

"Well, I yelled and screamed and carried on to some extent — not all the time. But once in a while, it would get under my skin, and I would. Bill never stood when he could sit, and he never sat when he could lie down."

In tasks that he did undertake, he was, as usual, ingenious. Lois recalled one of them:

"A pump, in its tiny house down the hill, pushed water from the spring all the way up to a tank under the porch and then through the pipes in the house. But it had a hard time getting the water upstairs, where our bedroom was. So Bill purchased from Sears Roebuck an open tank for cattle and put it up in the attic. Because of the weight of the water, he felt it wise to reinforce the attic supports in that area. The tank was filled periodically by the pump, and then gravity supplied the house with water. Bill worked out a Rube Goldberg system for knowing when the tank was empty and when the pump had filled it: A float in the tank turned on a red light in the kitchen when the water reached a low level; when the pump had filled the tank, a bell rang and kept ringing until the pump was turned off.

". . . One day . . . Bill was afraid there wouldn't be enough water in the tank for company on the weekend. He turned on the pump 'only for a short time.' But friends unexpectedly invited us out for the evening, and we forgot all about the pump.

"On our return, we could hear the alarm bell ringing before we entered. Our hearts sank. Inside, water was cascading down the stairs."

Helen, Bill's half sister, who lived for a time with the Wilsons, talked about how Bill solved the problem of getting the furnace started in the morning:

"That house is heated from a furnace in one big register in the middle of the floor. Well, in those days, it was coal, and you had to go down and shovel it, and in the morning it would be cold, and somebody would have to go down and open the door and — drafts and whatever — so the heat would come up. That was a little too much, so he got an alarm clock. Remember the old Rube Goldberg things? Well, he rigged an alarm clock and some string and a big cement block and attached it to the furnace door, and the alarm clock would go off and move this string, which did something, and this big block would fall down and the furnace door would open. This was great, except that of course we had coal dust — you got coal, you're going to have coal dust— and that got in the clock, and it didn't work.

"So he cleaned up the clock. My room [was] on the first floor. Bill and Lois were upstairs. He bored a hole right by my bed, brought the alarm clock up, set the alarm clock. So in the morning about six o'clock, the alarm clock would go off, and I'd reach over and pull the darn string, and all these things would happen, and the furnace door would open, and we'd have heat. When I stayed in town — why, everybody froze to death."

Lois's domestic streak in no way interfered with her adventurous nature. Another woman, after two full years of wandering, might have settled immovably into her nest. Not Lois. On April 20, nine days after she and Bill had moved into the new house, Lois left on a six-week cruise.

Horace C., generous lender of the Green Pond summer camp, was the nephew of the Moore half of the Moore-McCormack Lines. It was his mother who invited Lois to accompany her on a cruise to South America and back. Never one to decline an adventure, Lois left Bill to struggle alone with the vicissitudes of their new dwelling. Ever a romantic (by her own admission), Lois wrote in her diary on Sunday, April 20: "Bill and I waved in unison until I could not see him anymore."

It was sometime during 1941 that Bill abandoned the idea of "getting a job," though the Wilsons' income of $55 per week (from the Rockefeller fund and the Big Book royalties) hardly removed all financial worries. "Bil-Lo's Break" (the "working title" for the new house) cost them $40 per month; that left about $200 a month to cover all other living expenses. Even in pre-inflation 1941, $200 a month did not go far. Lois continued to try to augment their income. Again, she tried writing; while working on the furniture floor of Loeser's in Brooklyn, she had written and sold an article on veneers to *House and Garden*. Perhaps she could be successful once more at writing. So she squeezed in as much time as possible writing an imaginary tale for the magazine *Romantic Stories*, but it was soon returned. Not discouraged by these failures, she concentrated on putting her "Hoboes' Diary" of their 1925 motorcycle trip into better shape.

The year 1941 appeared to mark a turning point in the Wilsons' lives: They had a house; they had enough money to support themselves; and the Fellowship finally seemed assured of a future. Now, as they settled into a more permanent routine, some of the temporary quality of their lives seemed to disappear.

The house made a big difference. For the first time since the founding of A.A., Bill and Lois were able to have some measure of private life, separate from the Fellowship.

During the days of the Oxford Group meetings, the Wilsons had started the practice of holding a "quiet time" each morning. Now, when they could expect to wake up in the same place each day, they strengthened the practice. Lois described these quiet times:

"They'd last 15 minutes or so. We were in bed and we'd get

up and I'd make coffee and we'd have coffee in bed, and then we'd say a prayer together. And then we'd be quiet for a little while. Then we'd talk. This Oxford Group practice is a very, very helpful thing. Even though nothing very world-shaking comes to you at all, the quiet and thinking about the day and being grateful for all that comes is a very helpful thing.''

This is the prayer composed by Bill and recited by the Wilsons at these times:

''Oh Lord, we thank Thee that Thou art, that we are from everlasting to everlasting. Blessed be Thy holy name and all Thy benefactions to us of light, of love, and of service. May we find and do Thy will in good strength, in good cheer today. May Thy ever-present grace be discovered by family and friends — those here and those beyond — by our Societies throughout the world, by men and women everywhere, and among those who must lead in these troubled times. Oh Lord, we know Thee to be all wonder, all beauty, all glory, all power, all love. Indeed, Thou art everlasting love. Accordingly, Thou has fashioned for us a destiny passing through Thy many mansions, ever in more discovery of Thee and in no separation between ourselves.''[2]

For Alcoholics Anonymous as a whole, this was hardly a ''quiet time.'' In 1941, the Fellowship could be likened to a noisy, robust infant; to extend the metaphor, an infant in the midst of ''the terrible twos.'' It called for limitless energy, constant feeding, and uninterrupted overseeing to ensure that it not only survived but thrived.

No one was more aware of this than Bill. A good parent, he willingly gave his unruly offspring all the attention it required — and demanded. He never doubted that it would be a great success; he even believed it would change the world. So he gladly worked tirelessly to make it as sturdy as possible.

The infant was already demonstrating its personality. It had many of its father's traits: sociability, democracy, fairness, humor, warmth, optimism, and a sort of down-home funniness — some might even call it corniness. Now began the long, slow evolution of its character and integrity; as the fledgling Fellowship grew and strengthened, it needed guidelines by which to conduct itself. Bill now began the shaping of A.A. in terms of its ethics and values.

Questions and requests for help flowed into the office in a steady stream. Everywhere, groups were sprouting like crocuses in springtime.[3]

Los Angeles A.A. was a case in point. Kaye M., an attractive woman of 29, headed east from Milwaukee in 1939 with her alcoholic husband, Ty. By the time Ty arrived in Akron and "got" the program under the sponsorship of Dr. Bob and Wally G., another Akron A.A., the marriage was finished. Kaye continued alone to New York, where she planned to catch a freighter back to Los Angeles via the Panama Canal.

The high point of her New York stay was a conversation she had with Bill. "Ty is no longer your business," he said. "You are probably the worst wife he could have had." Kaye gasped at his bluntness. "You kept him out of jail. You fished him out of everything. You were always there to break his fall for him. And that was wrong. His life belongs to him. So don't worry anymore about what happens to him. The main thing now is to put Kaye on an even keel."

With only three other passengers on the freighter to Los Angeles, and the Big Book her only reading material, Kaye finished the book by the time she reached there — and it changed her life. Back "on an even keel," she took the book to Johnny Howe of the Los Angeles Probation Department, and the two nonalcoholics dug up the alcoholics who started A.A. on the West Coast. Just when the new group seemed to be faltering, Mort J. — another "book convert" — arrived from Denver and went into energetic action.

As Bill had once predicted, a single copy of the Big Book or a single enthusiastic member was all that was really required to start a group. In November 1941, on the eve of Pearl Harbor, A.A. had 200 groups and a membership of 6,000 — most of

The featured speaker wherever he went, Bill nearly always told his own story to an eager and tireless audience.

whom had never seen Bill. He would spend most of the next three years, 1941-44, on the road, out in the groups, getting to know the members, making himself available to the individuals, talking, listening, counseling, sharing, and above all, giving of himself to nurture this being, this embodiment of his compelling vision.

He traveled (Lois was usually with him) primarily by train, but occasionally by plane or car from one city to the next, sometimes staying overnight, sometimes for two nights at each stopover. Everywhere he went, he was the center of attention. The recovering alcoholics received him as a messiah; he had literally saved their lives, and they couldn't get close enough to him, physically and emotionally. He was mobbed wherever he went. John L. Norris, M.D., first met Bill during one of these early 1940's trips. "Dr. Jack," who later served A.A. as a trustee for 27 years, talked about this phenomenon:

"One of the amazing things to me about Bill was the amount of devotion and real adoration he was getting almost everywhere he turned. How any human being could have been on the receiving end of the kind of devotion that he had from so many people, and keep any sort of personal humility was amazing."

No one was more acutely aware than the early membership of what a miracle Bill and Dr. Bob had wrought — no one knew better than those early A.A.'s just how hopeless their disease had been before Alcoholics Anonymous; no one except, perhaps, the medical profession itself. Said Dr. Jack of the alcoholics he had been called on to treat in pre-A.A. days, in his capacity as medical director of Eastman Kodak in Rochester, New York:

"I hated to see them coming, because I knew I was no use to them. If someone was sent to me from the plant — 'can't you do something about Joe, Jack, Jim? They're our best people, but they always show up missing when we need them most' — I would do a medical job on them, tell them to quit drinking (if they told me the truth). I didn't know how impossible that advice was. But what else did I have? There was no teaching in medical school.

"Or we'd have a wife call us: 'Joe hasn't brought home a paycheck in three months. The gas company's going to turn off the gas. The kids need shoes. The milk bill hasn't been paid. Can't you do something?' Well, we'd call Joe in and garnishee his wages and get some money to the family, and Joe would

"Dr. Jack" Norris's gentle wisdom and understanding gave A.A. leadership for his 27 years as a nonalcoholic trustee.

behave for a little while. And after three or four months, when they'd got in shape financially, we'd be back in it again.

"In general, the medical profession was not very active — '[Drunks are] just a damned nuisance. You can't do anything with them. You're wasting your time.' It was the rare physician who would knowingly accept an alcoholic."

With such memories still green in the minds of A.A. members, it's hardly surprising that Bill was given a hero's welcome everywhere.

He was the featured speaker at every meeting he attended, and his primary subject was almost always his own dramatic story: his Vermont background, his boyhood alienation, the boomerang, Bertha Bamford, Lois, World War I, the Roaring Twenties on Wall Street, his alcoholic misery, his extraordinary experience at Towns, the vision that followed in the wake of his spiritual rebirth, and the founding of A.A. He would tell some variation of this — soon, it came to be known as "the bedtime story" — and then speak, in addition, about whatever happened to be on his mind: in later years, the Traditions, the General Service Conference, and the trustee ratio change. His talks could take as long as two hours, but he never seemed to tire of telling his story, and no one was ever seen to leave while Bill was talking. His talks were always extemporaneous. His personal story, therefore, was slightly different each time in its details and in what he chose to emphasize. But it was always built around a central outline, and it always contained Bill's special brand of wry, self-deprecatory humor. For instance, he often referred to his enormous, intense, mystical, life-changing spiritual experience as a "hot flash." He did this so often that other A.A.'s began using the same term, never realizing that Bill was deliberately "deflating" his own experience (and his own ego) by describing it thus.

His humor and his gift for improvisation added to the mesmerizing effect he had on his audience; he was a charismatic personality and a hypnotic speaker. His magnetism hardly lay in the quality of his voice — he had a high tenor, a nasal twang, and spoke in a sort of monotone, a mixture, perhaps, of Jimmy Stewart and Arlo Guthrie. But the content of his talks, coupled with his unmistakable sincerity, authenticity, and above all, sanity, was irresistible to those who heard it.

Tom P., a lifelong friend, described the first time he heard Bill speak. The year was 1941; the locale, a meeting in Greenwich, Connecticut. "He was talking about himself. He was telling the bedtime story, a variety of it. I don't remember the details. I was real screwed up mentally, but my instincts were all right, and he really galvanized me. He was authentic, and he was sincere. But you know there are sincere fools in the world — the field is crowded. This guy was right on balance on the spiritual stuff. He was the first crack in my armor. Authenticity was a big part of it — I saw he was sane and was for real."

Dr. Jack Norris, who also first heard Bill in the early 1940's, described that occasion: "It was a meeting in Rochester, in the largest ballroom in town. The place was packed; of course, everyone worshiped him — 'I owe my life and my happiness to this man.' You can sense the emotional tones of that meeting.

"He spent most of his time talking about [what would become] the Second Tradition — God as the ultimate authority; 'our leaders are but trusted servants.' This would have been in about '43 or '44. In telling how the ideas came to him, he pictured Lois at the store, and they'd been put out of their flat in Brooklyn, and they were living in [one] little, dingy room over the 24th Street Clubhouse. It was about as depressing a picture as I could get. The Big Book had been written, and Bill wanted to be listed as author, because he thought the royalties would recoup the family fortunes, and Lois would be able to leave her job. For a man to be supported by his wife in those days — well, for a Vermont Yankee — was a disgrace. He had been offered the job by Colonel Towns, which would have given them money. And Bill said, 'I wanted these things. And the groups wouldn't have it. The groups were right, and I was wrong!'

"This was during the time when we, as a world, had been suffering from such a totally different kind of leadership. The picture that came to me was what a different world this could be had Hitler — and Stalin and Mussolini — been this kind of person. I was impressed. It really got to me. It was a part of my really high regard for Bill."

At the time of that talk, the United States was at war with Germany, Italy, and Japan. Bill was deeply concerned over the course of the war. He had maps on his office wall, and he daily charted the battlefronts with pushpins.

In his personal politics, Bill was a conservative Republican. ("We were appalled when F.D.R. won the [1944] election," said Lois.) But he had not belonged to the isolationist faction. "He was very much for preparedness," said Ruth Hock. "He thought the United States should have gone in sooner, that we should have been over there helping."

Since Bill had been raised in a tradition of military service and had served with honor during World War I, it came as no surprise that he now tried to enlist, although he was 46 when the United States entered this war. In March 1942, he had received a recommendation for the Supply Service from a Colonel Donovan in Washington, and had an interview with the briga-dier general in charge of the Army's Philadelphia Quartermaster Depot, who offered to accept him as a captain.

However, he had an Army physical that same month and was rejected, he wrote to a friend, "because of ulcers." Having made two other unsuccessful attempts to join the service, he noted, not without some bitterness, that his World War I experi-ence didn't seem to count for much. In a letter to Father Dowling dated May 25, 1942, his frustration is evident: "Still struggling to get in the Army. No luck yet. Maybe I'm supposed to be a missionary after all. *I wish I knew.*" (The emphasis is Bill's.)

He sought alternative ways to contribute to the war effort. In a letter dated the same day as the one to Father Dowling, he turned his attention to helping Lewis B. Hershey, then director of Selective Service:

"It well may be that there is some draft dodging by claimants who say they are chronic alcoholics. [But] we know for a fact that many chronic alcoholics are anything but draft dodgers. Hoping to serve and at the same time cure themselves, thousands of them are probably trying to break into the service by any hook or crook. Our experience suggests that these people will, as a class, only be in the way — their drinking will continue and lead only to a medical discharge.

"But there is still another class of alcoholic applicant for Army service. He is the man who has really recovered from his illness. This organization most emphatically thinks that if adequate proof of his recovery can be submitted, such a man ought to be allowed to serve.

"In fact, this letter is prompted by certain members of our San Francisco group who have been rejected upon the sole ground of their alcoholism, yet who have considerable sobriety time behind them and who would be recommended as reasonably well men by their own group.

"Therefore, would it be possible for the Army to relax its requirement in those cases where acute alcoholism can be proved to be a thing of the past? Some discrimination would be necessary, such as a doctor's certificate or, if the selectee happened to be a member of Alcoholics Anonymous, then the recommendation of his local group.

"It is our feeling that the Army is passing up many very able men for lack of just a little more discrimination.

"I would like to offer the Army the benefit of our experience in this field of alcoholism, to be used in any manner that might seem helpful."

The Army's official response reads, in part: "It is the considered opinion of this office that, notwithstanding the patriotic attitude of your organization and of these individuals, it would be manifestly unwise to subject these men, who have apparently made a satisfactory adjustment in their individual environment,

[to] one where stress and strain play an important part and where the temptation to resort to their former inclinations would be far more inviting.''

Like so many of his ideas, Bill's offer to assist the military was merely ahead of its time. It would come to fruition in the 1960's, when the U.S. military instituted alcoholism and drug abuse programs for military personnel (following the lead of the private sector), receiving strong support from the A.A. membership.

A.A.'s who did serve in the armed forces (by 1944, they numbered about 300) proved that they could stay sober, even under the additional stress of military life and without their regular meetings.

---

1. The ''Chinese job'' was with the American Bureau for Medical Aid to China, where Bill applied for a position as director of fund-raising. He did not get it.

2. Lois, who remained deeply in love with Bill for her entire adult life, said, years after his death: ''That business about no separation between ourselves is something that I cherish.''

3. Bill, with characteristic foresight, had retained a clipping service to keep track of A.A. publicity around the country. The decision to do this when funds were still so scarce suggests a premonition that the Fellowship would one day be interested in its own history. Most of these early clippings are now in the A.A. archives in New York City.

Chapter Sixteen

One of Bill's persistent fascinations and involvements was with psychic phenomena. His belief in clairvoyance and other extrasensory manifestations arose out of his conviction that our lifetimes on earth constitute what he liked to call ''a mere day in school''; that we are all pupils in a ''spiritual kindergarten''; and that life after life is a matter of fact as well as faith. This belief led to his attempts to get in touch with other lives in other lifetimes.

Because Bill was such a sensitive person in this world, it should come as no surprise that he believed himself able to pick up energy from another. He thought of himself as having some psychic ability; to him, spiritistic matters were no mere parlor game. It's not clear when he first became interested in extrasensory phenomena; the field was something that Dr. Bob and Anne Smith were also deeply involved with. Whether or not Bill initially became interested through them, there are references to séances and other psychic events in the letters Bill wrote to Lois during that first Akron summer with the Smiths, in 1935.

One of Bill's most dramatic tales of discarnate communication is this story, as he himself told it:

"Probably in 1947,[1] my wife and I visited Nantucket. We had never been there before. We only knew it for its sturdy Yankees and vanished whaling trade. After dark, our host met us at the boat, and we were driven a mile or so to his house near the beach.

"Next morning, I woke early, maybe six o'clock. I tiptoed to the kitchen and made coffee. While musing over the first cup, there was a sudden 'intrusion.' In came the words 'I want to go whaling.' Questioning the purported entity, he gave me a Scandinavian name, now forgotten. More questions developed that he didn't realize that he was 'dead.' He said he saw people dimly, that nobody paid any attention when he spoke. He complained of great loneliness and misery. Said he'd been a sailor and wished he could have a drink. I explained what had happened to him and inquired if he had any faith, which he said he hadn't. I told him there were plenty of people about him who would be his friends, but people he couldn't see or hear because he was still earthbound. Of course, this was a typical experience that our amateur circle had often had with those discarnates who seemed stuck in some sort of purgatorial state.

"Presently, another entity came along and announced his name to be Shaw, a storekeeper on the Nantucket of a hundred years before. Shaw thanked me for trying to help the Norwegian [whom] he and his friends had been trying to wake up and get going. Shaw then explained that he usually found several hundred old-time friends at Nantucket who liked to return there just as he did. Would I like to meet a few?

"He forthwith presented me to one who called himself David Morrow. My conversation with David Morrow disclosed that he had been a sailor during the Civil War when he had, as he said, been killed serving under Admiral Farragut at the Battle of Mobile Bay. Note in passing the name — David Morrow.

"I was then presented to another entity, who declared himself to be one Pettingill, master of a whaler out of Nantucket or

Martha's Vineyard, I now forget which. This conversation was without much significance except the name of Pettingill — not an ordinary one. Others came, whose names I now forget. I believe that one of these called himself Quigley, another whaling master.

"So ended, for the moment, my tryst with the Nantucket ghosts in my friend's kitchen. Every bit of the foregoing could, of course, be attributed to phantasy, or forgotten information; that is, if it hadn't been for those names, especially Morrow and Pettingill.

"Just for fun, I told this story at breakfast, making such pointed reference to the names I'd picked up that my host was later able to recall them. At first, though, my host thought I was ribbing him; he knew little of psychics and had heard nothing before this of my adventures. When I pressed matters, he began to be concerned for me. When I pressed more, he got downright annoyed. Here, of course, the subject was dropped.

"On the eve of going home, our host and hostess arranged a picnic lunch. We were to be joined by others. The rendezvous was to be at the head of Nantucket's main street, which terminated in a circle where four other streets converged. I hadn't before visited this spot.

"As we approached the circle, I observed in its center a small monument. Coming closer, I saw that it was dedicated to Nantucket's fallen in the War of the Rebellion. Chiseled around its base were the names of the dead. In a moment, I spied a familiar name — it was David Morrow. I called my host. He well remembered David Morrow from my description at the breakfast table. He was astonished, to put it mildly.

"Next day, my wife and I visited for the first time the Nantucket Whaling Museum, a place filled with relics of the bygone past. Just inside the door, we saw a large open book. It was filled with the names of ships' masters, and sailing dates for the whole period in which the whaling industry had flourished. Imagine our surprise when our search soon discovered [the] name Pettingill as master of a whaling vessel. One other name I'd received was also there. If I now remember correctly, this one was Quigley.

"And upstairs in the museum, we found a life-size painting of Admiral Farragut, and there was a plaque describing the part Nantucket sailors had played in the Battle of Mobile Bay. This confirmed Morrow's story.

"Therefore, the record shows that I had picked up pretty accurate descriptions of three quite obscure and long-dead Nantucket citizens, names no doubt gone from the minds of living people. There isn't even a remote chance that I had at some earlier time read or heard about all three of them, *ordinary* former *inhabitants* of the island. Maybe *one*, but certainly not *three*." (The emphasis is Bill's.)

As early as 1941, Bill and Lois were holding regular Saturday "spook sessions" at Bedford Hills. One of the downstairs bedrooms was dubbed by them the "spook room"; here, they conducted many of their psychic experiments. Of one session with a ouija board, Bill wrote this description:

"The ouija board got moving in earnest. What followed was the fairly usual experience — it was a strange mélange of Aristotle, St. Francis, diverse archangels with odd names, deceased friends — some in purgatory and others doing nicely, thank you! There were malign and mischievous ones of all descriptions, telling of vices quite beyond my ken, even as former alcoholics. Then, the seemingly virtuous entities would elbow them out with messages of comfort, information, advice — and sometimes just sheer nonsense."

Bill would lie on the couch in the living room, semi-withdrawn, but not in a trance, and "receive" messages, sometimes a word at a time, sometimes a letter at a time. Anne B., neighbor and "spook" circle regular, would write the material on a pad. Lois describes one of the more dramatic of these sessions:

"Bill would lie down on the couch. He would 'get' these things. He kept doing it every week or so. Each time, certain people would 'come in.' Sometimes, it would be new ones, and they'd carry on some story. There would be long sentences; word by word would come through. This time, instead of word by word, it was letter by letter. Anne put them down letter by letter.

"I had three years of Latin. I said, 'This looks like Latin to me.' So Bill asked Dick Richardson [of the Rockefeller Foundation], who was quite a student of Latin. He asked him what this said. Was this Latin? He said yes. (Bill knew no Latin except what he got in his law course. He always regretted it.)"

Bill continues the story:

"[Richardson] was a fine classical scholar. Astonished, he finally looked up and exclaimed, 'Where on earth did you ever get this?' I demurred, but asked him if the Latin was readable. 'Yes,' said he. 'It is perfectly good, though difficult. Looks like the beginning of what was probably intended to be an allegorical account of the founding of the Christian church in Italy.' I then asked if he saw any grammatical errors in the paragraphs. He looked again and reported that the Latin looked all right to him. Since he was an old friend, I told him the story of its production, at which he was deeply impressed."

Another of their "spooking" experiences was told by Tom P., friend and neighbor:

"We went over to my aunt and uncle's one night, and Lois and Bill went along and a couple of other people. Someone said, 'Have you got a table?' So they hauled this table in, and she said, 'Oh, this table's been sitting in the sunlight and it's all faded out, and I've been intending to have it refinished and never did.' So we sit down, and we're knocking the table around, and I don't know if it levitated or not, but the table would begin to spell out messages. It would raise and tap. One tap was 'a'; two taps were 'b'; and three taps were 'c.' It took quite a while, but by that means, it would give you messages. So the table was used primarily to astound by levitating but also, and more fundamentally, by rapping out these messages. Then, we sat around and turned the lights out and put our hands down, and it rapped around inconclusively, and we'd say, 'Oh, well, he'll find us another session,' and we all went home.

"The next day, Marian called up and said, 'A very strange thing has happened. We went to bed last night, and when we got up this morning, we found the table was refinished. The whole color is restored and the finish is perfect.' So we all went back to see the refinished table, and we had to take her word that she didn't do it."

Tom and his wife Ginny were regular members of the "spooking" circle. This is Tom's story of how he became involved with them:

"I was a problem to these people, because I was an atheist, and an atheist is, by definition, a materialist. I mean, you can't be an atheist unless you're a materialist, and a materialist is, by definition, someone who does not believe in other worlds. Now these people, Bill and Dr. Bob, believed vigorously and aggressively. They were working away at the spiritualism; it was not just a hobby. And it related to A.A., because the big problem in A.A. is that for a materialist it's hard to buy the program. I had a hell of a time getting on the program. Couldn't get it through my head that there was any God, because God was a supernatural being. And there ain't any supernatural beings, and everybody knows there isn't. So the thing was not at all divorced from A.A. It was very serious for everybody."

According to Tom, Bill never did anything that was not in some way was connected with A.A. and with his own spiritual growth. He was, as Tom put it, very "one-pointed."

Other sorts of spiritual activities also claimed Bill's attention. During the 1950's, he became involved with the experiments in precognition that were conducted at the time at Duke University's Rhine Institute.

It was through Fulton and Grace Oursler, now personal friends of the Wilsons (Fulton was the *Liberty* editor who had run the early A.A. piece called "Alcoholics and God"), that Bill was introduced to Fulton Sheen — then a monsignor, later to become a bishop. Monsignor Sheen was already a nationally popular man of the cloth — a sort of Billy Graham of the Catholic Church, whose radio program, "The Catholic Hour," had a weekly audience of over 1,000,000 loyal listeners. When the monsignor "offered to explain Catholicism to him — he didn't say 'converted' — Bill thought it would be very ungrateful not to at least try to learn," said Lois. Bill met with Sheen on Saturdays for the better part of a year.

Of his actual intention to convert to Catholicism, opinions vary widely. As early as 1944, Bill realized that his name was inextricably linked with that of the Fellowship, and although the Traditions had not yet been written down and accepted, his belief in nonaffiliation for the Fellowship had already been voiced. Looking back, Lois was sure that he had no intention of actual conversion, in any case. She said, "He never really had it in the back of his mind that he would be converted." Bob H., who was close to Bill during this period, believed otherwise: "I had the impression that at the last minute, he didn't go through with his conversion because he felt it would not be right for A.A."

Whatever his ultimate intentions, there can be no doubt that he took his instruction, as he took Catholic doctrine, very seriously. Many of his feelings about the church, pro and con, were voiced frankly to Father Dowling. In a letter dated September 9, 1947, Bill wrote to the priest:

"I'm more affected than ever by that sweet and powerful aura of the church; that marvelous spiritual essence flowing down by the centuries touches me as no other emanation does, but — when I look at the authoritative layout, despite all the arguments in its favor, I still can't warm up. No affirmative conviction comes.

"Of Monsignor Sheen's deep conviction, power, and learning — I'm gratefully impressed. He really practices what he preaches to a degree which ought to make me ashamed to differ with him at all. Yet I tremendously appreciate being with him so much. He is very generous of himself.

"P.S. Oh, if the church only had a fellow-traveler department, a cozy spot where one could warm his hands at the fire and bite off only as much as he could swallow. Maybe I'm just one more shopper looking for a bargain on that virtue — obedience!''

And in another letter dated two weeks later, he continued: "I'm not the least bit scandalized by the sins of the church or any of the people in it. I don't see how an ex-drunk could be scandalized about anything. The thing which is a little disturbing seems to be an inability of the church to confess its own sins. Historically, it's difficult to reconcile perfect infallibility at certain moments with very human carrying-on at other times. Did I not think so seriously of joining, I wouldn't even think of raising the question.''

To Sheen himself, Bill wrote: "Your sense of humor will, I know, rise to the occasion when I tell you that, with each passing day, I *feel* more like a Catholic and *reason* more like a Protestant!'' (The emphasis is Bill's.)

As in some other problematical areas of his life, Bill himself may have remained ambivalent, if not about his involvement, then about his ambitions regarding ultimate conversion. Because he was able to see many facets of any given issue, conflicting as well as harmonious, he may have spoken one day as if he was intending to convert, and the next as though his religious instruction was undertaken only in the service of his spiritual growth. It is probable that despite the contradictory thoughts being expressed, he was entirely sincere in what he said each time. He didn't change his mind easily, particularly on so serious an issue; rather, he saw things differently on different occasions. That may have been bewildering for those around him, but it appeared to make total sense to him.

One of the problems that preoccupied Bill was the relationship of A.A. with the community in general, and with the professional community in particular. The professions that most overlapped the sphere of A.A.'s interest were, of course, medicine and religion. Bill felt it would be unwise for A.A. as a fellowship to have an allegiance to any one religious sect. He felt A.A.'s usefulness was worldwide, and contained spiritual principles that members of any and every religion could accept, including the Eastern religions. (As Lois put it, Bill never had any small ideas.)

In the early 1940's, "cooperation without affiliation" had not yet been presented as an important A.A. policy. But that the thought had already occurred to Bill is evident from his correspondence of the time.

There were other reasons for Bill's refusal to ally himself with any formal belief system. One of these was his personal resistance to "man-made" authority. Some of this resistance was probably traceable to his New England background (American folk mythology has it that there is no American quite so independent-minded as a Vermont Yankee).

A 1948 letter to Clem L. reads in part: "The thing that still irks me about all organized religions is their claim how confoundedly right all of them are. Each seems to think it has the right pipeline — no mud in its spiritual water. To secure converts or punish unbelievers, the great religions have violated every known law of man or God. Just now, the Hindus and Moslems are at it.[2] Quite obviously, infallibility seems to be much more important than spirituality. The record of the Western world is no better. The Jews crucified Christ; and ever since, Christians have been crucifying Jews — and each other. No sooner had my own ancestors set foot on Plymouth Rock when they drove Roger Williams and Anne Hutchinson out into the New England woods to die. Sure, the sorrows of the Prince of Peace since His first crucifixion defy all description. The root cause: disputes over doctrine, clashing infallibilities. What else were they fighting about?

"Every time this dubious principle of religious rightness takes a firm grip on men's minds, there is hell to pay, literally. In a sense, it's worse than nationalistic rightness or economic rightness, those scourges of the moment. The ungodly might not be expected to know any better. But men of religion should. Yet history shows that they just don't. It seems to me that the great religions survive because each has a sound core of spirituality. They survive because of their spirituality and in spite of their infallibility.

"So, when a religious group claiming 100 percent perfection in faith and morals asks me to join, these thoughts do arise. I simply can't help them. At least not yet. But neither am I denying the doctrine of infallibility. I can't be so cocksure as that. For aught I know, it brought down through the ages and gave to me what little I have of Christ. Yet I cannot blind myself to the frightening perversions to which it has always been subject. I find it hard to believe that Christ would have ordained things that way. Your feeling that A.A. is already so strongly built that no action on my part could split us along religious lines makes me wonder, too. If the A.A. movement knew me as I really am, I agree no one would care very much what I did. But unfortunately, that is not the case. They believe in me as the symbol of the whole. And A.A. as a whole does not make any endorsements or commitments. There is the rub."

Whatever Bill's personal feeling, he nonetheless recommended to many of his friends and recovered alcoholics that they either join or rejoin a church. As he himself said:

"The fact is that I feel deeply the great power and spirituality which flows out into the world through the church. I know of no other source of like quality. Therefore, when people come to me questing, and I see they are at loose ends, I tell them how I feel about the church — without, however, any special emphasis on my own personal difficulties."

In addition to his predilection for a religious or spiritual life (after all, was it not a deeply religious experience, even though he nonchalantly called it a "hot flash," that had saved his own life?), he was closely connected with a number of men of the cloth

— in other words, some of his best friends were clergymen.

Bill never stopped seeking to improve his conscious contact with God, trying to find more direct routes to the source of healing. This search sometimes led him down strange paths, which intersected with those of some odd people. But that is jumping ahead; during the early 1940's, he was seeking more conventional ways to make the young Fellowship more available to more alcoholics, and more effective in carrying the message.

---

1. Bill was mistaken about the year; it was 1944.

2. It was the time of the partition of India and Pakistan.

Chapter Seventeen

On October 24, 1943, Bill and Lois set out on the first leg of an ambitious cross-country trip. The Los Angeles groups, which had been started with no personal help from Bill, were anxious to see him, to hear him, and to touch him.

The Wilsons' itinerary (they were traveling primarily by train) was strenuous and complicated by the fact that it was wartime: "Leave New York 6:30 p.m. Sunday 10/24; leave Chicago 5:30 p.m. Monday 10/25; leave Denver Friday p.m. 10/29; leave Williams [Arizona] 9:00 p.m. 11/1; arrive Los Angeles 11:45 a.m. 11/2."

At each of these stops, they were welcomed generously, and of course, Bill spoke. They had a three-week stay in Los Angeles, leaving on November 23 and arriving in San Francisco the next day. From San Francisco they went to Portland, from Portland to Seattle, and from Seattle to San Diego, where they planned to spend a three-week Christmas - New Year's holiday with Bill's mother. Then, they would go from San Diego back to Los Angeles, to Tucson, to Houston, to New Orleans, back to Houston, to Dallas, to Little Rock, to Oklahoma City, and back to Little Rock. They planned to return to New York on Wednesday, January 19. On their first major A.A. tour, the Wilsons would be on the road for three months.

With minor variations, the procedure on all these stopovers was similar. Bill and Lois were met at the station and taken to their lodgings — sometimes a hotel, sometimes a private home. Then, they met local A.A.'s for a meal. If the meal was lunch, the afternoon was often spent touring the local sights. If the meal was dinner, it was invariably followed by an A.A. meeting, at which Bill always spoke. Coffee and more conversation followed the meeting. After a few hours of sleep, they had breakfast with local A.A.'s — bacon and eggs, perhaps; more coffee and more conversation, certainly. All the A.A.'s were anxious to tell Bill their own stories and to hear his. If the visit was a one-night stopover, Bill and Lois would board their train sometime the next afternoon. From one stop, the journey to their next destination would last overnight; from another, only a few hours. In places where their stay was longer, they might get a chance to catch their breath and perhaps a few hours' sleep.

The Los Angeles membership had raised about $2,500 to cover their traveling expenses. Throughout these early years, it was more the rule than the exception that Bill and Lois received money for traveling expenses from the groups. It was no secret that the Wilsons were financially pinched, nor that the reason for this was Bill's total commitment to the demands of the Fellowship, from which he continued to draw only a small stipend.

Some highlights of the trip, as described by Lois in her diary:

"Tues., Nov. 2, 1943 — Arrive Los Angeles — 11:45 a.m. Dr. Forest H—— and Bill S—— met us at the station and took us to the Town House, where we have the most wonderful suite — bedroom, living room, kitchen and dinette, and bath. Two of the wives filling the larder and fixing flowers had lunch with the two men and ourselves. After lunch, the reporters and

photographers streamed in, and Bill had to give them an argument to prevent his name and picture getting in the papers. That
night, Doc H —— and his wife Merle, Bill and Agnes S ——,
and Mr. and Mrs. Montjoy, vice-president of the hotel organization, took us to dinner in a private dining room.

"Fri., Nov. 5 — Bill S —— stopped for us at 10:00 a.m.,
and we met Bud F —— at the Universal Studios in Hollywood.
Then met another A.A., who got us a guide, and we all went and
saw where pictures were being shot. We had lunch in the com-
missary and saw a number of stars. Then, we went to Warner
Bros. and saw Bette Davis and Claude Rains and several other
sets. By the time we got home, we didn't have time to change,
but there was an orchid there for me, and we met the H —— s,
the S —— s, and Mort and Francis J —— and Elinor and
Frank R —— , and went to the meeting where Frank S ——
introduced Mort J ——, and Mort introduced Bill, who talked
on A.A. for two hours. 800 present. The R —— s came home
with us, and we had coffee and sandwiches.

"Wed., Nov. 10 — some of the 'oldsters' came to have
lunch with Bill and me, but I stayed in bed rubbing oil of winter-
green on my sore muscles, without much effect. Then, Bill left at
5:00 p.m. and drove with H —— and S —— to Long Beach,
where there were about 400 present. He didn't get back until
1:30 a.m.

"Friday, Nov. 12 — Bill went to Psychopathic Court in the
a.m., and then he and I went to meet Bill's mother on the 2:30
train from San Diego. We went down to the Cape Cod Room for
dinner, and the H —— s called for us and took us to the second
mass meeting at the American Legion Post in Hollywood. There
must have been about 1,000 there. Bill was fine. He called on
Mother and me to take a bow. She was quite astounded at the
fuss they made over Bill, rising when he first stood up to speak.
She had had an accident two weeks ago and was made quite
nervous by it. Otherwise she seems fine, but lots older. The maid
rolled a bed into the living room for her.''

Bill's mother stayed with them until November 15, when, with some difficulty, she boarded a train back to San Diego. There were so many servicemen on the road that traveling was not easy for civilians.

On November 19, Bill, for the third time, gave a two-hour talk at a mass Hollywood meeting.

Their Los Angeles stay ended on November 23, when they boarded a train for San Francisco. There, the whole Los Angeles scenario was more or less repeated. One of the variations was Bill's trip to San Quentin; its liberal warden, Clinton T. Duffy, had permitted the founding of an A.A. meeting inside the walls of the maximum security prison. There, Bill spoke to an audience of about 420 inmates.

Bill also spoke at Folsom Prison in Sacramento. Of this event, Lois wrote:

"Because of the recent prison disturbance and investigation, the prison authorities only allowed one other man to go with Bill. Bill returned about 11:30, tremendously impressed and with an illuminated affidavit of appreciation of him and A.A. signed by 137 convicts. Folsom has some of the country's most desperate criminals. Bill said they all seemed sincere about A.A., and some of them even wept a few tears."

Bill and Lois spent Christmas and New Year's with Bill's mother in San Diego, where she lived in the Sandford Hotel. Of her life-style, Lois said, "It seems terribly pathetic for Mother to live this way, but she must like it, for she has always done it and could have it different if she wanted it." Dr. Emily owned and managed three apartment houses in San Diego. Although Lois did not spell out what she meant by "terribly pathetic," the implication is that Bill's mother, even though she could afford to live more comfortably, chose not to. (This inference is confirmed by Bill's nickname for his mother; he sometimes referred to her as "Hetty Green." The richest woman on Wall Street at the turn of the century, Hetty Green was famous for her miserliness — despite all the money she made, she always wore the same black dress and carried her lunch in a brown paper bag.)

Of their 13 married years together, the Strobels had spent much of it traveling. During a stay in Vienna, Dr. Emily studied under Alfred Adler, a former colleague of Freud's. When the Strobels settled permanently in San Diego, they opened joint offices. He was the consultant for medical and surgical cases; she, for those requiring osteopathy. But, Lois said, "It turned out she didn't get many patients. Her husband got most of them." Dr. Emily then became a lecturer and practitioner in the Adlerian school of psychoanalysis.[1] Dr. Emily's husband died in 1936.

Lois felt that Bill's relationship with his mother was not all it might have been: "Bill felt as if his mother had deserted him when she went into Boston to go to school. He almost hated her for a long time, until he got to know her." Lois believed that it was she, Lois, who brought Bill and his mother together, "but there was always something, a hitch in their relationship, something lacking."

On New Year's Day, the Wilsons journeyed south from San Diego to Trabuco, in the California desert. Trabuco was a college that had been founded by an English philosopher named Gerald Heard, whom Dave D., a California member, had been anxious for Bill to meet.

On the home journey east, the Wilsons were also able to bear witness to the A.A. tradition (as yet only a custom) of autonomy, as practiced by local groups. In Little Rock, Arkansas, for instance, the group leader ensured his anonymity by speaking to the 1,200-person meeting from behind a closed curtain. In New Orleans, at a dinner for 60 members, the A.A. chairman arrived "slightly squiffed," as Lois delicately termed it.

On January 22, 1944, the Wilsons returned home to their brown-shingled Bedford Hills refuge. The trip had been an unqualified success.

---

1. Part of the problem may have been Dr. Emily's feminism, which was a phenomenon in her time. When she first began her practice in Boston, while Bill was at Norwich, she refused to accept male patients. She was also very opinionated; she once declared that most of the world's troubles stemmed from sex and alcohol.

Chapter Eighteen

The Wilsons' three-month tour of the groups had been such a personal uplift for Bill and such a triumph in terms of the Fellowship that what happened upon their return must have come as a total surprise, an inexplicable blow. Hardly had they returned home when Bill was plunged into a depression so black that its effect on him was more debilitating than a physical assault.

He was not unfamiliar with depression; he had first experienced it as an adolescent. In his years as an active drunk, it had been his chronic if not constant companion. But this was virtually his first encounter with it as a sober, sane adult.[1] Its onset was the more unexpected because it followed the incredible joy of witnessing his vision as a lasting reality.

A connection between the tour and the onset of his depression was suggested jokingly by Al M. of Los Angeles. The way Al put it, "Bill saw himself that we didn't need him — all we needed was his book. As I understand it, he went into a five-year depression on account of it."

There are many and varied accounts of Bill's recurrent depression, and almost as many opinions about its nature, its causes, its intensity, its dynamics, and its manifestations. Thus it is virtually impossible to isolate a definitive account. The subject is further clouded by the fact that Bill, throughout his life, was subject to a variety of physical ills, and it was not uncommon for him to spend a day or more in bed with no clear diagnosis of what was ailing him. As Lois put it, ''He was almost a hypochondriac.'' The operative word is ''almost.'' Bill would frequently refer to his own ills as ''an imaginary ulcer,'' or ''the colliwobbles'' — in other words, he always retained a sense of humor about his own ailments. But there was nothing funny about his depressions; they were dark and crippling.

No one was more disturbed about his condition than Bill himself. Apart from the agony of the depressions themselves, the very fact that he had them disturbed him deeply. When, in the Big Book, written in 1938, he had described sobriety as ''a fourth dimension of existence of which we had not even dreamed,'' he had meant it in all sincerity. Now, scarcely five years later, he was plunged into an abyss of such bleakness and negativity as to make him suicidal.

Bill's depressions lasted for roughly 11 years in all, until 1955, when he was finally freed of them. During those years, however, they were not constant, nor were they always the same in intensity. The first two years, 1944-1946, were apparently the worst. Recalling them, Marty M. said, ''It was awful. There were long periods of time when he couldn't get out of bed. He just stayed in bed, and Lois would see that he ate. An awful lot of people believed he was drinking. That was one of the worst rumors we had within A.A.''

Nell Wing, Bill's secretary from 1950 until he died, said, ''He would come down to the office many times and sit across from me and just put his head in his hands and really not be able to communicate, just almost weep. He used to talk about it. It baffled him.'' Herb M., general manager at G.S.O. for many years, echoed Nell's memory: ''There were some times when these horrible depressions would go on and on, for days and days. Then, it was pretty hard to make contact with him. He'd try and cooperate if you had a question, but to try and sit down and do any planning with him at that time was useless. His whole face would fall; he looked sad, sad, very sad.''

Lois was as baffled as Bill, as baffled as everyone else. Because his condition was so beyond her, she remembers herself as not very sympathetic. ''It was awfully hard for me to understand. I wasn't too sympathetic, actually. Or I didn't know how to be sympathetic, exactly. Or what to do differently.'' Lois was temperamentally so different from Bill that it is easy to understand her bewilderment; she herself could be upset or distraught over a specific person, event, or circumstance, but seemingly causeless, long-term depression was as alien to her as alcoholism.

Nell Wing, Bill's longtime secretary, filled many jobs at the Alcoholic Foundation, and became A.A.'s first archivist.

What was now happening to Bill was neither a mood swing nor a temporary loss of emotional equilibrium. It was a deep, lasting, and monotonous — in the sense that it was unvarying in color — period of blackness. For the first two years, 1944-1946, he had little if any relief.

Bill's own description of his mood is implied in ''Twelve Steps and Twelve Traditions'' (written during a time of depression):

''If temperamentally we are on the depressive side, we are apt to be swamped with guilt and self-loathing. We wallow in this messy bog, often getting a misshapen and painful pleasure out of it. As we morbidly pursue this melancholy activity, we may sink to such a point of despair that nothing but oblivion looks possible as a solution. Here, of course, we have lost all perspective, and therefore all genuine humility. For this is pride in reverse. This is not a moral inventory at all; it is the very process by which the depressive has so often been led to the bottle and extinction.''

If Bill's mood was darkened, his character remained unimpaired. It was never his style to let a circumstance, a tragedy, or even a disaster overwhelm him; rather, it was inherent in him to wring the good from every situation, no matter how hopeless it appeared. This depression was no exception. Using himself as a guinea pig, as usual, he set about finding a reason — and a cure — for his relentless black mood.

During the 1940's, psychoanalysis was much in vogue in this country. In 1944, Bill began to see Dr. Harry Tiebout, the Blythewood psychiatrist who had always championed A.A., and had brought Marty M. into the program. Psychiatric treatment was just one of many routes that Bill would investigate in an attempt to understand and heal himself of the negativity that was making his life such an intolerable burden. For someone in Bill's position — a founder of a lifesaving program that promised its adherents ''a new happiness'' — to openly undertake a course of psychiatric treatment was an act of courage.

Whether or not these psychiatric sessions ever satisfied him as to the cause of his depression is unknown; years later, he wrote to a friend: "I had some psychiatric attention years ago. That helped a good deal in my understanding, but I didn't find it especially curative. It took down my fear of these conditions [i.e., the depression], but the effect was not positive enough to fully overcome them."

What is known is that the depression remained long after he terminated the psychiatric sessions. Thus, even if he did learn what he had set out to learn, the cure did not follow promptly on

Dr. Harry M. Tiebout was the first psychiatrist to see in A.A. a significant approach to the treatment of alcoholics.

the heels of this knowledge. Bill was an acutely intelligent man. The simplicity of his writings for publication may have given — to those who did not know him — the impression that there was nothing complex about his personal attitudes and philosophies. Nothing could be farther from the truth. The fact seems to be that he deliberately conveyed this impression. Because he was a man with a vision and a message, everything he did at the public level was in the service of more effectively conveying the message, of sharing his vision.

Among his confidants, he was not reticent about revealing his deep perceptiveness regarding himself and other people. He did this frequently and generously. To judge from letters to friends and from their memories of personal conversations with him, it seems probable that nothing emerged from his psychiatric sessions of which he was not already aware. Said Dr. Jack Norris: ''I think Bill was too sharp. He could see through part of the mystique of psychotherapy. (This, I think, is part of the need for continuing, repetitive surrender.)''

Whether or not Tiebout helped Bill psychiatrically, he and Bill remained firm friends, and he a staunch supporter of Alcoholics Anonymous. Tiebout himself may have learned a great deal from Bill; he made important contributions to the psychiatric knowledge of alcoholism, particularly in the areas of surrender and ego reduction in A.A.

Bill, in the meantime, was not content to investigate a single avenue of relief. He addressed his depressions from every angle he could think of, and explored every potential solution — physical, psychological, and spiritual. Following are excerpts from letters he sent to some of the many people who petitioned for his help with their own depressions:

''Recently, an osteopath gave me a tremendous lift. He found a lesion in my spine near the base of the skull which had seriously interfered with the circulation of the blood in my brain. When this was righted, my capabilities of resistance increased tremendously. This side of the causation needs exploration in each of us. But we mustn't think it's a cure for neurosis; it's just a blowout patch.'' . . .

''Years of neurosis and emotional strain tend to throw the glandular system out of order. In my own case, I found that I had a very overactive pancreas and [was] getting a more or less constant insulin shock. When I cut my sugar consumption to about one-third, this was largely relieved with excellent results. I found that my neurosis and my surroundings could not hurt me nearly so much. There was a slight thyroid deficiency, easily corrected by an eighth of a grain a day.'' . . .

''I have had a really savage depression for about two years, during which there has been psychiatric care, physical examinations, osteopathic treatments, and a real good look at the hormone possibilities. The examination showed, however, no sex hormone deficiency. Quite the reverse. I had a great excess of one of them — not the sex hormone, but a related one. My metabolism was under par, though not badly so. About two months ago, my doctor started to give me thyroid, which is of course a hormone, in relatively small quantities. The depressions were greatly lightened.'' . . .

''I would set myself a small stint. I would determine to *walk* and *breathe* for a *quarter of a mile*. And I would *concentrate* to the extent of *counting* my breathing — say six steps to each slow inhalation and four to each exhalation.

''Lots of times, I had to beat myself to do even this much. But I had learned that the penalty of quitting entirely — just looking at the wall — was far greater. So I would do the quarter mile. Having done this, I found that I could go on, maybe a half mile more. Then another half mile, and maybe another.''

Bill always concentrated heavily on walking and breathing as an antidote to depression. When he could, he walked five miles a day on the wooded trails around Bedford Hills.

Above all, Bill believed that his depressions were perpetuated by his own failure to work the A.A. Steps.[2] Thus the already painful depression was deepened by this added sense of guilt. He wrote: "I used to be rather guilt-ridden about this. Why, I asked myself, considering all the advantages I had, should I be subject to this sort of thing? At other times, I blamed myself for inability to practice the program in certain areas of my life. These, and many more reasons for self-downgrading, constantly put in an appearance."

The prescription he kept returning to: "Part of the answer lies in a constant effort to practice all of the A.A. Twelve Steps. Persistence will cause this to sink in and affect that unconscious from where the trouble stems. I used to be ashamed of my condition and didn't talk about it. But in recent years, I freely confess I'm a depressive, and that attracts other depressives to me. Working on them has helped a great deal. In fact, it helped me more than it did them.

"Then, too, there is the physical side of the equation. Constant depression, tension, or aggression obviously throws the glandular system out of gear. Mild tonic doses of some of the modern drugs — B-12, male hormones, ACE and the like — help. They don't cure the personality defects, but they take the heat off."

Bill was learning, starting with the revelation of some truths about himself, that alcoholic drinking may in some people mask deeper psychological and emotional disturbances. He was also learning that the A.A. program might not be the answer for every alcoholic. There might be people who could not "get" the program because of various perceptual or psychological obstacles.

Those two pieces of information, coming to Bill through the vehicle of his own depression, now sent him on a quest to find greater enlightenment, to find healing for sober alcoholics for whom sobriety alone, even when they worked the Steps, was insufficient to provide a comfortable life. The search would eventually lead him in a direction apparently away from A.A., and would have consequences of major proportions.

But in this period, Bill simply shared everything he knew

about depression — and its symbolic significance. He wrote to a fellow sufferer: "You must have often asked yourself the very question so frequently in my own mind. Why all this pain? What have I done to merit this suffering? The answer I get is that pain, quite as much as pleasure, is in God's providence. In the long run, everything evolves for the better, not because of pleasure, but because of pain."

Other people who knew Bill had their own speculations as to what caused his depressions. Dr. Earl M., psychiatrist, A.A., and close friend, said: "I felt that he had no one he could talk with about his far-out spiritual ideas. When I listened to him, he would turn on and become vibrant, and his eyes would shine. I had the feeling that what Bill needed was someone who could really validate what he said. You know, the thing that brought A.A. into being was [Dr. Bob's saying] to Bill, 'I drink like that!' at that meeting at Henrietta Seiberling's.

"Tiebout was trying to analyze, and here Bill had some new ideas about spirituality, and maybe there was an afterlife or another life, and right or not, the guy was looking all the time as to how he would bring this to A.A. members."

Said Dr. Jack Norris: "You can't separate an organic depression from a psychological depression." He added, "In the excitement of success, he brought up a tremendous amount of energy, so that you have an organic element in it. I don't think the organic is all of it. But I think [it] is part of it. It's a matter of energy. If I get a lot of pats on the back and everything goes well, I feel wonderful; I have a tremendous amount of energy. But when the pats on the back aren't there, when I have to settle back as a normal human being — what's wrong?"

Another proponent of the energy theory was Tom P., who had started his A.A. career as a confirmed atheist but changed his mind. Tom had his own theory of Bill's depressions. He

Boyhood achievement, as first violin in the school orchestra, turned into satisfying recreation in later years.

said that they were the result, though indirect, of the "hot flash"; Tom interpreted both in terms of mystic experience. Of Bill's experience in Towns Hospital, Tom said: "The thing Bill had was a perfectly clear case of *satori* or *somate*.[3] You know by the fruits. The guy goes out and starts to act like an enlightened man. No one ever went further to prove it than that man did — he led a life of total service.

"It is the aim of every religion — spiritual experience."

Tom (sometimes speaking of the late co-founder in the present tense, 12 years after his death) linked Bill's spiritual experience to his later depressions: "Bill is a man of enormous capacity of will. People think they understand what will is, but they don't very well, and people vary in their endowment of will. They think it's puckering yourself up mentally or something, but it isn't. Will and intelligence come right off spirit.

"This guy is very heavily endowed that way. It's his chief characteristic before and after anyone. After A.A., he's a guy with a mission. All enlightened people have a mission. But it's real. He's a tough man physically, but not so tough nervously. But he just went out to do this job. That's okay the first year or two. But what about when the damned thing began to burgeon, began to spread? After they picked up on the newspaper stories, it was a different thing, and the job was much harder. This guy learned a lesson that all enlightened people learn, according to the biographies. St. Francis of Assisi, who was Bill's patron saint, said: 'Since the day of my conversion, I have never been well.'

"When the thing started to grow up in California, he went to California. And you know what drunks are like — they all like to sit up all night and drink coffee, and talk! And this guy would go on, and they'd all land on him, and he'd stay up and drink coffee. It's fun to hear someone's story, then to tell your own story, but if you do that all night . . .! He would come back from one of these trips like he'd been dragged from one end of New York to the other by a wagon. He was a big, tough fellow, but you never saw anybody so beat-up. And the depressions were largely exhaustion — I mean spiritual exhaustion. That guy wasn't just making conversation.''

It's probably not coincidental that the years of Bill's depressions — 1944-1955 — were also the years when he did the most exhausting and intensive work for A.A. After World War II, he embarked on the enormous undertaking of establishing a service structure for A.A. — a ten-year task. After 1955, the year he declared A.A. of age, pronounced the service structure complete, and turned the Fellowship over to its members, he was free of depression.

During that decade (years he himself characterized as ones of ''immense stress and strain''), Bill was always beating upwind emotionally. All his work during this period was done with and in spite of the burden of his depression — sometimes so heavy and black that it took a heroic effort to get out of bed in the morning. Were this one fact all the evidence we had, it alone would be measure of the depth of Bill's vision and commitment. It was the boomerang incident all over again, but this time on a worldwide, life and death scale.

---

1. Ruth Hock once said that Bill had had a bout of depression in February 1942.

2. Many A.A.'s agreed. Not a few of them suggested to Bill that he try working the Steps.

3. The characteristic Zen Buddhist teaching of sudden enlightenment, or *satori*, goes back to the seventh century. It is defined as the direct seeing of one's own ''original nature.''

Chapter Nineteen

In the woods near Stepping Stones, Bill and a friend built a small cement-block studio. This he called "Wits' End," and here he spent much time writing. He commuted into the Manhattan office a couple of days a week, except when he was on the road or ill. Often, he stayed overnight in town, spending those nights at the Bedford Hotel.[1] With some variations, he would continue these habits for the rest of his working life.

By 1944, A.A. was "official," with 360 groups and an estimated membership of 10,000 people. Alcoholism, too, was official; 1944 was the year Bill was invited to address the New York State Medical Society; he was one of the few lay people ever asked to speak to its members on a serious medical problem. In that talk he referred to alcoholism as a disease. In 1944, A.A. moved uptown—from Vesey Street to 415 Lexington Avenue, near Grand Central Station.

Ruth Hock was gone; she had left in 1942 to remarry — a member of the Fellowship — and had moved to Ohio. She was replaced by Bobbie B., a former dancer and an A.A. member.

There were more paid assistants in the office; often, translators were brought in to handle inquiries from abroad.

The Grapevine, A.A.'s monthly periodical, had commenced publication with the June 1944 issue. Originating independently of Bill, it was founded by a group that he affectionately termed "six ink-stained wretches." An eight-page bulletin at the start, intended to get A.A. news to members in the armed forces, it soon expanded and became the Fellowship's official magazine. Over the years, the Grapevine would publish about 100 pieces by Bill. It was one of his most important vehicles for communication with the membership.

Much of Bill's work at the office was taking care of the correspondence. Since the publication of the *Saturday Evening Post* article, mail had been arriving in a steady stream. Many of the letters asked for assistance in forming new groups, or requested advice on various problems and circumstances in the groups. It was from having seen similar questions arise again and again that the idea of devising clear guidelines for the groups first evolved. This need had been discussed since 1943, when the headquarters office began to collect information, requesting of the groups a list of their membership rules and requirements. Listing them, Bill recalled, took a great many sheets of paper. "A little reflection on these many rules brought us to an astonishing conclusion. If all these edicts had been in force everywhere at once, it would have been practically impossible for any alcoholic to have ever joined A.A. About nine-tenths of our oldest and best members could never have got by!"

Bill described the problem as it existed in mid-decade:

"The solution of group problems by correspondence had put a large volume of work on Headquarters. Letters to metropolitan A.A. centers filled our bulging files. It seemed as if every contestant in every group argument wrote us during this confused period.

"The basic ideas for the Twelve Traditions of Alcoholics Anonymous came directly out of this vast correspondence. In late 1945 a good A.A. friend suggested that all this mass of experience might be codified into a set of principles which could offer tested solutions to all of our problems of living and working together and of relating our Society to the world outside. If we had become sure enough of where we really stood on such matters as membership, group autonomy, singleness of purpose, nonendorsement of other enterprises, professionalism, public controversy, and anonymity in its several aspects, then such a set of principles could be written.''

It was testament to Bill's genius that he thought to call them Traditions. Had they been called "laws," "rules," "by-laws," or "regulations," they might never have been accepted by the membership. Bill knew his fellow alcoholics well; he knew that no self-respecting drunk, sober or otherwise, would willingly submit to a body of "law" — much too authoritarian!

The name "Traditions," however, would come a bit later. At first, he dubbed them "Twelve Points to Assure Our Future," because he saw them as guidelines necessary to the survival, unity, and effectiveness of the Fellowship. Under that title, they were first published in the April 1946 issue of the Grapevine. In subsequent issues, Bill wrote an editorial for each point, explaining its origin and why it was necessary.

As Bill set about his task, it became obvious that some of the Traditions were already in place. That made them truly traditional, inasmuch as their practice within the Fellowship was already customary.

To say that Bill was the sole author of the Traditions is both true and untrue. He was certainly not the sole author of the experiences from which they evolved, but he was the person who interpreted and culled meaning from these experiences. The meanings, as derived by Bill, subsequently became the backbone of the Traditions.

The best-known (if not, at the time, the most secure) — in terms of its importance and also in terms of the publicity it had already received — was the tradition of anonymity. The term had been appropriated when the Big Book was named; prior to that, the Fellowship had been a "nameless bunch of drunks," not secret in terms of the work it did — that had never been secret — but in terms of who belonged to it. "Alcoholics Anonymous" had always referred to the members, never to the message, which Bill had been trying to pass on since his spiritual awakening.

Anonymity was originally practiced for reasons that had to do with the experimental nature of the Society and with the prevailing stigma on alcoholism. To make public one's A.A. membership and then to go out and drink again was to jeopardize the reputation and ultimately the survival of the entire Fellowship. Anonymity at the level of the public media was vital to the welfare of the group. This attitude would be one of the major determinants of the Eleventh Tradition: "Our public relations policy is based on attraction rather than promotion; we need always maintain personal anonymity at the level of press, radio and films."

The anonymity break by Rollie H. caused Bill to examine his own feelings, and in the process of so doing, he realized the greater significance of the anonymity principle. For Bill's own response to Rollie's "transgression" was to seek out publicity for himself. Bill then concluded that the deeper purpose of anonymity was "actually to keep those fool egos of ours from running hog wild after money and public fame at A.A.'s expense."

Early on, Bill had realized that the limelight — something that most A.A. members, himself included, craved — was an experience that most had little tolerance for. To lose one's bid for the limelight could be as disastrous as to win it. Power-driving was a potentially dangerous activity for an alcoholic; Bill said he believed it to be the source and cause of all his own troubles (see his letter to Yale University, page 311). It was much better, then, to rely on principles and ideas, which were constant, stable, and dependable, than on the unstable and quixotic ups and downs of personal relationships. Thus was born the Twelfth Tradition: "Anonymity is the spiritual foundation of all our Traditions, ever reminding us to place principles before personalities.'' Bill knew that ''life among the anonymi,'' as he characterized the spats that were sometimes a part of A.A. life, were the surface manifestation of a fragile sense of self. In the ''civilian'' world, these might be seen as a demonstration of ordinary ego desires, but because they could be sufficient to get an A.A. drunk, the gratification of such desires must be sacrificed in the ongoing quest for across-the-board sobriety.

He would write, in his essay on the Twelfth Tradition: ''The spiritual substance of anonymity is sacrifice. Because A.A.'s Twelve Traditions repeatedly ask us to give up personal desires for the common good, we realize that the sacrificial spirit — well symbolized by anonymity — is the foundation of them all. It is A.A.'s proved willingness to make these sacrifices that gives people their high confidence in our future.''

These are sophisticated concepts, and it took a mind like Bill's to distill them. Another person might have interpreted the experiences from which they evolved quite differently — and not arrived at the crucial generalizations.

Anonymity breaks were one of the biggest stresses on the Fellowship at this time. A.A. was by now a household word; it had gotten almost unanimously good reviews in the national press; and if it had not quite become ''smart'' to be a member, at least to confess your membership publicly was to evoke admiration. A film star had gone so far as to break her anonymity on celluloid with the filming of her life story. (She broke it first in 1946-47; her autobiography appeared in 1954; the film, in 1955.) She subsequently drank again. Bill described what happened next:

''[She] got hold of a letter which she thought damaged her professional reputation. She felt something should be done about this and so did her lawyer, also an A.A. They assumed that both the public and A.A. would be rightfully angry if the facts were known. Soon several newspapers headlined how Alcoholics Anonymous was rooting for one of its lady members, named in full, of course, to win her suit for libel.''

There was, as well, the noted radio commentator who broke his anonymity on the air and in the press, to an estimated audience of 12,000,000.

Bill's reactions to these violations exhibited his usual patience, compassion, and humanity. He was, as many said, the most forgiving of men. Some excerpts from a letter he wrote to Jack Alexander on the subject of the radio announcer:

''Of course, this looks like wonderful publicity to folks outside A.A. But to 99 A.A.'s out of 100, it is a danger signal. Most of us deeply realize that enough repetition of such blasts could alter the whole character of our Society. We would become one more example of personal ballyhoo; we invite every A.A. promoter — and there are many — to use the A.A. name on his own behalf. And, more seriously, we would enable all those who choose to break anonymity at the general public level to hire out in other fields of work and draw the A.A. implied endorsement along with them.

''As the value of the A.A. name for money raising and publicity purposes increases, so will the temptation. A.A. opinion can and does restrain most of our personal publicists. But not the few like N——. Only public opinion counts with him. He really thinks he is doing us a favor; he hasn't the slightest idea that he is busting the best protective gadget our Fellowship will ever have. As to the immense spiritual implications of anonymity, poor old N—— just doesn't know.''

Or, as he later paraphrased it in the Grapevine: ''. . . we alcoholics are the biggest rationalizers in the world, and . . . fortified with the excuse that we are doing great things for A.A., we can, through broken anonymity, resume our old and disastrous pursuit of personal power and prestige, public honors, and money — the same implacable urges that when frustrated once caused us to drink, the same forces that are today ripping the globe apart at its seams. These lessons make clear, moreover, that enough spectacular anonymity breakers could someday carry our whole Society down into that ruinous dead end with them.''

An earlier anonymity break that caused an uproar was that of Marty M. Her case was a particularly sensitive one, because she was a close personal friend of Bill's. In addition, Bill strongly supported her work in alcoholism education. Now in her early 40's and personally attractive, Marty made excellent newspaper copy as she toured the country on behalf of her National Committee for Education on Alcoholism. Newspaper clippings began arriving at A.A. headquarters; she was often photographed full face and identified as a member. When *Time* magazine did a piece on her committee in 1944, her background as an A.A. was described.

Bill was on the spot. He seemed at first to believe that the importance of Marty's work overrode the importance of the anonymity principle. In a letter to a Georgia A.A. who had asked permission to break his own anonymity, Bill wrote: ''I still feel that it was right for her to do exactly as she did. Though the risk of a precedent for other A.A.'s to drop their anonymity was serious, and may still be, the gains to A.A. and to the cause of education have apparently outweighted this consideration by far.''

Soon, Bill had other proposals to consider. A member began to publish a magazine devoted to the cause of Prohibition. He thought A.A. ought to help the world go dry. In public, he freely used the A.A. name to attack the evils of whiskey and those who made it and drank it. Bill said: ''He pointed out that he too was an 'educator,' and that his brand of education was the 'right kind.' ''

As other proposals and ideas continued to reach Bill, he came to realize that no matter how good Marty's cause, it nonetheless set precedents for others who sincerely believed their causes equally good. Bill finally admitted that he had made a mistake, and that he had learned from it. Witness this 1948 letter to a Florida member:

''[In] this particular matter, I confess a great deal of fault myself. Several years ago, we did not realize the protective value of anonymity to the A.A. movement as a whole. When, for educational purposes, Marty broke hers, I consented to it. In the light of later events, that has proved to be a mistake. In our Traditions pamphlet, you will find an acknowledgment of that error.''

Bill's own behavior, with regard to reaping the recognition, fame, and prizes that were offered him for his A.A. work, was a model of modesty. As he put it: ''My record respecting public honors is so far very much on the conservative side.'' He himself said he turned down six honorary degrees: ''My estimate was that the precedent of not personally taking such degrees would be more valuable than the taking of them — from the viewpoint of Alcoholics Anonymous.''

Perhaps the most significant of these was his refusal of an honorary Doctor of Laws degree from Yale University, an event that deserves description in some detail, as it so perfectly exemplifies the concerns Bill was trying to espouse. Although he would have loved to accept, he decided that he would decline. His letter of refusal was a masterpiece of humility, tact, and intelligence. Dated February 2, 1954, it read in its entirety:

''Mr. Reuben Holden, Secretary, Yale University, New Haven, Connecticut

''Dear Mr. Holden,

''This is to express my deepest thanks to the members of the Yale Corporation for considering me as one suitable for the degree of Doctor of Laws.

''It is only after most careful consultation with friends, and with my conscience, that I now feel obligated to decline such a mark of distinction.

''Were I to accept, the near term benefit to Alcoholics Anonymous and to legions who still suffer our malady would, no doubt, be worldwide and considerable. I am sure that such a potent endorsement would greatly hasten public approval of A.A. everywhere. Therefore, none but the most compelling of

reasons could prompt my decision to deny Alcoholics Anonymous an opportunity of this dimension.

"Now this is the reason: The tradition of Alcoholics Anonymous — our only means of self-government — entreats each
member to avoid all that particular kind of personal publicity or
distinction which might link his name with our Society in the
general public mind. A.A.'s Tradition Twelve reads as follows:
'Anonymity is the spiritual foundation of all our Traditions, ever
reminding us to place principles before personalities.'

"Because we have already had much practical experience
with this vital principle, it is today the view of every thoughtful
A.A. member that if, over the years ahead, we practice this anonymity *absolutely,* it will guarantee our effectiveness and unity by
heavily restraining those to whom public honors and distinctions
are but the natural stepping-stones to dominance and personal
power.

"Like other men and women, we A.A.'s look with deep
apprehension upon the vast power struggle about us, a struggle
in myriad forms that invades every level, tearing society apart. I
think we A.A.'s are fortunate to be acutely aware that such
forces must never be ruling among us, lest we perish altogether.

"The Tradition of personal anonymity and no honors at the
public level is our protective shield. We dare not meet the power
temptation naked.

"Of course, we quite understand the high value of honors
outside our Fellowship. We always find inspiration when these
are deservedly bestowed and humbly received as the hallmarks
of distinguished attainment of service. We say only that in our
special circumstances it would be imprudent for us to accept
them for A.A. achievement.

"For example: My own life story gathered for years around
an implacable pursuit of money, fame, and power, anticlimaxed
by my near sinking in a sea of alcohol. Though I survived that
grim misadventure, I well understand that the dread neurotic
germ of the power contagion has survived in me also. It is only

dormant, and it can again multiply and rend me — and A.A., too. Tens of thousands of my fellow A.A.'s are temperamentally just like me. Fortunately, they know it, and I know it. Hence our Tradition of anonymity, and hence my clear obligation to decline this signal honor with all the immediate satisfaction and benefit it could have yielded.

"True, the splendid citation you propose, which describes me as 'W. W.,' does protect my anonymity for the time being. Nevertheless, it would surely appear on the later historical record that I had taken an LL.D. The public would then know the fact. So, while I might accept the degree within the letter of A.A.'s Tradition as of today, I would surely be setting the stage for a violation of its spirit tomorrow. This would be, I am certain, a perilous precedent to set.

"Though it might be a novel departure, I'm wondering if the Yale Corporation could consider giving A.A. itself the entire citation, omitting the degree to me. In such an event, I will gladly appear at any time to receive it on behalf of our Society. Should a discussion of this possibility seem desirable to you, I'll come to New Haven at once. Gratefully yours,"

Bill himself realized that he could reap more rewards for refusing this singular honor than the honor itself would have bestowed on him, had he accepted it. Therefore, he asked those who knew about the Yale offer not to talk about it. As he put it: "I don't want to capitalize on humility." Lois said: "Bill felt very strongly that of all things, he should not set himself up as superior in any way to other alcoholics. So to emphasize this, he took every opportunity reasonable to exaggerate his own defects. He was a tremendous egotist. But he recognized this, and I believe that the triumph of his life was his victory over himself and his becoming truly humble."

Yale's response to Bill's refusal shows the corporation members' deep respect for his integrity. The letter from Reuben Holden reads, in part: "After hearing your magnificent letter, [the committee members] all wish more than ever they could award you the degree — though it probably in our opinion isn't half good enough for you. . . . We understand completely your feelings in the matter, and we only wish there were some way we could show you our deep sense of respect for you and A.A. Someday, the opportunity will surely come.''

When *Time* magazine wanted to put Bill on its cover — that is, put the back of his head on the front of the magazine — Bill declined, and declined the cover story as well. He reasoned:

''For all I know, a piece of this sort could have brought A.A. a thousand members — possibly a lot more.

''Therefore, when I turned that article down, I denied recovery to an awful lot of alcoholics — some of these may already be dead. And practically all the rest of them, we may suppose, are still sick and suffering. Therefore, in a sense, my action has pronounced the death sentence on some drunks and condemned others to a much longer period of illness.

''But I went well over on the conservative side, because the requirements of the piece would have tended to create a clear and colorful public image of me as a person. This would have created for the future, I am sure, a temptation in our power-driving people to get like pieces — presently with full names and pictures. For this reason, I estimated that it would be better for some to die and others to suffer, rather than to set such a perilous precedent. Therefore, I declined the publicity, and I must confess it wasn't easy.''

As to the other ''points to assure our future,'' Bill, with his genius for making the best of what was in any case inevitable, formulated a tradition designed to make his own presence, if not obsolete, at least only marginally important and by no means indispensable to the continued well-being of his own creation. In 1942, even before his eye-opening trip to Los Angeles, he had written:

''The realization has come strongly in the last year or so that we older folk are actually getting less important to the movement. Though it's a little hard on the old ego, I begin to see how truly providential that is. Here are people lifted up by their principles rather than by their preachers. How well this all [augurs] for the long future.''

Rather than deplore the time ahead when he would have outlived his own usefulness, he assured the Fellowship that the most desirable state of affairs was that individual members, himself included, should always be less important to A.A. than the principles of the program itself. By making A.A. primarily dependent on idea, spirit, and concept, rather than on any temporal force or individual personality, Bill's ''Twelve Points to Assure Our Future'' did exactly that.

The Tradition that evolved from the second of the ''Twelve Points'' specifies as much: ''For our group purpose there is but one ultimate authority — a loving God as He may express Himself in our group conscience. Our leaders are but trusted servants; they do not govern.''

Bill's first published experience with the notion of group conscience had been the events surrounding the offer he received, early on, to work professionally as a lay therapist at Towns Hospital. This was an anecdote that Bill always enjoyed telling.

If ''for our group purpose there is but one ultimate authority — a loving God as He may express Himself in our group conscience,'' it follows logically that A.A. leaders are not authorities in the usual sense of the word, but are rather servants and instruments of the group conscience. Their tenure will be brief, as it is in the evolutionary nature of A.A. that they are replaced by those coming up behind them.

Of the other Traditions, Tradition One says: ''Our common welfare should come first; personal recovery depends upon A.A. unity.'' Discussing this Tradition, Bill paraphrased it by stating that ''the group must survive or the individual will not.''

Tradition Three says: ''The only requirement for A.A. membership is a desire to stop drinking.'' The trial-and-error method produced all the Traditions; failed attempts to impose other requirements underlay this one. For instance, even Dr. Bob had expressed uneasiness about admitting women to A.A. membership when the first few appeared.

The principle that would be expressed concisely in Tradition Three might have been generally accepted, but putting it into practice was not so easy. One of the obstacles was that it was sometimes seen to contradict the Fourth Tradition, which says, "Each group should be autonomous except in matters affecting other groups or A.A. as a whole." In a 1943 letter, Bill deplored this and confessed his frustration and feelings of futility about the situation:

"Along with you, I feel very deeply about this race business. Save this one question, I suppose A.A. is the most democratic society in the world. All men should have an equal opportunity to recover from alcoholism — that is the shining ideal.

"But, unhappily, my own experience suggests that it may not be achieved in our lifetimes. In all the South and in most of the North, whites refuse to mingle with blacks socially. That is a stark fact which we have to face. Nor can they be coerced or persuaded to do so, even alcoholics! I know, because I once tried here in New York and got so much slapped down that I realized that no amount of insistence would do any good. It would be bound to do harm. Compared to the white alcoholics, the number of blacks is very small indeed. Suppose that some of us tried to force the situation in the South. The prejudice is so great that 50 white men might stay away from A.A. in order that we save one colored. That's the principle of the greatest good for the greatest number. It falls grievously short of our ideal — but practically speaking, what can be done about it? I don't know — I'm still looking hard for the answer.

"As I long since learned that no man can dictate to an A.A. group, I tell each fellowship to abide by the wishes of the majority of its members. And if a group refuses Negroes socially, it ought to make a superhuman effort to help every single colored case to start a group of his own and permit him access to a few open meetings as an observer.''

As early as 1940, Bill had drawn fire for inviting two black alcoholics to attend meetings in the New York area. After hearing him speak at an institution, they asked him whether, on their release, they might join A.A. Bill said yes, and a few weeks later, they appeared at a local meeting.

"I remember it well because I was there," Bobbie B. said. "Immediately, a reaction started up within the group. We had some Southerners with us who strongly felt that Bill had overstepped in making this decision before consulting the group. They were ready to secede from A.A. and walk out. On the other hand, there were some Northerners who thought the Negroes should come in as full members with full privileges. And of course there were those who were on the fence."

Bill realized immediately that he had made a mistake. "So he asked those who objected if they would agree that Negroes had the right to A.A. just the same as any other human being," continued Bobbie. "On the basic principle, there was complete agreement. So it was more or less decided then that Negroes should be invited to attend open or closed group meetings as visitors."

The compromise method of permitting blacks to come to meetings as "observers" worked. By the mid-1940's, a number of black alcoholics had found sobriety in the program. Jim S., a physician, was called the originator of A.A.'s first black group. ("Jim's Story" appears in the second and third editions of the Big Book.)

Barry L., who joined the Manhattan Group in 1945, remembered what happened upon the arrival of a person who not only was black, but also had other obvious and startling differences.

In 1945, Barry was doing desk duty at a clubhouse on 41st Street. "A man came in needing help. He was black, and we had no black members then. He was an ex-convict. He had all his earthly belongings on his back. His hair was bleached blond; he had on makeup; and he told us he was a dope fiend.

"We didn't know what to do about the guy. I got together with some of the older members, and we talked to the man, and about him. What could we do?"

When no satisfactory group-conscience decision was forthcoming, Barry did what many another A.A. would have done: He called Bill, to whom he described the prospective member. After a silence, Bill asked Barry to run over the list again. Barry did so.

"Now," said Bill, "did you say he was a drunk?" "Oh yes," Barry replied. "There's no question about that. He's certainly a drunk." "Well, I think that's all we can ask," said Bill.

The prospect was invited to attend meetings, and although he soon disappeared, his presence created a precedent for the Third Tradition.

Says Tradition Five: "Each group has but one primary purpose —to carry its message to the alcoholic who still suffers." Or, as Bill paraphrased it with an old saying, "Shoemaker, stick to thy last."

To illustrate the principle of Tradition Five, Bill tells an anecdote about "a member" (obviously, Bill himself) who went to Towns Hospital and twelfth-stepped an alcoholic described by Dr. Silkworth as "an awfully tough Irishman. I never saw a man so obstinate. He shouts that if his partner would treat him better, and his wife would leave him alone, he'd soon solve his alcohol problem."

After Bill explained the purpose of his visit, the patient "demanded, 'Do you really mean the only reason you are here is to try and help me and to help yourself?'

" 'Yes,' I said. 'That's absolutely all there is to it. There's no angle.'

"Then, hesitantly, I ventured to talk about the spiritual side of our program. What a freeze that drunk gave me! I'd no sooner got the word 'spiritual' out of my mouth than he pounced. 'Oh!' he said. 'Now I get it! You're proselyting for some damn religious sect or other. Where do you get that "no angle" stuff? I belong to a great church that means everything to me. You've got a nerve to come in here talking religion!'

"Thank heaven I came up with the right answer for that one. It was based foursquare on the single purpose of A.A. . . .

"Finally, he saw that I wasn't attempting to change his religious views, that I wanted him to find the grace in his own religion that would aid his recovery. From there on we got along fine. . . .

"Years later, this tough Irish customer liked to say, 'My sponsor sold me one idea, and that was sobriety. At the time, I couldn't have bought anything else.' "

In almost no other of Bill's writings is his gift for simplifying complex issues more evident than it is in the Traditions. First, he was able to name the potential threats to the survival of the Fellowship: Simply, they were problems of property, prestige, and power. The complicated problems of property could be eliminated if A.A. owned none and was also self-supporting. Thus Traditions Six and Seven: "An A.A. group ought never endorse, finance, or lend the A.A. name to any related facility or outside enterprise, lest problems of money, property, and prestige divert us from our primary purpose," and "Every A.A. group ought to be fully self-supporting, declining outside contributions."

By 1946, the Fellowship had already had sufficient experience for Bill to believe that a solid tradition of nonaffiliation, with no exceptions, was the only way to keep A.A. free of controversy and distractions. The most famous and telling of these experiences had to do with another mistake Bill made regarding Marty M. — this time, in his own public endorsement of her work.

In 1943, richer by four years of A.A. experience, Marty had attended the first session of the newly founded Yale School of Alcohol Studies,[2] the country's first such educational program. That summer marked a turning point in her life; she became convinced that public attitudes toward the disease and its sufferers needed to be changed, and that it was her calling to work in the field of alcoholic education. She particularly wanted to help women alcoholics, who she felt suffered "a double stigma."

The National Committee for Education on Alcoholism, Inc., the organization Marty founded, opened its offices on October 2, 1944. N.C.E.A. — eventually to become the National Council on Alcoholism — received an enthusiastic endorsement from the Grapevine, itself only four months old. It also received the support of many prominent (and some not so prominent) people, whose names, including those of Bill Wilson and Dr. Bob Smith, appeared on the committee's letterhead. N.C.E.A. was not officially affiliated with A.A., but the A.A. co-founders' names on its letterhead gave the impression that the two groups were connected. To confuse matters further, Marty, as she spoke across the country on behalf of her new organization, was breaking her anonymity.

The resulting confusion was heightened when, in 1946, N.C.E.A. mailed a large-scale public appeal for funds — on its letterhead. The appeals letter was sent to some A.A. groups, and Dick S., a trustee, wrote to Bill (who was away from New York at the time): "If this letter should ever go out to the A.A. mailing list quoting A.A. throughout and soliciting funds on a letterhead that carries both your name and Bob Smith's as sponsors, no little hell would be popping."

Adding to the problem of separating N.C.E.A.'s work from A.A.'s and to the problem of anonymity breaks was the fact that N.C.E.A. had to get most of its operating funds from the public (and those in public life).

Bill was finally persuaded that total nonaffiliation was the only solution. Within a year, he and Dr. Bob withdrew from N.C.E.A., and Marty said she would discontinue publicly identifying herself as an A.A. member.

While Bill was formulating the principles that arose from these experiences, he often traveled to Akron to consult with his co-founder. Dr. Bob's ability to keep it simple always served as a guide to Bill, who had a more complex perception of things. In some ways, he conveyed to Bill the A.A. vox populi. If Dr. Bob liked it, then so, probably, would the conservative element of the Fellowship.

Bill also tried out work in progress on the 30 or 40 people who would customarily "drop by for coffee" at Stepping Stones during the course of a typical weekend. The visitors would sit around and talk about the latest problem or issue. Bill would read what he had written; everybody would contribute ideas or suggestions; and he would scratch out his words and start all over.

It was hard to get him to talk about anything else when he was at work on a project; he was always totally immersed in and preoccupied with that single topic. Bill's half sister Helen, living at Stepping Stones at the time, had this memory of his monomania: "We'd get him to the table to eat lunch, and he'd just sit there, and you could see his mind was going around. And he'd pick up a fork to eat the soup with, or something. And Lois and I would get absolutely hysterical, and he'd sit there and look at us like 'What's the matter with you? You're out of your minds!' He really had a one-track mind. He saw one thing at a time through to the end."

It was much the same at the office. Bob H., general manager from 1968 to 1974, recalled that the characteristic persisted into Bill's last years: "If you'd gone in his office, and you'd never seen him in your life before — he'd never heard of you — you were just someone who'd wandered in — if he had something on his mind, you'd hear all about it. You'd sit there for an hour or two hours while he discoursed about it."

For all his single-mindedness, Bill never lost his sense of humor. Marion Weaver, a non-A.A. who was working at the office, recalled a not-untypical day there:

"Bill was writing the Traditions. He wrote them and polished them, and he wrote them, and I typed them. One day, he couldn't find them, and what did I do with them? I didn't have them. I said, 'I don't have them, Bill.'

" 'Yes, you have them.'

" 'No, I don't have them. You had them.'

" 'Well then, who's got them?'

" 'I don't know who's got them, but I don't have them.'

" 'Well, they're lost. You must have lost them. Nobody cares about them. Nobody cares what happens to me; all my life's work, and nobody cares what happens to me!' And he was crying. 'Nobody cares what happens to Bill!' And he left.

"And then the door opened again, and he stood across the room. He got down on his hands and knees and put the manuscript in his mouth, and he crawled across the floor like a little puppy dog, handed them to me. They'd been jammed in the back of his desk drawer."

It is commonly known that the Traditions evolved from Bill's personal experience and the experience of the Fellowship, as well as from the mistakes made by earlier institutions and movements, the history of which Bill had studied.[3] But not so many A.A.'s are aware that Bill did not use every experience relayed by the groups, nor did he always use the group conscience as his guide. He was selective, using only those experiences that went to the heart of A.A. problems. Since his desire was always the best interest of A.A., his so-called manipulations always worked for the good of the Fellowship. (As he put it, "My personal life may not be exemplary, but I have never made a mistake about A.A.")

A case in point is that of the co-founders' royalties from the sale of the Big Book. Had Bill listened to the group conscience at the time the book was published, it would not have been sold at all, but given away. But in this matter, Bill overrode the group conscience, insisting that the book be offered for sale. In a letter written some years later, he explains his reasoning in light of subsequent events:

"Our history proves that the sometimes idealistic majority of that day was seriously mistaken. Had there been no book earnings for the Headquarters and no royalties for Dr. Bob and me, A.A. would have taken a very different and probably disastrous course. Dr. Bob and Sister Ignatia could not have looked at those 5,000 drunks in the hospital pioneering at Akron. I would have had to quit full-time work 15 years ago. There could have been no Twelve Traditions and no General Service Conference. Financially crippled, the Headquarters could not have spread A.A. around the world; indeed, it might have folded up completely. Lacking close attention, our public relations would certainly have gone haywire. Anonymity at the public level, our greatest single protection, would have evaporated. Consequently, our unity would have been lost.''

Tradition Eight solved, once and for all, the difficult issue of Bill's own position in the Fellowship, and the income he derived from A.A. It had taken ten years to work it out. The group conscience, plus the experience of writing the Big Book, plus his and Dr. Bob's other A.A. labors, were the precedents for Tradition Eight: ''Alcoholics Anonymous should remain forever nonprofessional, but our service centers may employ special workers.'' Bill was without a doubt in this regard a ''special worker.''

Bill had this to say about ''paid missionaries,'' and why he didn't want them: ''Now, it is an undoubted fact that professionalism in spiritual matters has too often limited the spread of real understanding and practical application. The modern world has little time for paid emissaries of God, notwithstanding a deep yearning for the Rock of Ages.''

Bill, more than anyone, deserved to be paid for the unique service, he rendered the Fellowship. The book royalties he received were not payment for Twelfth Step work; they were payment for special services; but the money nonetheless freed his time to do the Twelfth Step work that he unceasingly did. Tradition Eight also made acceptable the proper compensation, in years to come, of other special workers. A.A. was becoming an institution, as well as a publisher of its own literature.

Functional and important lessons were culled from the aftertaste, bitter and sweet, of experience.

Though the "Twelve Points to Assure Our Future," basis of the Traditions, had now been published, they still had not been accepted by the membership. In keeping with the Second Tradition, Bill still had to "sell" them to the "constituency," and this he now set out to do. During the last three years of the decade, 1947-1950, still coping with his depression, he was out in the groups, "selling" the Traditions, whether his audience wanted to listen or not. Sometimes, they did not. Bill remembered: "I received letters like this: 'Bill, we would love to have you come and speak. Tell us where you used to hide your bottles and tell us about that hot-flash spiritual experience of yours. But please don't talk any more about those damned Traditions.' "

This was only one of a number of circumstances where Bill found himself "force feeding" independence of autonomy to the members of A.A. During these years on the road, he was also talking about his ideas for an A.A. structure of elected representatives; leaders who were "trusted servants" were Bill's fondest wish for A.A. In the time to come, Bill was to find himself in the curious position of having to persuade the Fellowship to take its care and welfare out of his hands. He would spend the next years trying to turn the Fellowship loose — against the wishes of the very people whom he was trying to free from himself.

---

1. The name Bedford was one of a number of clusters of coincidence in the Wilsons' lives. Bill had been stationed in New Bedford, Mass., in 1917, when he took his first drink. The Wilsons bought a house in Bedford Hills. For years, Bill stayed at the Bedford Hotel. They had friends in Brooklyn named Bedford.

The disproportionate number of doctors in their combined families was another coincidence. Bill's mother was a doctor, as was her second husband. Bill's sister Dorothy was married to a doctor. Lois was the daughter of a doctor and the sister of a doctor. Bill's co-founder was a doctor.

Yet another set of coincidences clustered around January 24. It was their wedding day; it was the date of Lois's 1954 heart attack; and it was the date of Bill's death.

2. The Yale Summer Studies program was founded by Howard W. Haggard, M.D., and Elvin M. Jellinek, a biologist. In 1962, it was transferred to New Jersey and became the Rutgers School of Alcohol Studies.

3. See his comments in the "Twelve and Twelve" (pages 178-179) about the Washingtonian movement, and how its decline helped him formulate the principles embodied in the Tenth Tradition.

Chapter Twenty

Bill knew that if a central headquarters and the board of trustees were to survive, they would need moral and financial support from the groups. His suggestions to Dr. Bob were: (1) that the groups be given full control of their own affairs and (2) that they be officially linked with the board and with headquarters through what Bill called a general service conference. The membership of this conference would comprise representative, elected delegates from the groups themselves.

His first proposal was sent to the nine Alcoholic Foundation trustees in the form of a memo, which he called "A Suggested Code of Traditions for A.A. General Headquarters." He wrote this memo following a sudden release from depression early in the summer of 1946. His relief was immense; in a letter to Dr. Tiebout dated June 1, 1946, he described what happened:

"Until recently, there has been almost no relief from depressions for two years. And when I used to feel better, it was only that I had less of the blues than usual.

"About six weeks ago, I canceled every single speaking engagement and completely withdrew from the office situation. We then went to Vermont.[1] Regime: sleeping, eating, walking, fishing, reading. Lois and me alone at an old farmhouse near Brattleboro. One morning, after about ten days of this, while she sat reading to me in the living room, I suddenly went 'quiet.' No elation, nor was there any special sensation of peace. I just became very quiet inside. Neither was it inertia or apathy. It was as though someone had moved the gearshift lever into neutral, the car coming to a slow stop. But — this is very important — the engine was still running. I could hear it there under the hood, fully alive, but idling quietly. I never had a feeling of quite this quality before. And this undertone has since persisted, under all conditions.

"Coming back to New York, I got heavily involved, at the office, in a Hollywood movie project.[2] I got tired; once, I got mad. But I became thoroughly interested and outgoing. Not a vestige of the frustration collapse phenomena to be sensed. I have had the feeling of coming alive again — mentally, physically, and emotionally. The reaction to all this is gratitude rather than ecstasy. Very interesting — eh what?"

The "Code for General Headquarters" that Bill submitted to the trustees had 12 sections, like the Steps and the "Twelve Points to Assure Our Future" recently published in the Grapevine. Bill's "code" and the memorandums he later wrote to the foundation in its support brought about no major changes — except, perhaps, to put the trustees on the defensive. They were injudicious preludes to the proposal he now sought support for — the conference of regional representatives from the groups.

Most of the trustees wanted to keep the status quo. They were confident of their own ability to handle whatever situation might arise, and they did not agree with Bill about the need for change. There was also opposition from the old-timers in New York, Akron, Cleveland, and Chicago, who felt that they could and should supervise the affairs of those arriving after them.

Bill knew that the newer members would not continue to

accept this supervision; his mail regularly turned up letters that scolded him for "exceeding his authority." If the members were critical of Bill, with his enormous prestige in the Fellowship, there was little chance they would accept direction from oldtimers, much less from trustees they did not even know!

In his campaign for the general service conference, Bill found little support on the board. Only Bernard Smith, the chairman, backed him. Said Bill: "The majority of the board . . . felt that creating a conference . . . would entail unnecessary politics and expense. The foundation had done well for ten years, so why could it not go on in just the same way?"

With a wry eye to his own behavior, Bill tells what happened next: "Typically alcoholic, I became very excited, and this turned the passive resistance of my fellow workers into solid opposition. A serious rift developed between me and the alcoholic members of the board, and as the months went by the situation became worse and worse. With much reason, they resented my sledgehammer tactics and my continued violence. As the tempest increased, so did my blistering memorandums to the board. One of them was an amazing composition. Following a long plea for an elected A.A. conference and other reforms, and after having pointed out that the trustees had all the authority there was, with no responsibility to anyone, even to Dr. Bob and me, I finished the memo with this astonishing sentence: 'When I was in law school, the largest book I studied was the one on trusts. I must say, gentlemen, that it was mostly a long and melancholy account of the malfeasances and misfeasances of boards of trustees.' I had written this to a group of the best friends I had in the world, people who had devoted themselves to A.A. and to me without stint. Obviously I was on a dry bender of the worst possible sort."

Now Bill decided to sound out the feelings of the membership. On February 6, 1948, he and Lois left on a tour of the groups. Traveling by train across Canada, they stopped to visit groups in Toronto, Winnipeg, and Calgary. Crossing the vast

Canadian land, they were awakened in Regina, Saskatchewan, at 4:00 a.m. by the lone A.A. there, who boarded the train to say hello. He had been to New York City with the National Horse Show, to exhibit his sheep dogs!

In British Columbia, the Wilsons made a stop to visit Bill's father. Gilman and Christine still lived in the tiny town of Marblehead, and Bill's father still worked around the quarries there. Getting to them turned out to be an adventure in itself. It was February, and the road to Marblehead was impassable except by foot; snowslides blocked it for three miles. Local A.A.'s lent Bill and Lois ski pants, woolen socks, and flashlights, and off they trudged. Lois's feet kept coming out of her shoes. "It was exciting in the dark and cold and snow, alone on a strange road," she said.

On the other side of the snowslides, a truck was waiting to get provisions from a boat, and to take them the additional five miles to the home of Gilman and Christine, who, Lois said, were not surprised to see them, having suspected that they would persist.

Bill had seen his father only about a dozen times since 1906, and it was usually at Bill's instigation (although Gilman had come to New Bedford when Bill and Lois were first married, to "see what kind of a girl his son had picked"). Bill, though, apparently felt no resentment against his father; on the contrary, as an adult, he expressed gratitude to his father, a gesture typical of Bill.

Lois believed that when Bill and Dorothy were children, Gilman had sent support money "only occasionally," a cause of some bitterness on Dr. Emily's part. But, added Lois, "I think by degrees he [Bill] began to feel sorry for his father. They found they had something in common. But they didn't have enough background of companionship for them to be really true pals."

Bill and Lois stayed in Marblehead for a week, resting, walking, talking, and playing violin-piano duets on borrowed instruments. (Bill was never attached to any specific instrument;

he would play whatever violin — or cello — was at hand. He was also extremely fond of tinkering with the instruments.) They left Marblehead on February 21, having extracted a half promise from the older Wilsons to come East in spring to attend their daughter Helen's wedding. She was planning to marry Ralph R.

Two days later, Bill and Lois arrived in Vancouver, where Bill spoke about the Traditions to a meeting of about 1,000.

Everywhere they went, they were greeted with gifts, many of beauty and value (a cameo, a large inscribed silver tray, a Royal Crown Derby coffee set, a pair of inscribed pen and pencil sets, a silver gravy boat and ladle, an illuminated parchment of the Steps), and with flowers for Lois (usually orchids). Reporters and often photographers were on hand.

At the end of this trip, which lasted three whole months, Bill was convinced beyond doubt that the groups also wanted a general service conference.

Dr. Bob, like the board, was conservative in his reaction to Bill's proposal. In May 1948, he wrote Bill the following: "However desirable many of these changes may be, I have the feeling that they will be brought about without too much sudden upheaval. If the trustees are wrong, they will hang themselves. I am just as interested in A.A. as you are, but am not 100 percent sure as to the wisest course to follow and the wisest ultimate setup. It does seem that for the moment, perhaps, 'Easy Does It' is the best course to follow. . . . Keep your shirt on for a bit, and remember that whatever happens, we love you a lot."

Bill was unable to let the matter go. His persistence — perhaps in spite of himself — is obvious in a letter to Dr. Bob written two months later:

"Though for the time being I have quit pressing the conference business, it did seem wise to set down on paper an outline of the material I have been presenting [to] the groups and the trustees. This outline could later become the basis for experimentally setting up the conference.

"So I wonder if you would look over the enclosed material

carefully, and then let us talk on the telephone about it. Maybe you will have some suggestions in mind. Or perhaps you will conclude you don't like the general idea at all. If the latter is the case, I'm perfectly willing to forget about the whole business.''

But he wasn't. "On the other hand, if we can both agree what sort of a program for a conference we wish to see someday inaugurated, I will then attach to this material a letter that such is our joint wish. If the undertaker got both of us while our trustees and friends are still thinking matters over, there would exist a clean-cut record of how we felt the conference ought to be got under way.

"Meanwhile, please be assured that I shall sit tight.''

Bill, despite his assurances to his partner, was unable to ''sit tight.'' His desire to see the conference established now took on greater urgency. Dr. Bob had been operated on for cancer; Bill understood that this illness would probably be terminal. That knowledge must have evoked thoughts about his own mortality and about the practical relationship of the foundation and its trustees to the membership.

In Robert Thomsen's biography of Bill, these words describe the child Bill Wilson had been: "Bill hated to do things that were difficult, but it was as if the boy sensed he had to go at them, as if he understood he would find no peace until he conquered them.''

So it was with Bill now; it was as though he had demons driving him. He simply had to see the general service conference established. He was convinced that the Fellowship would not survive without it.

And so, despite his avowed intention to let the matter rest, he was unable to do so, and the dispute continued.

A letter to Dr. Bob written in February of 1949 indicates Bill's frustration, urgency — and sense of helplessness:

"Dear Smithy: Surely, the time is here when you and I shall need to make decisions concerning the future of the Alcoholic Foundation and its eventual relation to the A.A. movement. We shall need to determine what our remaining responsibilities are; also when and how we are going to act upon them.

"Nothing could afford me more personal relief than to retire from the situation completely, and now. Could I only comfort myself with the tempting alibi that God will do all; that you and I have no further agency and hence no further responsibility in this matter. To surrender all ill will is an imperative; to turn away from clear-cut responsibility may be to fail Alcoholics Anonymous.

"Do we not have the clear duty to see that the foundation, Grapevine, and office are put in good order and delivered into the direct keeping of A.A. as a whole?

"The stark fact is that you and I still head Alcoholics Anonymous. By common consent, we remain the only two individuals in A.A. actually entitled and expected to speak for the whole. You and I know how unsound for the future this condition is. Neither of us wants it; we don't like it. But we simply can't walk from under yet. Nor can we successfully transfer all this burden to a small and unknown board of trustees, no matter how willing they may be to assume it. Like us, they will at some point crack up, and then our vital services to the 'million drunks who don't yet know' would be in sore jeopardy. The only place we can safely go with our full responsibility is to A.A. itself. Lock, stock, and barrel, the foundation will have to be transferred into the direct custody of regional representatives of the A.A. movement.

"Naturally, the groups do not at all realize how solidly their vital affairs are lodged in a legal and independent trusteeship on which neither they nor we are in a position to exert the slightest direct action.

"So, Smithy, if we do not take the lead in mending this impractical state of affairs, then the groups will one day discover these things for themselves. All too late, it may be learned that the penalty for drift and surrendered responsibility is often far more shattering than the passing discomfort of timely action.

"Everywhere, the groups have taken their service affairs

into their own hands; local founders and their friends are today on the sideline. Why we forget that, when thinking of the future of the foundation, I shall never understand.

"There is now some reason to think that all the nonalcoholics and at least one of the alcoholic trustees have become desperately tired of that highly inflammable nonsense which has characterized the foundation scene these many critical months. I can have no doubt our friends are dismayed and hurt as they see the whole course of our business, perchance our destiny, deflected by drunks on benders — both wet and dry.

"Your presence and influence are badly needed by all, especially me. Your calm disposition and firm support may mean everything. Let us take no more chances; time flies. Affectionately,"

Dr. Bob was terribly ill. His response to Bill's continued importuning was to defer the issue. A letter dated March 14 read:

"Dear Bill: Have been quite painfully ill since you were here. Do not have the feeling that this is a particularly guided thing to do now. Maybe I am wrong, but that is the way I feel. Love, Smithy"

There the matter rested — more or less — for the time being.

As if all this wasn't enough sadness and grief, Anne Smith's health was failing. Nearly blind from cataracts, she had three operations to correct the condition, but then refused further surgery.

Everything clamored for Bill's attention. A.A.'s First International Convention was to be held in Cleveland in July 1950. There had already been regional and state conventions, but the possibility of an international convention had been first raised in a June 1949 letter from a Houston member to the New York office. Bill's reply endorsed the idea without making a commitment to Houston as the site. There was no representative body to approve or reject such a proposal, he said (never missing an opportunity to underscore his point!), and he suggested the wisdom of not billing it as an "international" gathering — such a title might seem to carry the endorsement of headquarters.

It soon became clear that Cleveland could be used as a site without drawing fire from other parts of the country. It was a large A.A. center, and it was only 35 miles from Akron, so that Dr. Bob, now in the last stages of illness, would be able to appear. He had undergone his first operation in 1947; by 1948, he was diagnosed as having terminal cancer.

As plans for the Convention were laid, Earl T., founder of the Chicago group, suggested that the "Twelve Points to Assure Our Future" would benefit from revision and shortening. In 1949, Bill set out to do this, in time for the Cleveland event. And, of course, he never really let go of his idea of a general service conference; memorandums to the trustees and letters to Dr. Bob continued to fly from his fertile brain.

On May 24, 1949, at the invitation of Rochester's Dr. Kirby Collier, one of A.A.'s earliest admirers among psychiatrists, Bill was invited to participate in an alcoholism symposium to be presented at the American Psychiatric Association meeting in Montreal. A number of A.P.A. members were unenthusiastic about being addressed by a layman. About this, Bill liked to tell an anecdote on himself: After his talk, a past president of the A.P.A. had declared that "outside of the few A.A.'s in the room, and myself, I do not think a single one of my colleagues believed a word of your explanation." When Bill expressed surprise at this and mentioned how much applause he had received, the man replied, "Well, Mr. Wilson, you A.A.'s have a hundred thousand recoveries, and we in the psychiatric profession have only a few. They were applauding the *results*, much more than the *message*." (The emphasis is Bill's.)

On June 1, barely a week after Bill's Montreal talk, Dr. Bob's wife Anne died.

Bill's emotions must have been a virtual roller coaster. He was still seeing a psychiatrist; now, it was a doctor named

Frances Weekes. He saw her once a week on Fridays, and Msgr. Sheen for Catholic instructions on Saturdays. Of the help the psychiatrist was giving him, he wrote to a friend:

"Her thesis is that my position in A.A. has become quite inconsistent with my needs as an individual. Highly satisfactory to live one's life for others, it cannot be anything but disastrous to live one's life for others as those others think it should be lived. One has, for better or worse, to choose his own life. The extent to which the A.A. movement and individuals in it determine my choices is really astonishing. Things which are primary to me (even for the good of A.A.) are unfulfilled. I'm constantly diverted to secondary or even useless activities by A.A.'s whose demands seem to them primary, but are not really so. So we have the person of Mr. Anonymous in conflict with Bill Wilson. To me, this is more than an interesting speculation — it's homely good sense."

To indicate some of the other kinds of demands that were regularly made on Bill, here is an entry from Lois's diary for a not-untypical day:

"Bill, Helen, and Eb left for town. Bill left saying that if anyone came to him with another problem, he'd scream. Soon after they left, Dot [Bill's sister] phoned saying she had the most awful letter from her mother, who had been told the March issue of the Grapevine said we were on our way out there (which it does not), that we had not let her know, that she had borrowed $75,000, etc., etc., etc. Dot said she thought she should fly right out, as she was afraid of suicide. Bill pulled ropes and got her a plane reservation for 2:30. She missed the train to N.Y., and Kitty drove her all the way. Everybody was phoning everybody else. I wired Freddy B. about Mother. Dot should arrive in L.A. in 12 hours. Helen came home, and Zerelda spent the night again. Bill sandwiched in getting Dot on the plane and Sibley out of Bellevue and off to High Watch Farm."

People sensed a strength and a larger-than-life quality in Bill; it was to him that they — family, friends, A.A.'s — turned for emotional, physical, and spiritual succor. Not only was he unwilling or unable to refuse them, he went out of his way to offer his help to all sorts of people: a former nonalcoholic trustee who had fallen on hard times; Mark Whalon, his childhood friend from East Dorset, who was ill and needed support; Dr. Bob's daughter Sue, who was having emotional troubles. For the last years of Gilman's life, Bill sent him checks regularly. He invited his half sister Helen to live at Stepping Stones; he made sure his sister Dorothy had help (he got her to Dr. Tiebout) when, in mid-life, she had an emotional crisis. He kept a constant eye on his mother in San Diego, and in her last years, insisted that she come East to live. And, of course, there was Ebby.

Bill's behavior toward Ebby — even given his generous nature and his debt of affection to the man he called his sponsor — went beyond the comprehension of many of his friends. Bill simply could not do enough for Ebby. This, given the fact that Ebby (after his family money had run out) could do very little for himself, meant that Bill undertook major responsibility for him until Ebby died — sober — in 1966.

In addition to all this, Bill maintained an endless running correspondence with the dozens of letter writers who communicated with him weekly, asking his advice and counsel on every manner of problem — alcoholism, depression, schizophrenia, rage, faith, no faith, everyday problems.

Despite all distractions, Bill's focus on building a service structure for A.A. remained constant, starting in 1945 and continuing until 1967, when the last piece of the process was finally completed. He was determined to liberate A.A. from its "parents" — himself and Dr. Bob — and to link the trustees more responsibly to the A.A. movement.

But Bill had not reckoned on the feelings of the members, who saw no need for such separation — or linkage. For the most part, they wanted Bill, their leader, to continue to lead them. In contentions between parent and child, it is usually the child who desires independence and the parent who wants to hold on.

Here, the opposite was true. A.A. was growing, now truly international. There were groups as well as loners in the United Kingdom, in western Europe, and all over the world. And the more A.A. grew, the more, in a sense, it clung to Bill.

Most ironic in this extraordinary situation was the fact that Bill and Dr. Bob could now no longer avail themselves of their own program for maintaining recovery. That bastion of anonymity, that safe place where any drunk could sit and quietly retreat, be healed, and be truly anonymous, was not available to Bill. It was virtually impossible for him to attend an A.A. meeting as a regular member. Wherever he went, he was sooner or later spotted, named, and asked to lead. Looking closely at the details of Bill's day-to-day life, one realizes that he was in a constant process of emptying himself out through service to others, and that he had little opportunity to replenish his own energies — not even the benefit of meetings.

On May 11, 1950, about three months before the Cleveland Convention, Bill and Lois went to Europe — specifically, to visit A.A. in Europe. A letter Bill wrote to Dr. Bob from Dublin reads, in part:

"We have been gone not quite seven weeks now and have visited four cities in Norway, three in Sweden, one in Denmark, two in Holland, as well as Paris, London, and now Dublin, Ireland.

"Lois and I both wish, Smithy, that you could have seen and felt what we have on this journey. We need not tell you that A.A. has come to Europe to stay. With its usual ease, it is breaking down all barriers of race, creed, language, and tradition. Without much of any A.A. literature, a great job is being done, strongly reminiscent of our pioneering time at Akron, Cleveland, and New York. Though they have the advantage of our background of success, the groups start here under very different circumstances than a new group starts up shop at home. Like us in the early days, they can take nothing for granted. The public still knows nothing about them; the clergy and doctors, with a few exceptions, still wonder. The usual debates whether God made man, or man made God, rage on. They fear all sorts of calamities which you and I know won't happen, and yet they press on. It makes us relive old times.''

Bill dubbed the upcoming 15th anniversary celebration A.A.'s "coming of age" party. A.A. is generally thought to have "come of age" five years later, at St. Louis, but Bill's inner timetable was, as usual, five years ahead of other people's.

The Cleveland Convention was a memorable event, the more so because it set the precedent for International Conventions to come. Since then, they have been held every five years in a major North American city, and all indications are that this practice will continue. It was Bill's idea that each Convention should have a specific purpose. The first two did: The main agenda at Cleveland was to accept the Traditions and to allow Dr. Bob to say farewell; the second, at St. Louis, would mark A.A.'s "coming of age" — Bill's turning A.A. over to the membership.

On Friday, July 28, 1950, the First International Convention opened, with approximately 3,000 people in attendance. Registration was $1.50 per person. The weekend consisted of a series of meetings, held from Friday through Sunday at several Cleveland hotels — the Carter, the Hollenden, the Cleveland — plus one meeting in the Music Hall. Saturday afternoon was reserved for the business of offering the Twelve Traditions (the shorter, more digestible form of the "Twelve Points to Assure Our Future") to the membership. Bill presented them as a natural corollary of the Twelve Steps, representing them as points necessary for the unity of the Fellowship.

"He asked for full discussion on the Traditions, and none was forthcoming," a member reported. "Then, he suggested as there were no comments, we should adopt them officially for A.A. by standing vote. Everyone in the crowded room rose. Bill Wilson said: 'These Traditions are now adopted as part of our A.A. doctrine.' " Support for the Traditions was unanimous, because by that time their sense was well understood and widely accepted.

The weekend's grand event was the Sunday afternoon meeting. Held at the Cleveland auditorium, it had two speakers, Bill and Dr. Bob. Dr. Bob's talk was the last that he gave. Many in the audience knew that he could not live much longer.

In the year since Anne's death, Dr. Bob's health had been steadily deteriorating, but with his characteristic stoicism and faith, he had apparently accepted this with neither fear nor self-pity. He had been resting to save his strength for the Convention. As the date drew near, Dr. Bob was terribly weak, and on the day he was to leave for Cleveland, he was hardly able to sit up. Al S., a member from New York and editor of the Grapevine, drove Dr. Bob to Cleveland. "I didn't think he was going to make it," said Al.

He did make it, and he did give his talk. Some who were there remember the waves of love that seemed to give Bob energy to deliver his farewell message. It was a short talk. He said, in part:

"I get a big thrill out of looking over a vast sea of faces like this with a feeling that possibly some small thing I did a number of years ago played an infinitely small part in making this meeting possible. . . .

"There are two or three things that flashed into my mind on which it would be fitting to lay a little emphasis. One is the simplicity of our program. Let's not louse it all up with Freudian complexes and things that are interesting to the scientific mind, but have very little to do with our actual A.A. work. Our Twelve Steps, when simmered down to the last, resolve themselves into the words 'love' and 'service.' We understand what love is, and we

Next two pages: Left, *Dr. Bob's quiet spirituality and "keep it simple" approach were ideal complements to Bill's vision and promoter instincts.* Right, *Bill's humor, homespun and even corny at times, was part of the personal magnetism A.A.'s found irresistible.*

understand what service is. So let's bear those two things in mind."

A few minutes later, Dr. Bob left the auditorium. After his departure, Bill gave his hour-long talk. On the way back to Akron, Al S. remembered, Dr. Bob was so exhausted that Al wondered whether he could complete the trip.

About three months after the Convention, on a Sunday at the beginning of November, Bill went out to Akron. Although Dr. Bob was very ill, he was still on his feet. Bill recalled, "I realized that I must press for his consent to the conference."

Bill, with his extraordinary persuasiveness, put it to his cofounder that if the two of them did nothing, their silence would in later years be interpreted as approval of the status quo. He "ventured the idea" that they should try the conference. If it was a failure, they could always cancel; they were not locked into anything. As Bill later relived his "pitch":

"The movement's delegates could come down to New York and see what A.A.'s world affairs were really like. They could then decide whether they would take responsibility or whether they would not. That would make it a movement decision, rather than one taken in silence by Dr. Bob and me.

"He continued to reflect, and I waited. Finally he looked up and said, 'Bill, it *has* to be A.A.'s decision, not ours. Let's call that conference. It's fine with me.' "

At last, Bill had his partner's consent.

A few hours later, Bill said goodbye: "I went down the steps and then turned to look back. Bob stood in the doorway, tall and upright as ever. . . . This was my partner, the man with whom I never had a hard word. The wonderful, old, broad smile was on his face as he said almost jokingly, 'Remember, Bill, let's not louse this thing up. Let's keep it simple!' I turned away, unable to say a word. That was the last time I ever saw him."

Dr. Bob died at noon the following Thursday, November 16. According to his wishes, no unusual monument or marker adorns his grave. At Akron's Mount Peace Cemetery, a single headstone identifies Dr. Bob Smith and his wife Anne.

---

1. Bill loved Vermont and went back there as often as possible for "rest and rehabilitation."

2. Several studios had approached Bill and the office about making a movie on A.A. Interest was high because of the success of "The Lost Weekend," released in 1945. (Although "The Lost Weekend" was strictly fiction, many details about the hero's life resembled Bill's drinking career.) Interest and negotiations continued for a number of years. Since that time, there have been numerous films made in which A.A. has played a major part. Notable among these are "Come Back, Little Sheba" and "Days of Wine and Roses."

Chapter Twenty-One

Bill always gave credit for the Conference to nonalcoholic trustee Bernard Smith, whom he dubbed "the architect of the General Service Conference." It was Smith who finally managed to convince the other trustees of the rightness of Bill's idea, and to get them, slowly, to begin to change their minds.

Now, finally, at their fall 1950 meeting, the trustees endorsed the conference plan and authorized Bill to proceed with it. After more than four years of discussions, dispute, conflict, and memorandums — four years that included three trustee resignations — Bill sat down to work out the details of the plan. He himself did not know exactly how it would operate.

As he set about this task, he kept reminding himself of the major objections to the conference. Not one to ride roughshod over the feelings of others, he attempted, in the details of the plan, to compensate for as many of the objections as he could.

First and most vehement of these had been the cost of holding such a conference. With A.A. membership now into six figures (in 1951, the records showed 111,765 members and 4,052 groups), this objection no longer had much validity; the expense could be absorbed easily. "Even if the outlay might be $20,000 annually, this would be only a few cents extra for each A.A. member, and well worth it," Bill said.

However the conference developed, it had to reflect the Traditions; therefore, it had to avoid political infighting. That possibility had been one of the major objections of many who had opposed a conference, fearing that it would offer an opportunity for the creation of political factions, for lobbying, for cliques and

Bernard B. Smith, trustee from 1944 to 1956, was influential in the decision to hold the First General Service Conference.

arguments and the defense of vested interests.

At that time, 1950-51, there were 48 states and ten Canadian provinces. In Bill's original plan, each state and each province was assigned one delegate, although areas with heavy A.A. populations could have additional representation. To give the conference continuity, the body of delegates would be divided into two panels. An odd-numbered panel, Panel 1, elected for two years, would be invited for the first year, which would be 1951. Panel 2 would be seated in 1952. Thereafter, one panel would be elected and one retired yearly. Thus the conference would rotate and still maintain continuity.

Bill wanted the delegates to be truly representative of their areas, but he also wanted to avoid the "hotly contested close election, which nearly always left behind a large and discontented minority." The problem of how the delegates were to be elected was a perplexing one. The solution suggested was to provide for the submission of written ballots, and to require that any single candidate receive a two-thirds majority of the vote for election. In the event that there were several strong contenders and no single one received a two-thirds majority, the names of the front-runners could be placed in a hat and the winner chosen by lot.

The next problem was how much authority would be held by the conference. Nothing less than real authority would truly serve the purpose of either the conference or the Fellowship. A tentative charter, therefore, made this relegation of delegates' authority: By a two-thirds vote, the delegates could issue "flat directives" to the trustees, and even a simple majority could issue a "strong suggestion" to the trustees. (Bill explained that such suggestions could be very powerful, because, were they not carried out, the discontented majority could return home and see to it that contributions to headquarters were cut.)

The trustees made the proviso that the service conference be given a five-year probationary tryout.

Together with a temporary scheme for financing the operation, all these ideas and suggestions for their best implementation were incorporated into a booklet called "The Third Legacy," put together by Bill with the help of Helen B. of the office staff.

Bill's idea was that the co-founders' First Legacy to A.A. was Recovery, embodied in the Big Book, in the Steps, and in person-to-person Twelfth Step work.

The Second Legacy to A.A. was Unity. This Bill had realized when he said, "We can do together what I cannot do alone" — it was vital that A.A.'s stay together. To insure A.A. unity, Bill had written the Twelve Traditions.

And now, with his penchant for symbolism, he had coined a third term to make the A.A. Legacies three in number. The Third Legacy was — what else? — Service. The general service conference would be the means by which the Fellowship would be autonomous, operating through the instrument of a truly democratic, representational, elected form of self-government.

The Third Legacy, as defined by Bill: ". . . an A.A. service is anything whatever that helps us to reach a fellow sufferer — ranging all the way from the Twelfth Step itself to a ten-cent phone call and a cup of coffee, and to A.A.'s General Service Office for national and international action. The sum total of all these services is our Third Legacy of Service."

Fifty thousand "Third Legacy" pamphlets were printed and distributed to the groups, which were then asked to form assemblies for the election of committeemen and delegates. Bill set out to stump the country for the Third Legacy plan, talking to large groups and watching assemblies select their delegates in more than two dozen states and provinces. When the oldtimers in Boston, after examining the plan in its every aspect, predicted that the conference would work, Bill felt very comforted, "since these folks in Boston knew politics as few of the rest of us did."

Bill had developed a format for his talks that he usually pretty much stuck to, whether he was speaking to A.A. groups or to non-A.A.'s. He would go right back to the very beginning and tell the now-familiar "bedtime story" — his own drinking, his "hot flash," his recovery, and how A.A. was born and grew. His Third Legacy talks combined that format with his new subject, the conference plan and how he envisioned it would work, and he sometimes spoke for two hours.

Mel B. remembers one of those talks:

"It was a frozen night in January or February, but I think I would have walked the 25 miles to Detroit for a chance to hear Bill Wilson. I expected him to be a dazzling person, about ten feet tall and expressing [such] profound truths that all of us would have a spiritual experience right on the spot. I was disappointed when he came loping onto the platform and slouched in a chair in a rather offhand manner. I had expected his speech to be stunning oratory that would leave us wrapped in flames. His voice was slow and twangy, and he was apparently suffering from a cold. He was more human than I wanted him to be.

"But the Detroit crowd was over a thousand, and the members were so interested in Bill's message that nobody left the building when Bill called the cigarette break after one hour.

"There was perfect logic in everything he said, although I remember feeling that Bill was unduly concerned about A.A.'s future. Like many A.A. members, I took our success for granted and didn't really see the need for a general service conference. But I was willing to accept the idea simply because Bill Wilson said it was a good thing."

Chuck C. of Los Angeles remembers local members being no more interested in the Third Legacy "than they were in a pig learning to speak." To them, it was just organization, and what did that have to do with staying sober?

Had Bill heard that comment, he might have made a joke, but it probably would have upset him. Himself a product of a "town meeting" society, Bill fretted when people did not exercise their political options. He realized, too, that apathy and indifference were threats to A.A.

In April 1951, a few months after Bill completed his speaking tour, the First General Service Conference met in New York City. Its theme, chosen by Bill, was "Not to Govern, but to Serve." There were 35 delegates on the first panel, and their general meetings were held at the Commodore Hotel. (The U.S./Canada General Service Conference still meets every April, in New York City, most frequently at the Hotel Roosevelt.) Bill was gratified to note that about a third of the delegates were real oldtimers, and the rest were active members sober four to eight years. Best of all, he was encouraged that the majority of them had been chosen by the two-thirds vote provision; only a few of the elections had had to "go to the hat."

Of that First General Service Conference, Bill remembered: "We all sensed that something momentous was happening; that this was a historic moment.

". . . The delegates inspected A.A.'s finances and listened to reports from the board of trustees and from all of the services. There was warm but cordial debate on many questions of A.A. policy. The trustees submitted several of their own serious problems for the opinion of the Conference. With real dispatch the delegates handled several tough puzzlers about which we at headquarters were in doubt. Though their advice was sometimes contrary to our own views, we saw they were frequently right. They were proving as never before that A.A.'s Tradition Two was correct. Our group conscience could safely act as the sole authority and sure guide for Alcoholics Anonymous. As the delegates returned home, they carried this deep conviction with them.

"For example, at its very first session the Conference had suggested that the Alcoholic Foundation ought to be renamed the General Service Board of Alcoholics Anonymous. . . . To their minds the word 'Foundation' had stood for charity, paternalism, and maybe big money. What had been good for our infancy would be no good for our future."[1] The success of the 1951 Conference and the promise it held out for the Fellowship's continuing unity were tributes to Bill's persistence and foresight.

In that same year, he turned down two honors offered to him —
as an individual — by organizations outside A.A.

In January, he was nominated for inclusion in "Who's
Who in America." He refused the nomination, declining to be
listed (his mother had also refused an invitation, earlier).

In the summer, the Lasker Award was offered to him. Established in 1946 by the Albert and Mary Lasker Foundation
and administered by the American Public Health Association,
the award honored exceptional achievement in the field of medical research and public health administration. Its previous recip-
ients had been scientists, public health leaders, and medical
groups. It was now proposed for Bill.

Bill's response was to refuse the award for himself personally, but to suggest that it be given to A.A. as a whole. The
Lasker Foundation replied favorably (a reaction that Bill probably had in mind when he later made the same suggestion in the
matter of the Yale degree). A.A's trustees, at their July meeting,
voted to accept the award — but not the cash grant of $1,000 —
subject to the approval of the General Service Conference delegates. The delegates, polled by mail, were overwhelmingly in
favor. Bernard Smith, chairman of the board of trustees, was
designated to accept for A.A. at the October awards ceremony in
San Francisco. Bill would also say a brief thank-you — not as a
co-founder, but as an early member. (The statuette and citation
are now in the archives at the General Service Office in New
York.)

---

1. The name change was not actually made until 1954.

Chapter Twenty-Two

Although money was never a motive for any of Bill's A.A. work, he was not without his practical side. In a 1952 letter, he outlined his plans for his immediate future:

"Now, I'm getting down once more to serious writing. A small book will appear in the fall. This will be followed by a short history of A.A. Then, I expect to do a book which will cover the application of the Twelve Steps to the whole problem of living — the problem of happy sobriety. After that, there will come a manual on A.A. services. So I am beginning to get on paper our whole experience of the last dozen years.

"This, if successfully finished, will of course bring me a substantial income — far more, perhaps, than I shall ever need myself. This will mean that out of my own earnings, I shall be able to pay off my former creditors.[1] That would, I think, set the best possible example to other A.A. members."

Bill may have written in that vein simply because his correspondent had offered him a generous financial gift ("Ab" A., a wealthy Oklahoman, wanted to give Bill $60,000). The letter also indicates, not only that he was an idealist so far as his life's work was concerned, but that he was thinking in practical terms.

With the service structure in place, the Traditions accepted and entrenched as part of the A.A. structure, Bill now breathed easier, feeling free to turn his attention to projects he had been obliged to hold in abeyance.

First, there was the writing of "Twelve Steps and Twelve Traditions." For some time, he had been planning to produce a volume of essays, one essay for each Step and one for each Tradition. These essays would expand, expound, and explain the meaning and applications of each principle.

If "Twelve Steps and Twelve Traditions" is a small volume in terms of length, it is large in its depth and content. Whereas the Big Book, written in 1938, radiates Bill's joy and gratitude at having finally found a way to stay sober, the "Twelve and Twelve" reflects an entirely different mood. In 1951 and 1952, when Bill wrote the second book, he was suffering almost constant depression and was forced to confront the emotional and spiritual demons that remain "stranded" in the alcoholic psyche when the high tide of active alcoholism recedes. The "Twelve and Twelve" provides a highly practical and profoundly spiritual prescription to help exorcise those demons.

During Bill's 15 sober years, he had had ample opportunity to become intimately acquainted with some of the unproductive and often negative attitudes and traits that are frequently part of the disease of alcoholism — continuing into sobriety. By now, he knew well that apart from alcohol, alcoholics have other problems, for which they must find solutions if they are to live comfortably. It is a further testament to Bill's genius that he had been able to write the actual Steps themselves when he was barely "dry behind the ears," for the Steps apply precisely to the problems common to so many alcoholics after they stop drinking. Now, Bill set out to write the essays that explained the Twelve Steps. He made no revisions or amendments in the Steps themselves; they remained exactly as he had written them years earlier.

The "Twelve and Twelve" discusses frankly some matters not even mentioned in the Big Book. As to God, for instance, whereas the Big Book says, "When we drew near to Him He disclosed Himself to us!," the "Twelve and Twelve" talks about the times when "the hand of God seemed heavy or even unjust." It continues, "All of us, without exception, pass through times when we can pray only with the greatest exertion of will. Occasionally we go even further than this. We are seized with a rebellion so sickening that we simply won't pray. When these things happen we should not think too ill of ourselves. We should simply resume prayer as soon as we can, doing what we know to be good for us." Those are extraordinary statements from a man who once had a spiritual experience like "the wind on a mountaintop." But Bill and other A.A.'s had learned that sober living does not necesssarily bring instant immunity from rejection, grief, guilt, rage, or jealousy. In the new book, Bill discussed such problems without promising quick or easy solutions.

In fact, he hit so hard on negative matters in the "Twelve and Twelve" that he apparently felt obliged to add an explanation — or apology — near the end of his essay on Step Twelve: ". . . it may appear that A.A. consists mainly of racking dilemmas and troubleshooting. To a certain extent, that is true. We have been talking about problems because we are problem people who have found a way up and out, and who wish to share our knowledge of that way with all who can use it. For it is only by accepting and solving our problems that we can begin to get right with ourselves and with the world about us, and with Him who presides over us all."

He started writing as soon as the First General Service Conference had come and gone. The Traditions essays came first; indeed, much of the work on the Traditions had already been done for Grapevine publication as the "Twelve Points to Assure Our Future." After these were finished and revised, he undertook the essays for the Steps.

Bill knew what he was taking on. It was one thing to write

the Steps themselves — not easy, but they were, after all, broad suggestions. It was another and far more difficult matter to enlarge upon them, and to interpret them to the many different kinds of people who suffer from alcoholism. In a letter to Father Dowling dated July 17, 1952, he described the dilemmas he was facing:

"The problem of the Steps has been to broaden and deepen them, both for newcomers and oldtimers. But the angles are so many, it's hard to shoot them rightly. We have to deal with atheists, agnostics, believers, depressives, paranoids, clergymen, psychiatrists, and all and sundry. How to widen the opening so it seems right and reasonable to enter there and at the same time avoid distractions, distortions, and the certain prejudices of all who may read, seems fairly much of an assignment."

His physical method of writing the "Twelve and Twelve" was much the same as that used to write the Big Book. He would assemble the second edition of the Big Book, and later "Alcoholics Anonymous Comes of Age," in similar fashion. These three books, all written during the 1950's, occupied him in immediate succession. The "Twelve and Twelve" was published in 1953; the second edition of the Big Book, in 1955; "A.A. Comes of Age," in 1957.

He wrote a section at a time and sent it to friends and editors for their comments. Then, he revised the original material according to suggestions that came in. He also used trusted A.A.'s to help him with the three projects: Betty L. worked on the "Twelve and Twelve"; Tom P., on the "Twelve and Twelve" and "A.A. Comes of Age"; and Ed B., on the second edition of the Big Book.

Jack Alexander, *Saturday Evening Post* reporter, was also one of the friends to whom Bill sent material. Of the Twelve Traditions essays, Alexander had this to say:

"The only serious (in my view) defect is that you have treated the old Washingtonian Society too briefly; most people never heard of it.[2]

"You should have no worries at all about your writing style. More than anyone else, you are qualified to speak the A.A. language, and you do it nobly. If you were to professionalize your style, the juice of the message would be lost.[3] It would read as snappily, and [be] as unconvincing, as the chromium-plated stuff produced in such appalling quantity by the Madison Avenue boys in the tab collars."

Bill's reply to Alexander:

"Besides my natural tendency to procrastinate, I've had a dreadful hex about further writing. Figure I had been so beat up by the events of these last years that I could never bring anything more off that would be worthwhile. So the comment from you was a real lift. Them were very kind words indeed, my friend.

"Just now, I'm doing a similar series on the Twelve Steps. The pitch and tone of them is somewhat different. Perhaps this is because the Traditions job was more in the nature of objective reporting, while the one on the Steps is definitely subjective."

Of the material Bill sent six months later, Jack Alexander wrote:

"The Twelve Steps script is fascinating. Only trouble with your writing style is mechanical; you rely too often on the clause or phrase set off by dashes. I started off by trying to reduce them, but gave it up. I think you ought to have someone go through the script seeing how many dashes, thus used, can be reduced to simple commas. It would make for smoother reading.

"The same person should remove most of your exclamation points, just to get another mechanical gimmick out of the readers' eyelashes. They are cries of 'Wolf! Wolf!' and their impact gets less with each repetition.

"Otherwise, the text is splendid. It has real authority and conviction, and I stayed with you to the end, which is more than I can say for Hemingway's 'The Old Man and the Sea.' "

"Twelve Steps and Twelve Traditions" was first published in two editions — one for distribution through A.A. groups, and a second edition, costing 50¢ more ($2.75 instead of $2.25), intended for sale in commercial bookstores and distributed through Harper & Brothers (by arrangement with A.A.'s old friend Eugene Exman). A.A. made a contract with Harper that enabled the Fellowship to retain full control and copyright ownership of both editions.

The book was an immediate success. In a letter dated October 5, 1953, Bill wrote: "At first, I was dubious whether anyone would care for it, save oldtimers who had begun to run into life's lumps in other areas than alcohol. But apparently, the book is being used to good effect even upon newcomers. We have shipped more than 25,000 to date, a figure that speaks for itself."

The Fellowship's demands on Bill had eased by now. Headquarters was functioning smoothly, and the Conference was in place, at least on its five-year trial basis. Bill was able to accomplish a great deal during this period. Two years after publication of the "Twelve and Twelve," the second edition of the Big Book was published. By 1955, the first edition had gone through 16 printings, and some of the personal stories were somewhat dated. The Fellowship now had the experience, and the members, to include more stories by women, more "high bottom" stories, and more stories from younger members.

For the second edition, Bill went out of his way to include one personal story that had been conspicuously missing from the first — that of Bill D., "Alcoholic Anonymous Number Three" ("the man on the bed"), who had never submitted his story for the first edition. As Bill D. himself said, he had not been interested in the book project at that time. Bill was one of those conservatives whom Bill Wilson regarded as vital to the Fellowship; they were the members who would not themselves launch new ventures, and would always protect the Fellowship from rash, new, and sometimes harmful plans for A.A. devised by other members. Bill D. did not share Bill Wilson's vision of A.A.'s future. He had not supported the idea of the General Service Conference, although he performed conscientiously when members in his area elected him their first delegate. In 1952, when

Bill D.'s health was failing, Bill Wilson persuaded him to record his story.

Published in 1955, in time for the St. Louis Convention, the second edition was designed to show the broader range of the membership. Many people had been asked to write or record their stories for possible inclusion in this edition; these were later donated to the archives. Bill was responsible for getting many of the stories himself, often going to a group with the express purpose of taping the drunkalog and recovery experience of this or that oldtimer. Now, these stories were thoroughly screened. In addition to the editorial help of Ed B., Bill had the assistance of Nell Wing, his nonalcoholic secretary. The brunt of the work, as with the other two books, was borne by Bill himself.

Unchanged in the new edition was the original text of the first 11 chapters, dealing with the principles followed by early members to achieve sobriety. In addition to Bill's story and Dr. Bob's, six others were carried over from the first edition; 30 new stories were included; and the present division of the story section into three parts was instituted.

The appearance of the new edition was well timed, for it was at the Second International Convention that Bill gave A.A. its formal release into maturity. Over the years, he had used various examples and analogies to illustrate the nature of his relationship to the Fellowship, and he was well aware that maturity for a child meant a changed role for the parent as well. He used a simple parable to describe this, calling it "The Case of the Cook in Trouble": "Let's suppose a 17-year-old boy gets the family cook in trouble. His father has a clear responsibility to help settle the matter, even though it was the boy's fault. The father should help him, because the boy is underage.

"But suppose the boy reaches the age of 21 and gets the cook in trouble. Should the father then come to his aid? I think not. The father can justifiably say to the son, 'This is your responsibility, and you'll have to take care of it yourself.' "

Through such parables, and through Bill's own behavior,

he had made it clear that A.A. must take complete responsibility for its own affairs. By 1955, the end of the General Service Conference five-year trial, he was assured that the Conference members could take charge of all matters affecting the Fellowship. With the advice and consent of those around him, Bill decided to make the Second International Convention the occasion for announcing A.A.'s "coming of age." Here, for once, Bill seems to have met with no opposition to his plan for letting go.

This Convention was held at St. Louis, another centrally located city. For Bill personally, St. Louis had the added advantage of being the hometown of Father Dowling, his spiritual sponsor. Other people important to Bill were also at the Convention: Ebby was there as his special guest; Dr. Emily came from San Diego; non-A.A.'s invited to speak at the occasion included not only Father Ed, but Dr. Sam Shoemaker, Dr. Harry Tiebout, Leonard Harrison, Bernard Smith, Dr. W. W. Bauer of the A.M.A., psychiatrist O. Arnold Kilpatrick, penologist Austin MacCormick (between his two terms as trustee), Henry Mielcarek, corporate personnel expert, and Dr. Jack Norris.

While Bill dedicated much of the St. Louis Convention to giving full recognition to non-A.A.'s who had aided the Fellowship in its early years, he was at pains to complete, before the Convention met, a major piece of writing for the benefit of the membership. Entitled "Why Alcoholics Anonymous Is Anonymous," it appeared in the January 1955 Grapevine.[4] It reflects Bill's deepest and most mature thinking on the subject of anonymity, literal and spiritual, and why anonymity is the heart and core of all that is best about A.A.

The St. Louis Convention ran from Friday morning, July 1, until late that Sunday afternoon. Titles of some of the weekend sessions give some indication of how widely A.A. had cast its net by now (membership had risen to 131,619 people; groups, to 5,927): "Helping the Young Alcoholic," "A.A. and Industry," "Linking the Group to General Service Headquarters," "The Children of Alcoholics," "Problems of A.A. Clubhouses,"

"Reaching the Alcoholic in Institutions," "A.A. and the Medical Profession," "Problems of Central and Intergroup Offices," "Money and Its Place in A.A.," "How to Form an A.A. Group." In addition, there were A.A. meetings and Al-Anon Family Group meetings. (While it is not within the scope of this book to detail the evolution of Al-Anon, it should be noted that the first Al-Anon service office had been opened four years previously.)

Bill gave three major talks. The first, on Friday evening, was "How We Learned to Recover." The second, on Saturday evening, was "How We Learned to Stay Together"; the third was "How We Learned to Serve." Four o'clock Sunday afternoon was reserved for the final meeting of the 1955 General Service Conference, which had begun its deliberations earlier in the week. This was the occasion on which Bill formally turned over the stewardship of A.A. to the General Service Conference, relinquishing his own official leadership and acknowledging A.A.'s responsibility for its own affairs. As he would later summarize it: "Clearly my job henceforth was to *let go* and *let God*. Alcoholics Anonymous was at last safe — even from me."

If Bill was a tired man at St. Louis, it was because he was somehow everywhere during those three days. But after 1955, the depression that had plagued him for so long lifted, and he regained his bright outlook.

Two years later, A.A. published Bill's "diary" of the proceedings of the St. Louis Convention, which he had gone to great lengths to have documented. Bill wrote it, he said, because he wanted to make sure that nobody misunderstood what had happened at St. Louis.

In many ways, "Alcoholics Anonymous Comes of Age" is a masterpiece. Deceptively simple in its guise as a log of the three-day proceedings, it is actually an entire history of the Fellowship and its place in society, with whole sections given over to the vision of A.A. as held by those in society at large — men of industry, doctors, ministers, and trustees — who lived in close relationship to the Fellowship. Published in 1957, it is Bill's penultimate book.

His last, published in 1967, is ''The A.A. Way of Life,'' the title of which was changed in 1975 to ''As Bill Sees It.'' It consists entirely of excerpts from Bill's other writings, suggested and edited (with Bill's word-by-word approval) by Janet G. Bill did some editing of his own, exercising the writer's prerogative of polishing his work.

Although Bill's health was now relatively stable, this was not true of family and close friends. During the early 1950's, Bill was sending his father $100 a month. His sisters also contributed, as did a nephew on the West Coast. How the elder Wilsons might best be cared for was a constant concern and worry to Bill. Letters flew back and forth between British Columbia and New York as Bill tried to find a solution to their myriad problems. At one juncture, he had investigated the possibility of having Gilman and Christine return to Vermont to live out their lives; but because such a move would cost the small pension they did have, the plan was abandoned. A.A.'s in Canada, however, were a great support to Bill, both practical and moral, as he attempted to care for his father and stepmother long-distance. In 1953, they came to Bedford Hills on a visit; but by that time, hardening of the arteries had impaired Gilman's speech and memory.

When they returned to Marblehead, he had to be watched constantly lest he ''wander off in the woods and get lost.'' With the help of A.A. members in Vancouver, he and Christine were moved to a Vancouver boardinghouse run by a retired nurse. Later, Gilman was moved again, this time to a nursing home.

In Bedford Hills, there was trouble, too. On January 24, 1954 (a meaningful date for Bill and Lois), Lois, who was never ill, had a heart attack.

On January 23, she shoveled the snow from their long driveway. The next day, their 38th wedding anniversary, she went into the city to meet Bill, who was already there; they had plans to celebrate. His note, written to her the day before, reads: "Come any peril, we know that we are safe in each other's arms because we are in God's."

Her diary for that day describes what happened next: "I had bad pain in my chest which continued for about 1/2 hour, while I did shopping. After a bite of lunch, I went to see 'The Living Desert' movie at Sutton Theater. Pain again and down left arm and then very bad down right arm. Sat till end of picture thinking pain would leave but it continued. Took taxi to Bedford Hotel where there was a message in our room box which I thought was for me and I called several places trying to find Bill and getting weaker and weaker. Did phoning in lobby. A.A. office finally told me Bill was at hotel. Called Leonard who arrived in about half hour. He called Doctor Regnikoff of N.Y. Hospital and an ambulance. About the time Leonard arrived, my pain stopped. When ambulance arrived they would not let me even go to the bathroom but carried me on stretcher into private room at N.Y. Hospital. So all following dates were canceled."

Lois believed health was a "moral issue," and she felt vaguely guilty, she said, for getting sick.

She turned out, to everyone's surprise (her own included), to be a model patient. Told to do nothing for a year, she was scrupulously obedient, despite the unaccustomed inactivity it forced on her.

From a letter from Bill to Father Dowling dated March 3 of that year: "The report on Lois continues very good. She has been home about ten days, and it's very evident that the attack was a light one. She gains strength by the hour, has a wonderful frame of mind about the whole business, and shows every sign of being amenable to the denials that will be required of her in months to come and to some extent, indefinitely. I am delighted with her beyond measure.

"I am looking forward, too, in the hope that I can now do for her what she once did for me. When I was sick, she was always there and saw me through. Now it is her turn. More than most any of the other women, she has been grass-widowed by A.A. May God forgive my part in all this and let me now even up the score.''

On February 14, just three weeks later, Gilman Wilson died. On Bill's behalf, Vancouver A.A. members helped supervise Gilman's funeral arrangements and services. His ashes were returned to East Dorset for burial in the small country cemetery with his Wilson relatives. Christine would later be buried beside him, although she had never lived in Vermont. (She died the following year, on January 6, 1955.) It fell to Bill to inform his mother, the woman who had so long ago been his father's wife.

Gilman's obituary, sketching the colorful life of a rugged individualist, appeared in the *Kootenian*, Kaslo, British Columbia, on Thursday, February 25, 1954:

''G. B. Wilson, age 84 years: Gilman Barrows Wilson was born in East Dorset, Vermont. He inherited his father's vast marble quarries at an early age, and took over management soon after graduating from Albany College, N.Y. These quarries were first opened by his grandfather, and were the first operated in America. Mr. Wilson's first big job was getting out marble for the Soldiers and Sailors Memorial, which still stands on Riverside Drive, New York City. About this time he also got out hundreds of marble doorsteps and stairways that are still gracing palatial homes in New York and Philadelphia.

''By friends, he was lured into construction work at the time there were bids out to construct the Boston subway. He accomplished this feat of engineering to perfection, which later brought him the superintendency of the Lackawanna tunnel and other projects. His skill in handling these operations called him to the attention of the Patch Manufacturing Co., who recognized him as a man with a future, and he, being still a marble man at heart, readily consented to go on a tour of states and provinces, and he became familiar with the different types of marble and travertines, as well as those of the Italian, their textures, and where they were found. It was on one of these inspection tours that he came to the Kootenay Valley to find merchantable stone. This he found at a place called LeBlanc. A Montreal firm developed it and later sold it to Mr. Wilson, who rechristened it 'Marblehead.' During these years a lot of marble was quarried here. The Great West Life Building in Winnipeg, a theater in Edmonton, and numerous other buildings were constructed from this marble.

"Early in the Roosevelt administration, he was called to Florida to construct arches for the Overseas Highway to Key West. These were to be sawn from native coral rock, the work to be done by veteran bonus-seekers that were camped on the White House lawn. The first 600 of these had been sent to Matecumbe Key, with more to follow as soon as housing facilities were available. This, however, never came to pass. A Caribbean hurricane blew in, and before a train could reach them, over 450 were swept into the sea and drowned. Although of stout heart and towering strength, this was more than Mr. Wilson could gracefully accept from the elements, and he returned to his old home in the quiet hills of Marblehead to semiretirement. He had already sold the plant and quarries to an Edmonton firm.

"When asked how he could endure the loneliness of the Lardeau after such an active career, his reply was: 'It is not so much where one lives as how.' When asked which his greatest achievement was, he replied, 'I believe it is the fact that I owe no man anything but goodwill.' Today many beautiful structures stand as a monument to his accomplishments. The big white columns in the Lincoln Memorial in Washington, D.C., are perhaps the best known.

"A man of quiet dignity, always kindly encouraging his crew of men, lending a hand to the weak, generous to those in need. 'He folded his tent like the Arab, and as silently slipped away,' at early dawn, February 14, at Vancouver."

Two years later, Bill had another major loss. When his good

friend Mark Whalon died, in 1956, Bill was clearly broken-hearted. From a letter he wrote to a mutual friend, shortly after returning from Mark's funeral:

"Only a week back from the West Coast, I was in a state of almost complete collapse. I had left orders at the office 'no messages under any conditions.' We were at the hideaway we have in the country near Brewster. I had called the office from a farmhouse only because it was urgent. Nell told me of Mark's death and your desire to reach me. This all hit me so hard that I got into a hysteria and felt that I simply couldn't face it. At no time the next day did I think I could do anything about it, either."

About this time, Bill received a letter from Caryl Chessman. The notorious Chessman spent 12 years on death row in San Quentin; the length of that period was due primarily to his own amazing ability to win himself stays of execution. His case became nationally known after the publication of his autobiography, "Cell 2455, Death Row."

Jack Alexander had suggested to Chessman that he write to Bill, for Alexander felt, "There is a close resemblance between the criminal psychopath and the alcoholic mind. Both are grandiose, resentful, defiant, and hating of authority; both unconsciously destroy themselves trying to destroy others." Alexander wondered whether criminals could also "recover" through a surrender similar to that experienced by A.A.'s.

Chessman wrote to Bill that he "woke up to the fact I'd been nothing more than a cynically clever, aggressively destructive, and sometimes violent damn fool." He decided he could do something about it besides feel sorry for himself: "I could tell my story and plead, not my personal cause, but society's cause and the cause of those who — in my opinion, needlessly — are criminally damned and doomed." Referring to his soon-to-be-published book, he said, "I am most hopeful it will make a very useful contribution to a most vexing social problem."

Bill was clearly moved by Chessman's letter, and he knew that Chessman was scheduled to die on May 14. His reply, dated

March 31, praised Chessman for endorsing the concept that "no personal calamity is so crushing that something true and great can't be made of it."

Then Bill continued:

"I think that society is only beginning to catch on to the fact that its own neurosis is tearing it apart. It still looks on people like you and me as dangerous or wicked freaks who ought to be punished or maybe killed off. This natural approach, it is thought, will make the world a safer place for the respectable and the sane.

"Therefore, alcoholics, criminals, and the like, whose symptoms are violent and menacing, are apt to be set off as a class apart. Society can't yet identify itself with us at all.

"Being better behaved, on the surface at least, society does not take in the fact that it has become just about as sick as we are. It can't think of itself as destructively neurotic, nor can it see us as merely the grotesque and dangerous end products of its own defects."

A few weeks later, Bill continued in the same vein: "I'm sure that my identification with you — in the sense of childhood inferiority, the generation of rebellion, the implacable urge to notoriety and power of a sort — is fairly complete. This despite the fact that my pursuit of that goal took, except for alcohol, a seemingly more respectable course. That the underlying malformation was identical, I have no doubt at all.

"Like you, I seemed to be living in a pretty senseless and hostile world, though one out of which fleeting satisfactions and prizes could be won by the strong, the contriving, and above all, the lucky. Possessive love of glory and self was the compelling demand, reckoning no consequences and brooking no opposition. And even in transient periods of ecstatic success, there was always that nagging and hopeless question 'What in hell is it all about, anyway?' "

Three days before his scheduled execution, Chessman wrote to Bill: "I cannot thank you enough for your May 3 letter. It helped me explore the crucial question you framed so aptly:

'What in hell is it all about?' Frankly, I still don't know the answer; yet I do feel I'm a little nearer to a personal solution. And in any case, I'm now quite prepared to die, and not disturbed or upset over what faces me Friday morning.

"I join you in the belief that surely there must be a purpose in this brief span of ours. That I have failed to perceive it in entirety I attribute only to my intellectual or spiritual blindness. I've caught glimpses of purpose, and those glimpses confirm my belief that behind reality is a larger truth."

On May 13, Chessman received an unexpected stay of execution. In fact, it was not until May 2, 1960, six years later, that he was actually executed. His correspondence with Bill was cut short, however; San Quentin inmates were permitted to correspond only with relatives and friends of long standing — a rule that had been temporarily eased because of Chessman's imminent execution. Even a copy of the "Twelve and Twelve" sent to the convict was returned. An appeal to the San Quentin warden for special consideration was refused; thus ended Bill's correspondence with Caryl Chessman.

Chessman was not the only offbeat celebrity whose life intersected briefly with Bill's. Others were drawn by the wideness of his personality, his capacity to respond to many different types of people, and the generosity that allowed him to identify with them.

---

1. Bill had incurred a large personal debt during his drinking years. While most of these debts had been outright forgiven or paid back, or had ceased to exist because of the statute of limitations, Bill himself did not forget them, and there is correspondence, over the years, to indicate that Bill continued to make good on these old debts.

2. The Washingtonian Society was an organization that flourished in the 1840's but quickly failed because of some of its own practices. Bill wrote: "At first, the society was composed entirely of alcoholics trying to help one another. The early members foresaw that they should dedicate themselves to this sole aim. . . . Had they been left to themselves, and had they stuck to their one goal, they might have found the rest of the answer. . . . Abolition of slavery, for example, was a stormy political issue then.

Soon, Washingtonian speakers violently and publicly took sides on this question. . . . [They] completely lost their effectiveness in helping alcoholics.'' Bill saw Traditions Ten and Five as A.A.'s safeguards against the Washingtonians' fate.

3. Herb M., A.A. and a G.S.O. general manager, always said that Bill's love of ''high-flown language'' was a great asset to him. ''It was the language of two generations back. The reason for that would be that we run such a gamut of educational levels in A.A. I think it's very important, because it makes his talks extremely impressive yet completely understandable.''

4. ''Why Alcoholics Anonymous Is Anonymous'' remains available in the pamphlet ''A.A. Tradition — How It Developed'' and the book ''Alcoholics Anonymous Comes of Age.''

Chapter Twenty-Three

Bill's prodigious labor to put together a truly representative service structure for the Fellowship did not go unnoticed in the rest
of the world. Aldous Huxley, author (''Brave New World''),
teacher, philosopher, and pioneer of New Age consciousness, was
the man who called Bill ''the greatest social architect of the
century.''

Bill met Huxley through their mutual friend Gerald Heard,
the British radio commentator, anthropologist, and metaphysi-
cian[1] whom the Wilsons had first visited at his Trabuco campus
in the winter of 1943-44. Bill and Huxley had an immediate rapport, a rapport that Bill, incidentally, was immensely proud of.
They had much in common, although Huxley was not an alcoholic.

Through the same connection, Bill was introduced to two
English psychiatrists whose field was of immediate interest to
him. These two men, Drs. Humphry Osmond and Abram Hoffer, were working with alcoholics and schizophrenics in a mental
hospital in Saskatoon, Saskatchewan, trying through various

methods to break through these patients' resistance, so that they could be reached and helped. While Bill had discovered a way to break through resistance — or, as he called it, that often impenetrable and always thick wall called ego — through spiritual surrender and deflation at depth, Drs Osmond and Hoffer had been trying to reach the same end through chemical means.

At the time Bill met them, they were using an experimental synthetic chemical called lysergic acid diethylamide, manufactured in Europe by Sandoz, a Swiss pharmaceutical company. This substance would later become known — and notorious — by its nickname, LSD. In 1954, when Osmond and Hoffer began their experiments, no one had ever heard of it; it was so new and so experimental that no regulations or restrictions governing or controlling its usage existed.

The two psychiatrists' original theory about why it might work for their particular purpose was quickly abandoned when they saw what in fact was happening. This is how Humphry Osmond describes both theory and actual experience:

"In 1954, Abram Hoffer and I, using LSD and mescaline [for] schizophrenia, conceived the idea that they represented something very similar to delirium tremens — that a good many people who really give up alcohol do so on basis of the fact that they've had an attack of D.T.'s and been impressed by them. We [thought] it might be a very good idea to give a person an 'attack' before he'd been completely destroyed. This was our original theory. We found, in fact, that this wasn't quite how it worked. [It was] really not unlike Bill's experience, which I later heard about — it gave a number of people pause for thought, not on the grounds of how terrifying it was, but how illuminating it was. Rather different!

"I went down and was introduced to Bill and told him about it, and he was extremely unthrilled. He was very much against giving alcoholics drugs."

Later, however, Bill became interested when he heard that the two doctors were getting results. As he observed the work closely, he arrived at this conclusion: It was not "the material itself [that] actually produces these experiences. It seems to have the result of sharply reducing the forces of the ego — temporarily, of course. It is a generally acknowledged fact in spiritual development that ego reduction makes the influx of God's grace possible. If, therefore, under LSD we can have a temporary reduction, so that we can better see what we are and where we are going — well, that might be of some help. The goal might become clearer. So I consider LSD to be of some value to some people, and practically no damage to anyone. It will never take the place of any of the existing means by which we can reduce the ego, and keep it reduced."

With that attitude, Bill undertook further investigation of the possible uses of LSD in treating alcoholics. Nell Wing remembers the sequence of events: "There were alcoholics in the hospitals, of whom A.A. could touch and help only about five percent. The doctors started giving them a dose of LSD, so that the resistance would be broken down. And they had about 15 percent recoveries. This was all a scientific thing."

Dr. Jack Norris followed the progress of these experiments, too. Of the psychiatrists, he said: "They felt that most alcoholics, or a high percentage of alcoholics, were also schizophrenics, and that this was one way of foreshortening the process of psychotherapy."

Nell continues the story: "Anyway, Bill wanted to see what it was like. He was intrigued with the work that Osmond and Hoffer were doing in Saskatoon with alcoholics. And he thought: 'Anything that helps the alcoholics is good and shouldn't be dismissed out of hand. Techniques should be explored that would help some guy or gal recover who could not do it through A.A. or any other way.' He gave his full enthusiasm [to] what other people were doing along that line. That's why he took it himself. He had an experience [that] was totally spiritual, [like] his initial spiritual experience."

Bill first took LSD in California, under the guidance of

Gerald Heard. Also present, and guiding, was Sidney Cohen, psychiatrist at the Los Angeles Veterans Administration Hospital. The date was August 29, 1956. Tom P. was there, and he and Gerald Heard took notes about the events of the afternoon.

Bill was enthusiastic about his experience; he felt it helped him eliminate many barriers erected by the self, or ego, that stand in the way of one's direct experience of the cosmos and of God. He thought he might have found something that could make a big difference to the lives of many who still suffered. Soon, he had a group of people — psychiatrists, ministers, publishers, and friends — interested in further experiments with the substance. Far from keeping his activities a secret, he was eager to spread the word. (Secrecy was never Bill's strong point. His candor, certainly an important part of his great charm and credibility, also had its drawbacks. As Nell said, if you did not want something to be publicly known, you were well advised not to share it with Bill. In a word, he was open about his own affairs and those of others.)

He invited many of his closest associates to join him in the experience. Those invited included Father Dowling, who accepted, Dr. Jack, who did not,[2] and Sam Shoemaker. Bill reported to Shoemaker: "You will be highly interested to know that Father Ed Dowling attended one of our LSD sessions while he was here recently. On that day, the material was given to one of the Duke precognition researchers,[3] a man now located in New York. The result was a most magnificent, positive spiritual experience. Father Ed declared himself utterly convinced of its validity, and volunteered to take LSD himself.''

Bill even persuaded Lois to try some: "Even acute heart cases can take the material with impunity, as the uniform effect — no matter what the emotional reaction — is to reduce the heart action slightly. Therefore, I have felt free to give it to Lois, and she had a most pleasing and beneficial experience. It was not the full dose, and I expect shortly to try that on her. Though she doesn't necessarily connect it with the LSD, there is no doubt she is undergoing a very great general improvement since even this mild administration.''

Lois herself had this to say about her experience: ''Bill gave me some. Actually, I could not tell any difference. I don't know. I looked down, and I saw things that were clearer, but they weren't any greener — it's supposed to make your perception greater. But I'd always been an observer of nature anyway and looked carefully at things.''

It was, in fact, about clearer perception that Huxley had written his now-famous book ''The Doors of Perception.'' Dr. Osmond had given him mescaline, an organic substance that produces effects similar to those of the synthetic LSD. Of this experience, Huxley wrote: ''The man who comes back through the Door in the Wall will never be quite the same as the man who went out. He will be wiser but less cocksure, happier but less self-satisfied, humbler in acknowledging his ignorance yet better equipped to understand the relationship of words to things, of systematic reasoning to the unfathomable Mystery which it tries forever, vainly, to comprehend.''

That is certainly not A.A. language, but the thought is the same as that expressed by Bill when he wrote about deflating the ego to permit ''the influx of God's grace.''

As word of Bill's activities reached the Fellowship, there were inevitable repercussions. Most A.A.'s were violently opposed to his experimenting with a mind-altering substance. LSD was then totally unfamiliar, poorly researched, and entirely experimental[4] — and Bill was taking it.

Bill was generous and openhanded, typically forthcoming in the way he personally acknowledged every complaint directed at him. But he was angry; again, he was facing one of the most irksome problems regarding his relationship to A.A. The name of the problem was Bill's Right to Lead His Own Life vs. A.A.'s Claim on Bill. That was part of his reason for wanting to give A.A. its formal release into maturity at the St. Louis Convention. He had stepped down at St. Louis, but as Dennis Manders, longtime controller at the General Service Office, so succinctly put it: "Bill would spend the next 15 years stepping down." In other words, everybody — Bill included — was having difficulty letting go.

In a long letter to Sam Shoemaker, written in June 1958, Bill aired his most eloquent and personal thoughts about his relationship to the program, LSD, personal ambitions for his own future, and the nature of the universe. Here are some pertinent excerpts:

"I often write letters to clarify my thinking and to ask advice. In this spirit, I am now turning to you.

"St. Louis was a major step toward my own withdrawal, [but] I understand that the father symbol will always be hitched to me. Therefore, the problem is not how to get rid of parenthood; it is how to discharge mature parenthood properly.

"A dictatorship always refuses to do this, and so do the hierarchical churches. They sincerely feel that their several families can never be enough educated (or spiritualized) to properly guide their own destinies. Therefore, people who have to live within the structure of dictatorships and hierarchies must lose, to a greater or lesser degree, the opportunity of really growing up. I think A.A. can avoid this temptation to concentrate its power, and I truly believe that it is going to be intelligent enough and spiritualized enough to rely on our group conscience.

"I feel a complete withdrawal on my part should be tried. Were any major structural flaws to develop later that I might help to repair, of course I would return. Otherwise, I think I should resolutely stay away. There are few, if any, historical precedents to go by; one can only see what happens.

"This is going to leave me in a state of considerable isolation. Experience already tells me that if I'm within range of A.A. requests or demands, they are almost impossible to refuse.

"Could I achieve enough personal freedom, my main interests would almost surely become these:

"(1) To bring into the field of the general neurosis which

today afflicts nearly everybody, such experience as A.A. has had. This could be of value to the many groups working in this field.

"(2) Throughout A.A., we find a large amount of psychic phenomena, nearly all of it spontaneous. Alcoholic after alcoholic tells me of such experiences and asks if these denote lunacy — or do they have real meaning? These psychic experiences have run nearly the full gamut of everything we see in the books. In addition to my original mystic experience, I've had a lot of such phenomenalism myself.

"I have come to believe proof surely exists that life goes on; that if better strategy and modern instrumentation were applied to the survival problem, a proof could be made to the satisfaction of everybody. To my mind, the world badly needs this proof now. So I would like to participate in some of these efforts and experiments.

"I realize that both science and religion have a really vested interest in seeing that *survival is not proved*. They fear their conclusions might be upset. Despite the demonstration of Christ Himself, theologians still argue that blind faith, excepting for Christ's demonstration, is the better thing. They say that people sometimes get into trouble through fooling with psychics. I've seen this happen, too.

"There is the argument that proof of survival would be of no value anyway, especially if it were actually revealed that in our Father's house there are really 'many mansions.' People could then get the idea they still have a long time to work things out, so they would continue to shilly-shally, to their detriment.

"Everything considered, I feel that full proof of survival would be one of the greatest events that could take place in the Western world today. It wouldn't necessarily make people good. But at least they could really know what God's plan is, as Christ so perfectly demonstrated at Easter time. Easter would become a fact; people could then live in a universe that would make sense.

"I've taken lysergic acid several times, and have collected

considerable information about it. The public is today being led to believe that LSD is a new psychiatric toy of awful dangers. It induces schizophrenia, they say. Nothing could be further from the truth. It was Dr. Humphry Osmond who first gave the drug to Aldous Huxley. The interest then spread to Gerald Heard and thence to Dr. Sidney Cohen, psychiatrist [at] the Veterans [Administration] Hospital in Los Angeles. Subsequently, this group then took on Dr. Keith Ditman, a research psychiatrist in the University of California. There is no question of their competence or good faith. They have with them a biochemist, also of U.C.L.A.

"In the course of three or four years, they have administered LSD to maybe 400 people of all kinds. Extensive tape recordings have been taken. The cases have been studied from the biochemical, psychiatric, and spiritual aspects. Again, no record of any harm, no tendency to addiction. They have also found that there is no physical risk whatever. The material is about as harmless as aspirin. It was with them that I took my first dose two years ago.

"[There is] the probability that prayer, fasting, meditation, despair, and other conditions that predispose one to classic mystical experiences do have their chemical components. These chemical conditions aid in shutting out the normal ego drives, and to [that] extent, they do open the doors to a wider perception. If one assumes that this is so — and there is already some biochemical evidence of it — then one cannot be too concerned whether these mystic results are encouraged by fasting or whether they are brought on by [other means].

"At the moment, it can only be used for research purposes. It would certainly be a huge misfortune if it ever got loose in the general public without a careful preparation as to what the drug is and what the meaning of its effects may be. Of course, the convictions I now have are still very much subject to change. There is nothing fixed about them whatever.

"And do believe that I am perfectly aware of the dangers to

A.A. I know that I must not compromise its future and would gladly withdraw from these new activities if ever this became apparent.''

By 1959, Bill had personally withdrawn from the LSD experiments.[5] He did so gracefully. He and Dr. Jack had had some correspondence on the subject of Bill's responsibility as a living founder, and these words from Dr. Jack doubtless helped to assure Bill that his decision had been right:

''You cannot escape being 'Bill W.' — nor would you, really, even though at times you will rebel. The best bets are made with all possible information in hand and considered. I am reminded of a poem written by the mother of a small child, in which she says, 'I am tied down' and goes on to list the ways she is captive, ending with the phrase 'Thank God I am tied down.' To few men has it ever been given to be the 'father image' in so constructive a way to so many; fewer have kept their stability and humility, and for this you are greatly honored. But you are human, and you still carry the scars of alcoholism and need, as I do, to live A.A. The greatest danger that I sense to the Fellowship is that you might lose A.A. as it applies to you.''

---

1. He also wrote dozens of mysteries, which he published under the pseudonym H. F. Heard.

2. Dr. Jack did, however, correspond with Osmond and Hoffer. As scientists, he said, they were less exuberant than Bill: ''They were guardedly enthusiastic in their correspondence with me, saying that it had to be given under very careful auspices, and with a considerable amount of preliminary setting of the stage.''

3. One of a series of ESP experiments conducted at the Rhine Institute at Duke University.

4. LSD was first brought to national awareness in 1961 through the work of Drs. Timothy Leary and Richard Alpert (later better known as Ram Dass), at that time of Harvard. Leary had given LSD to some of his psychology students as part of a class experiment. With neither the proper ''guidance'' nor the controls that were required to make the experiment scientifically valid, two of the students (both minors) had distressing ''flashback'' experiences. The experiments, ''respectable'' and quiet un-

til that time, erupted into a scandal, and Leary left Harvard.

Leary had actually approached Bill during the late 1950's, asking to be included in the work Bill was doing. Bill, who did not want to include him, kept putting him off until Leary stopped asking.

5. By 1963, the Canadian government had banned LSD; in April of that year, Sandoz withdrew it from the market. During the flower-child, hippie, Haight-Ashbury era of the late 1960's, it was manufactured illegally and peddled as a street drug. The advice tragically taken by many LSD abusers was Timothy Leary's slogan, ''Turn on, tune in, drop out.''

Chapter Twenty-Four

During the late 1950's and the 1960's, Bill's A.A. activities became more limited than they had been at any time during the previous 20 years, so he was free to pursue a diversity of interests.

One of these was to return, in a small and limited way, to the Wall Street field that he had abandoned — and been abandoned by — three decades earlier. Once again, he could be found of a morning, his feet on his office desk, ashes from an ever-present cigarette dribbling unnoticed onto his vest, reading the financial page of the newspaper. As he wrote to Dave D.:

"I have returned to business, feeling that I ought to make the same demonstration as my fellows who must, for the large part, return to the world and try to relate themselves to it. So, of all places, I've gone back to Wall Street! This is proving to be very good for A.A., and an excellent therapy for me. I confess that I had rather gone broke emotionally on an overdose of good works, and curiously enough, the new activity seems to have recharged me."

It was some time during the early 1960's that Bill again became acquainted with Joe Hirshhorn, the brilliant financier who had employed him during the early 1930's when no one else would. Hirshhorn, now richer than ever, had also become famous for his art collection, and had endowed a museum — the Hirshhorn, now part of the Smithsonian Institution.

Robert Thomsen, author of "Bill W.," tells how the two reestablished contact one afternoon when Bill and Lois were hurrying to catch a plane. At La Guardia Airport, Bill and Hirshhorn bumped into each other, literally. They had not laid eyes on each other in 30 years, and they exchanged pleased and excited greetings. Then Joe asked Bill what he had been up to. Bill, a bit surprised, replied that he thought everyone knew: He had become America's Number One drunk. From Hirshhorn's response, it was clear that he had no idea what Bill was talking about.

" 'You know, Joe,' he said. 'A.A.'

" 'Oh,' said Joe. . . . He was delighted. Delighted! Because Bill Wilson was certainly one man who needed to find A.A. And with this, he rushed on to catch his plane."

They continued to keep in touch, meeting for occasional meals and otherwise communicating by mail or phone. There is a record of correspondence between the two men between 1962 and 1966, solely about financial matters. Hirshhorn was apparently able to help Bill at this time (in more than one letter, Bill expressed his gratitude — probably for Hirshhorn's earlier loyalty), and Bill, for his part, provided Hirshhorn with the fruits of his investigations and intuitions about the market.

Bill was eager to share his wealth, however meager or abundant that might be. His generosity was legendary around the program, and with good reason; it was bottomless. (One of the things he habitually did was to send out, as gifts, the newest pieces of A.A. literature. At the bottom of the carbons of countless letters written by him are reminders to also send a copy of whatever his latest book was. He autographed each before sending it out, and the inscription was always thoughtful and personal.)

He began including friends and family in the results of his financial research. His mother had taken to Wall Street so enthusiastically and had done so well with her investments that by the time she died — in contrast with Bill's father, who died penniless — she had accumulated an estate worth around $100,000.

Herb M., general manager at the A.A. General Service Office from 1960 to 1968, was a recipient of Bill's financial counsel. At Bill's suggestion, Herb and his wife bought 600 shares of British Columbia oil lands. Said Herb:

"Bill would come in and report on it; it got weaker and weaker. And then, when I retired, Bill insisted on buying and giving us enough British Columbia oil lands so that we could sell the whole batch, including all that we had, and get all our money back. It had bothered him all those years that it had paid no dividends. He had this funny, elliptical way of helping us recoup our losses."

In the early 1960's, Bill became involved in a new idea for converting heat into electricity. Although national concern about the energy shortage was still ten years away, Bill was, as usual, years ahead of his time. Stan Ovshinsky, a Detroit inventor, had developed what he thought was a new, cheap way of converting heat directly into electricity. Ovshinsky's company, Energy Conversion Laboratories, was formed to market the idea, and the inventor needed help with both capitalizing his project and selling it. Humphry Osmond introduced him to Bill; as Osmond said, Bill was one of the few people who possessed a combination of financial knowledge, scientific imagination, and altruism.

Ovshinsky summarized Bill's involvement with the project: "He saw what we were doing in those days, and became very excited about it. We were not really in business at that time; we were more of a research group doing something he was interested in, and he wanted to help out every way he could. He was involved in my thinking about energy conversion, photovoltaics, thermal electricity. He was very forward-looking and thought that we were going to make it someday. I wish he was alive to see what progress we have made. He really was one of the most exceptional and unique people ever in the world.''

Ovshinsky's company was speculative, but it still exists. In 1977, the *Wall Street Journal* ran a page one story about his theories; in addition, Standard Oil of Ohio invested heavily in his company.

Bill's involvement with J. Robert Oppenheimer was equally magnetic, if somewhat briefer. The two met at Trunk Bay in the Caribbean, where Bill and Lois were on vacation. They were immediately attracted to each other, probably each sensing in the other a kindred spirit. After some long walks and long talks, the physicist broached the idea of Bill's joining him at the Institute for Advanced Study, at Princeton. Oppenheimer wanted Bill to oversee and evaluate some work being done there on the chemical composition of neuroses — most particularly depression. While in the end nothing came of these preliminary suggestions, it seems that Bill, no matter what direction he turned, was being faced with the possible physiological and chemical aspects of a problem that he had earlier approached almost exclusively in terms of its psychological and spiritual ramifications.

One of the projects that Bill had planned for his ''retirement'' was to deal with an unfinished task: acknowledging A.A.'s indebtedness to the countless people he felt were responsible for its creation. At the top of his list was Carl Jung, the psychoanalyst who had pointed Rowland H. and subsequently Bill himself — via Ebby — in a spiritual direction.

Bill's letter to Jung, dated January 23, 1961, is among the most eloquent of the thousands of letters he wrote in his lifetime. After first introducing himself, Bill wrote:

''. . . I doubt if you are aware that a certain conversation you once had with one of your patients, a Mr. Roland [sic]H——, back in the early 1930's, did play a critical role in the founding of our Fellowship.

". . . Our remembrance of Roland H——'s statements about his experience with you is as follows:

"Having exhausted other means of recovery from his alcoholism, it was about 1931 that he became your patient. I believe he remained under your care for perhaps a year. His admiration for you was boundless, and he left you with a feeling of much confidence.

"To his great consternation, he soon relapsed into intoxication. Certain that you were his 'court of last resort,' he again returned to your care. Then followed the conversation between you that was to become the first link in the chain of events that led to the founding of Alcoholics Anonymous.

". . . First of all, you frankly told him of his hopelessness, so far as any further medical or psychiatric treatment might be concerned. This candid and humble statement of yours was beyond doubt the first foundation stone upon which our Society has since been built.

"Coming from you, one he so trusted and admired, the impact upon him was immense.

"When he then asked you if there was any other hope, you told him that there might be, provided he could become the subject of a spiritual or religious experience — in short, a genuine conversion. You pointed out how such an experience, if brought about, might remotivate him when nothing else could. But you did caution, though, that while such experiences had sometimes brought recovery to alcoholics, they were, nevertheless, comparatively rare. You recommended that he place himself in a religious atmosphere and hope for the best. This I believe was the substance of your advice.

"Shortly thereafter, Mr. H—— joined the Oxford Group, an evangelical movement then at the height of its success in Europe, and one with which you are doubtless familiar. You will remember their large emphasis upon the principles of self-survey, confession, restitution, and the giving of oneself in service to others. They strongly stressed meditation and prayer. In these surroundings, Roland H —— did find a conversion experience that released him for the time being from his compulsion to drink.''

Very long in its entirety, the letter went on to tell Jung how the message reached Bill at the low point of his own alcoholism; it described his own spiritual awakening, the subsequent founding of A.A., and the spiritual experiences of its many thousands of members. As Bill put it: ''This concept proved to be the foundation of such success as Alcoholics Anonymous has since achieved. This has made conversion experience . . . available on an almost wholesale basis.''

The closing of the letter was Bill at his most gracious:

''. . . As you will now clearly see, this astonishing chain of events actually started long ago in your consulting room, and it was directly founded upon your own humility and deep perception.

''Very many thoughtful A.A.'s are students of your writings. Because of your conviction that man is something more than intellect, emotion, and two dollars' worth of chemicals, you have especially endeared yourself to us. . . .

''Please be certain that your place in the affection, and in the history, of our Fellowship is like no other's. Gratefully yours,''

Jung's reply, datelined Kusnacht-Zurich, January 30, 1961, read, in its entirety:

''Dear Mr. Wilson,

''Your letter has been very welcome indeed.

''I had no news from Rowland H. anymore and often wondered what has been his fate. Our conversation which he has adequately reported to you had an aspect of which he did not know. The reason that I could not tell him everything was that those days I had to be exceedingly careful of what I said. I found out that I was misunderstood in every possible way. Thus I was very careful when I talked to Rowland H. But what I really thought about was the result of many experiences with men of his kind.

"His craving for alcohol was the equivalent on a low level of the spiritual thirst of our being for wholeness, expressed in medieval language: the union with God.*

"How could one formulate such an insight in a language that is not misunderstood in our days?

"The only right and legitimate way to such an experience is that it happens to you in reality, and it can only happen to you when you walk on a path which leads you to higher understanding. You might be led to that goal by an act of grace or through a personal and honest contact with friends, or through a higher education of the mind beyond the confines of mere rationalism. I see from your letter that Rowland H. has chosen the second way, which was, under the circumstances, obviously the best one.

"I am strongly convinced that the evil principle prevailing in this world leads the unrecognized spiritual need into perdition, if it is not counteracted either by a real religious insight or by the protective wall of human community. An ordinary man, not protected by an action from above and isolated in society, cannot resist the power of evil, which is called very aptly the Devil. But the use of such words arouse[s] so many mistakes that one can only keep aloof from them as much as possible.

"These are the reasons why I could not give a full and sufficient explanation to Rowland H., but [I] am risking it with you because I conclude from your very decent and honest letter that you have acquired a point of view about the misleading platitudes one usually hears about alcoholism.

"Alcohol in Latin is *spiritus*, and you use the same word for the highest religious experience as well as for the most depraving poison. The helpful formula therefore is: *spiritus contra spiritum*.

"Thanking you again for your kind letter, I remain yours sincerely, C. G. Jung

"* 'As the hart panteth after the water brooks, so panteth

my soul after thee, O God.' Psalm 42, 1''

Bill was overjoyed with Jung's letter. Not only was it gracious and meaningful, it answered in the affirmative a question that many thoughtful A.A.'s, beginning with himself, had often asked: Was not their excessive use of alcohol in itself a perverted form of search for some measure of enlightenment or higher consciousness? The emphasis in the Steps on a spiritual connection was here confirmed by one of the world's great psychoanalysts as the most appropriate — indeed, the only appropriate — antidote for intoxication.

Moreover, the letter arrived at a moment in Bill's life when he sorely needed it. In St. Louis, Father Dowling had died. Bill's spiritual sponsor, guide, and mentor had understood the nature and import of Bill's search in a way that no one else had. From the very beginning, he had endorsed and affirmed it without reservation.

As Bill's letters to A.A. members so often became talismans for them,[1] so now Jung's letter became a talisman for Bill. The original hangs in the library at Stepping Stones. As time passed, copies of it would be read at meetings or framed and hung on meeting-room walls, and it would be printed and reprinted in the Grapevine.[2]

Bill's reply to Dr. Jung's letter is dated March 20, 1961. It reads, in part:

''Your observation that drinking motivations often include that of a quest for spiritual values caught our special interest. I am sure that, on reflection, thousands of our members could testify that this had been true of them, despite the fact that they often drank for oblivion, for grandiosity, and for other undesirable motives. Sometimes, it seems unfortunate that alcohol, used in excess, turns out to be a deformer of consciousness, as well as an addictive poison.

''Years ago, some of us read with great benefit your book entitled 'Modern Man in Search of a Soul.' You observed, in effect, that most persons having arrived at age 40 and having acquired no conclusions or faith as to who they were, or where they were, or where they were going next in the cosmos, would be bound to encounter increasing neurotic difficulties; and that this would be likely to occur whether their youthful aspirations for sex union, security, and a satisfactory place in society had been satisfied or not. In short, they could not continue to fly blind toward no destination at all, in a universe seemingly having little purpose or meaning. Neither could any amount of resolution, philosophical speculation, or superficial religious conditioning save them from the dilemma in which they found themselves. So long as they lacked any direct spiritual awakening and therefore awareness, their conflict simply had to increase.

"These views of yours, doctor, had an immense impact upon some of the early members of our A.A. Fellowship. We saw that you had perfectly described the impasse in which we had once been, but from which we had been delivered through our several spiritual awakenings. This 'spiritual experience' had to be our key to survival and growth. We saw that the alcoholic's helplessness could be turned to vital advantage. By the admission of this, he could be deflated at depth, thus fulfilling the first condition of a remotivating conversion experience.

"So the foregoing is still another example of your great helpfulness to us of A.A. in our formative period. Your words really carried authority, because you seemed to be neither wholly a theologian nor a pure scientist. Therefore, you seemed to stand with us in that no-man's-land that lies between the two — the very place that many of us had found ourselves. Your identification with us was therefore deep and convincing. You spoke a language of the heart that we could understand."

There was no reply to Bill's second letter. Two months later, on June 6 of that year, Dr. Jung died. Bill, having waited a quarter of a century to write his thank-you note, had sent it just in time.

The fact that Bill never made a similar personal acknowledgment of A.A.'s debt to Frank Buchman, who also died in

1961, remains a sore point with some, a matter of bewilderment to some others.

Bill himself seriously regretted the omission. A month after Buchman's death, Bill wrote to a friend: ''Now that Frank Buchman is gone and I realize more than ever what we owe to him, I wish I had sought him out in recent years to tell him of our appreciation.''

Fear of controversy loomed large in Bill's thinking; he had even consulted Father Dowling and others before giving credit to the Oxford Group in ''Alcoholics Anonymous Comes of Age.''

It was also in 1961 that Dr. Emily died. During the last five years of her life, with both her physical and her mental faculties failing, Bill had persuaded her to move East. She was in a nursing home in Dobbs Ferry, New York, when she died on May 15, at the age of 91. Bill discovered after her death that she, a true eccentric, had kept no books — ''only scribbled and scattered memorandums, incomplete.''

Bill's complicated feelings toward her, as she intuitively sensed them, and their relationship — truncated in its way as had been his relationship with his father — were summarized in a letter she wrote to him:

''It seems that conditions in this life have prevented our spending much time together, in somewhat ironical disregard of the physical ties that should have bound us in a much closer companionship. But it is my dearest hope and belief that in our future existence, these earthly ties of flesh and blood will be strengthened and expanded to include closer ties of our mental and spiritual natures through a better understanding of enlightened Truth. I am looking forward to this time.''

She was laid to rest in the East Dorset cemetery — in the Griffith family plot.

Even though the LSD experiments were ended, Bill's friendship with Drs. Osmond and Hoffer continued. Bill had a great regard for them. Dr. Osmond once said: ''Bill told us that we were among the few people he had met who did not explain his work to him, but asked him to explain it to us.''

More important, Bill continued his intense interest in their ongoing work with schizophrenics and alcoholics. Whereas Bill's approach to alcoholism had always been primarily spiritual with psychological overtones, theirs had always been primarily biochemical.

The two doctors believed they were having some success in treating alcoholics who could not stay sober by giving them niacin, which is vitamin B-3. They felt that when they administered it as part of the detoxification process, the vitamin lessened the effects of alcohol withdrawal. They also felt that they had additional success when they used the vitamin to treat schizophrenics who did not respond to traditional psychotherapeutic methods — in other words, were inaccessible to any sort of "talking cure."[3]

To Bill's great joy, he believed Osmond and Hoffer had discovered the "exact nature" of the allergy Dr. Silkworth had talked about. Bill had always maintained that Dr. Silkworth, when he referred to an "allergy of body," knew the condition was not strictly an allergy; he simply used the word for want of a more specific one. As Bill described Dr. Silkworth's position:

"It was Dr. Silkworth who introduced the idea to me that alcoholism had a physical component — something he called an 'allergy.' He knew this was a misnomer; he used it to express his intuition that something was physically wrong with most of us, a factor perhaps causative and certainly an aggravation of the alcoholic's condition."

Dr. Silkworth's "allergy," said Bill, was the tendency of alcoholics to have some disturbance in their blood chemistry, often hypoglycemia — low blood sugar — which had an effect best described as a mild insulin shock.[4] Although the condition is usually controllable through diet (little glucose, sucrose, or other simple carbohydrates, low caffeine, high complex carbohydrates, and frequent feedings), Hoffer and Osmond thought that niacin (also known as nicotinic acid) could prevent, to at least some extent, a drop in blood sugar. And niacin was not a mood-changer. It was a v'tamin.

Bill grew wildly enthusiastic about his friends' niacin work. He read the literature, studied the statistics, pored over the studies they had done, took the substance himself, and professed a great benefit from it. Then, thoroughly persuaded of its effectiveness and benefit, Bill took it upon himself to bring the work of Osmond and Hoffer to the attention of the professional (medical) community and the great army of A.A. members who were, almost without exception, Bill's fans and followers. Marshaling his talents as a leader, his skills as an organizer, and his energies as a pioneer, he began to advocate B-3 with a zeal similar to that he had brought to the infant A.A. program 30 years earlier.

Bill put together three papers about B-3. Primarily intended as information for the "trade" — in this case, the medical profession (doctors in A.A.) — the first, dated December 1965, was prefaced with a letter to physicians in which Bill praised the efficacy of niacin in treating emotional problems and alcoholism.

When Bill got onto a new idea, there was no stopping him. In other situations, this ability to immerse himself totally in what he believed had been a strength and an asset; his enthusiasm was infectious.

The word about B-3 spread. Frank R., a trustee from the Boston area, had dinner with Bill after a board meeting on a Sunday evening in 1967. Frank remembers the evening:

"Bill and I went over to Stouffer's, and we no sooner get in the restaurant and order up, and he starts in on the B-3, extolling its virtues to me. The soup is still in front of him, and the waitress is prodding him. 'Mister, mister, are you going to finish your soup?' No, he's all wrapped up, selling me — a promoter! So I'm very patiently listening.

"I guess we got out of Stouffer's after about two hours, and then he invited me up to his room. And there he is, promoting me, and I'm very patient. He's got some papers from doctors backing him up on the proposition. I didn't get out of that room until one o'clock in the morning. He's telling me about how right he's been over the years in all the different phases of A.A. Now, he's getting into the medical department. I'm doing the listening. He went back into ancient times and took some of his ideas from the ancient philosophers. He's telling me how when they invented the wheel, this took a great burden off mankind, and they didn't keep it to themselves. And we found out a way to stay sober here, and we didn't keep it to ourselves. Here we are in A.A. We found out we could stay sober, so we passed it along.''

By way of afterthought, Frank added, ''But I do know that Bill was having some of the girls in the office taking it, and it was getting a little out of hand. 'Come on, girls, it won't harm you.' So they're taking it, and they don't even know what they're taking and whether it's doing them any good or not. And those girls over there, I never saw any of them in a depression.''

Soon, niacin advocates began voicing their enthusiasm in A.A. meetings, and those opposed to it were using A.A. meetings as a forum for their opinions. Some of the opinions were about the merits or nonmerits of niacin; most were about Bill's behavior. The most vocal members were loudly against what he was doing. ''He's pulled one miracle; now he's going for a second'' was the disgruntled consensus of some; '' He's got a messiah complex,'' said others. Almost everyone agreed on one thing: Bill was in direct violation of two of his own Traditions. Six says, ''An A.A. group ought never endorse, finance, or lend the A.A. name to any related facility or outside enterprise, lest problems of money, property, and prestige divert us from our primary purpose''; Ten says, ''Alcoholics Anonymous has no opinion on outside issues; hence the A.A. name ought never be drawn into public controversy.''

Really, there was no way to prevent Bill from endorsing and promoting niacin, or to stop him; all the Fellowship could do was insist that he not mix it up with the A.A. name, nor use A.A. facilities for the work. Accordingly, in the board report accepted by the 1967 Conference, there was a recommendation "to insure separation of A.A. from non-A.A. matters by establishing a procedure whereby all inquiries pertaining to B-3 and niacin are referred directly to an office in Pleasantville, N.Y. In order that Bill's personal interest in these items not involve the Fellowship, the board requested that Bill's stationery (used in such correspondence) carry an address other than G.S.O.'s and that no G.S.O. employee be involved."

This solution pretty much ended the uproar provoked by Bill's public involvement with vitamins; that it did not end his actual involvement was evidenced by the fact that his last paper about niacin was written shortly before his death, and distributed posthumously.

---

1. The following letter from Ginger G., of El Paso, Texas, is only one of many such letters Bill received: "Many, many years ago when I was new in A.A. and, I might add, quite confused, I wrote you a letter. You answered that letter with one that was enlightening, encouraging, and inspiring. I read your letter as frequently as I did the Big Book. Your letter made me understand why people act as they do, and I am tolerant of any action that might be taken.

"Your letter, which was a part of my daily inspiration, was destroyed by fire in my house a few months ago. If you are not too busy, would you write another? I feel entirely lost without it. It was a part of my daily routine — reminding me of a lot of things none of us should ever forget."

2. Beginning in 1963, the Grapevine has printed the correspondence — Bill's long letter and Jung's answer — four times. Each time, the issue has sold out; there are no copies left in the Grapevine's back-issue file.

3. This was before the introduction of the antipsychotics — Thorazine (chlorpromazine), Compazine (prochlorperazine), Stelazine (trifluoperazine), etc. — now used in the treatment of schizophrenia.

4. This description, as given by Bill, was an early and simplified explanation of hypoglycemia.

Chapter Twenty-Five

As Bill grew older, his long face grew somehow longer; his non-descript hair, now white, grew sparse; and his monotone be-came, if anything, flatter. His tall frame was as erect as ever, but now his clothes hung more loosely. He had a reputation for being a terrible dresser — but Frank R. remembers a day that was atypical. "I was in Herb M.'s office, talking to Herb one morn-ing, and Bill strolls in and says, 'Look, fellas, I got a new suit.' Now at this particular time of his life, Bill could have gone to Brooks Brothers and ordered five. But he was like a kid. I'll never forget 'Look, fellas, I got a new suit.' "

Always eloquent, Bill remained as able as ever to hold forth on his current cause. Over the years, the timbre of his voice had changed very little. But by 1968, his shortness of breath had be-come noticeable, if one was listening for it. His smoking had been an issue for years; Ruth Hock remembered Bill trying to give up cigarettes as early as 1940. In "quitting," he was a noto-rious smoker of other people's cigarettes — often wanting to take two at a time; Ruth said that it was not unusual to have her whole pack gone by the end of the afternoon. Dennis Manders described the top of Bill's desk, its edges scarred from the burned-down ends of countless cigarettes that Bill, over the years, had balanced there and then forgotten.

It's unclear when Bill first learned he had emphysema; in 1961, he requested that the General Service Conference make provision for Lois, should he predecease her. This was done without delay. Also during 1961, and again at Bill's request, provision was made for Ebby to receive a regular monthly check for the rest of his life. Ebby received $200 a month until his death in 1966.

Bill's royalty payments were his only source of income. He received royalties from the Big Book, "Alcoholics Anonymous Comes of Age," "Twelve Steps and Twelve Traditions," and "The A.A. Way of Life" ("As Bill Sees It"). According to an agreement made in 1963 between Bill and A.A. World Services, he was allowed to bequeath his royalties to Lois. She, in turn, was permitted to bequeath her royalties to "approved beneficiaries" as part of her estate, the main provision being that 80 percent of the royalties had to go to beneficiaries who had reached the age of 40 at the time of the agreement in 1963. Upon the death of these beneficiaries, their royalties would revert to A.A. At his own request, Bill received no royalties on any of the foreign editions of his books (nor has his estate).

Bill's A.A. work was still unfinished; there was a final coda that he felt he had to hear played; there would be no rest until the last chord had been harmoniously resolved. The issue of the trustee ratio was not a very complicated one, but it was Bill's last exertion of will against the conservative, occasionally reactionary opposition of the trustees. Because the change itself was minor compared to the fuss it caused, the symbolism of the issue stood out more clearly.

Bill's entire life had been dedicated to growth. He had always embraced, endorsed, and encouraged change and growth in himself and others, in events and circumstances — and in this regard he was highly unusual. Psychoanalysts agree that the condition resisted the most fiercely by most people is change; people will go to very great lengths to maintain the status quo.

When, in 1938, the board of trustees had originally been formed to oversee the affairs of the infant Fellowship, it had been Bill's idea to have on the board a majority of nonalcoholic trustees. At that time, no one knew whether the alcoholics could be sufficiently mature to take charge of their own affairs — even if they could stay sober.

After the St. Louis Convention, and after the ive-year probationary period of the General Service Conference was declared a success, Bill realized that it was time to reverse the original setup and to change the composition of the board to a majority of alcoholics. His efforts to see the ratio changed precipitated a wrangle that lasted through ten General Service Conferences. But now, the roles were reversed. Earlier, when Bill was lobbying for the establishment of the Conference, he had been in the role of parent trying to "wean" a child. Now, Bill (symbolizing the A.A. membership) was the child trying to convince his "parents" — in this case, the board of trustees — that the Fellowship was mature enough to have the final word in the management of its own affairs.

Historian Ernest Kurtz summarized the situation as follows: "Explicitly composed of a majority of nonalcoholics, the trustees and foundation were the most visible witness to the Fellowship's respectability. Such dependence upon nonalcoholics was to Wilson a denial of responsibility and evidence of immaturity. But . . . these men had given much, and most had become close personal friends. Appropriate gratitude . . . was also a responsibility of and a witness to maturity."

In a 1958 letter to Harrison Trice, a nonalcoholic trustee, Bill gave the following reasons for the proposed change:

"Because of the increased press of work with which we have no business to saddle the nonalcoholic members; because of the increasing importance of proper determination of the A.A. policy and its administration, which the nonalcoholics have, wrongly, I think, disclaimed all ability to handle; because of the need for a wider representation geographically of alcoholic trustees; and finally, because it is unsound psychologically for a movement of the present size and maturity to take a childish and fearful view that a majority of alcoholics cannot be trusted to sit on our most important board — well, these are the reasons for the change as I see them.''

The Conference was proving to be a conservative body. Some delegates did not share Bill's fears that the old ratio would bring serious future problems. But most resisted, they said, because of the way Bill went about his mission. Said Herb M., a trustee from 1956 to 1960:

"He approached it head-on and running, because in his own mind he was getting along, and he wanted to see this thing done. None disagreed with him as far as the ratio was concerned. There was no active opposition to doing this. There was active opposition to the way he was going about it.''

Said Dr. Jack, Bill was not above acting like a "bleeding deacon'' when he was thwarted. Bill's reaction to seeing his plan at first defeated was to say, "Will it be all right if I still have an office at headquarters?''

Even Lois found it difficult to understand why Bill was so heated on the subject. At St. Louis, he had formally passed authority to the General Service Conference, which then took the full responsibility for the makeup and policies of the board. Since the Conference delegates now had the power to change the trustee ratio whenever they wished, what did it matter if they waited a few years to do so? That was Lois's more relaxed view.

Year after year, the Conference turned Bill down. Here are just a few notices to that effect, as they appeared yearly in the summaries of Conference activities mailed to all groups:

1956: "Approved continuation of the present structure of the board of trustees (eight nonalcoholic members and seven alcoholics) until 1958, but asked that the matter be given further study at the 1957 Conference."

1957: "Tabling, for consideration at the 1958 Conference, a proposal to change the current (eight to seven) ratio of the non-alcoholic and alcoholic trustees on the General Service Board."

1962: "Accepted Bill's long-awaited manuscript on 'Twelve Concepts for World Service' and recommended that it be distributed initially as a supplement to, and eventually as an integral part of, 'The Third Legacy Manual.'

"Reaffirmed, by a 72-to-36 vote, decisions of earlier Conferences that the principle of having a majority of nonalcoholics as trustees of the General Service Board should be retained. (The present ratio is eight nonalcoholics to seven members of A.A.)"

Finally, in the 11th year, Dr. Jack said to Bill, "They're not reacting to your ideas — they're reacting to your method. Let me handle it." And then . . . "There was no problem at all. All I did at that meeting was say that the [alcoholic] trustees have come in from the movement. They've been great people; they've been very solid. There's never been an action on the board where there's been division between the A.A.'s and the non-A.A.'s, and I was very sure that the non-A.A.'s would accept the judgment [of the A.A.'s]. At the time the majority was set up, nobody had more than three years' sobriety in A.A., and they didn't trust themselves in the money department. I said, 'Give it a try. If it doesn't work, we can change it.' And it was that easy."

Thus ended Bill's long struggle to give alcoholic trustees majority control of the General Service Board. The board's report to the 1967 Conference, summarizing the past year's activities, stated: "At the quarterly meeting in April [1966], the board voted unanimously to accept the Advisory Actions of the Conference. Some of them were:

"1. That the board be increased to 21, seven nonalcoholic and 14 alcoholic. . . ."

This was Bill's last official business with the Fellowship. His satisfaction with the outcome was evident in this letter to Herb

M.: "You cannot imagine how happy and grateful I am that the decision was taken that A.A. should try to go on its own at the level of the board. Chief among my sources of happiness at this outcome is the remembrance that without your good offices, nothing might have been accomplished for years, if ever."

Bill's A.A. work was finished.

He had turned 70 in 1965, and he was still smoking. He had stopped many times and resumed many times. Said Nell Wing, "His breathing had become worse from maybe 1966 or 1967 on. Each year, he progressively slowed down. The emphysema took hold, and he was still smoking."

Pam B., of Red Bank, New Jersey, ran into Bill on vacation in the Caribbean during the winter of 1968. She, too, was trying to stop smoking, and when she and Bill met on the beach one afternoon, they made a mutual pact that neither would have a cigarette until they met again the following day. Every day, they met on the beach; and every day, they refrained from smoking until they met. The appointed hour of their rendezvous, however, grew earlier and earlier.

Bill began to carry a pocket inhalator. It was an L-shaped device; one end went into the mouth, and the other end was a plunger that was depressed with the thumb. On his walks on the trails around Stepping Stones (the Wilsons owned nine wooded acres), Bill now frequently stopped to rest, perching on the stumps of trees while he caught his breath. The neighbors, accustomed for years to seeing him on these daily walks, noticed that he was slowing down.

A turning point came in February of 1969. It had been a bad winter, and Bill climbed onto the low roof of his studio to survey the damage done by ice and snow, lost his footing, and began to slide off. Catching an overhanging branch, he managed to break his fall. He got to his feet, went inside for a meal, and soon returned to work. But he was badly bruised, and the bruises did not readily subside.

With that incident, the steady decline in Bill's health began.

By April of that year, he had actually quit smoking, and this time, he stayed stopped. Said Bob H.: "I can tell you exactly when it was, because — to my disbelief — he successfully tapered off. He was smoking fewer each day, and I can tell you exactly when it was — 1969, the winter of '69. A good deal of damage was done by that time."

For Bill, 1969 was a year of off-and-on illness, primarily pneumonia. He went into the office very seldom. When he did, he could hardly walk the few blocks to the station for the trip home; he'd have to stop every block and rest.

Al M. saw Bill for the last time at about that stage: "We were in New York, and we called Bill and said we would like to come out, and he told us he was not feeling very well, and wanted to invite us to stay overnight, but didn't think it would be a good idea. We got off that little train, and here's Bill with one foot outside of the car, hanging on the wheel and gasping for breath. He was that bad. He couldn't get out of the car."

Often, Nell Wing went to Bedford Hills to work. She was able to do much of the mail herself; by now, she could so well anticipate what Bill would say that she was able to write it — she could even imitate his handwriting and his style.

In early 1970, he rallied slightly. Although he was still going to New York irregularly, he was able to attend all the trustees' meetings. Many in the office were still not aware that he was seriously ill, although Bill spoke openly about his emphysema. Whether or not he realized that he was in the beginning of terminal illness is not known.

Every April, Bill spoke at the opening dinner of the Conference. In 1970, he was scheduled to speak as usual. Bob H. remembered what happened that night:

"He started to speak, and of a sudden he just stopped, right in the middle of the sentence. And he just stood there for a little bit, and then he said, 'I'm sorry. I can't continue.' And he went and sat down.

"Everybody was really taken aback at this, because if there

was one thing Bill could always do, it was speak — eloquently and articulately and persuasively.''

Dennis Manders, in charge of taping the Conference, remembered his own surprise when Bill apologized to him for messing up the tape by being unable to continue. (Nell, too, confirmed that during Bill's entire last illness, he remained the way he had always been: considerate of others.)

In April, G.S.O. moved to its present address at 468 Park Avenue South. Bill saw the new offices only once or twice.

Now, Bill was hurting in every way, and he was mentally groggy as well. But he wanted badly to attend the International Convention at Miami Beach in July. In May of that year, he went down to stay at the Miami Heart Institute; the director was

Bill in 1970 at the General Service Conference, by then a proven vehicle for the Fellowship's group conscience.

Dr. Ed B., fellow A.A., dear friend, and devoted physician. Bill had also spent a week with a vitamin and diet doctor in upstate New York.

Bob H. described the Miami Convention, which took place over the July Fourth weekend:

"He and Lois and Nell came down. As soon as they checked in, I went up to the suite. Bill was in a bad mood, and he'd gone into the bedroom and just thrown himself down on the bed, face down across the bed.

"Bill was scheduled to be at a press conference. There were about four things he was supposed to do; that was one of the most important. Of course, he was supposed to make a major talk, which he always did at these every-five-year Conventions.

"Lois asked me if I'd stay to dinner. They had dinner sent up, and Bill's mood improved a little. He came to table, but he didn't really eat. He went back into the bedroom and flung himself back on the bed. I was quite concerned about him, because it began to look that unless some miracle occurred, [it would] be somewhat of a risk to put him on in front of a lot of reporters.

"We had the press conference scheduled for the next morning, so first thing I did was to beat it up there and see how he was. During the night, they had gotten hold of Ed B. He was at that time the head of the cardiac clinic in Miami, and he said, 'We're going to have to take him right over to the institute' — Miami Heart Institute. So they got an ambulance, and he was taken over, and we had a couple people substitute for him, mostly Dr. Jack, I guess, at the press conference.

"And then he was going to speak at the big meeting on Friday night. He had his heart set on this. Ed, who admired him a great deal and was very close to him, said that they could work it out." It was physically impossible for Bill to speak on Friday, but he was not ready to give up.

"We had the [Sunday morning] meeting in Convention Hall," Bob H. continued. "There were 14,000 people. Bill was brought to the back entrance by ambulance. They had a hoist-lift truck there that just took Bill and the wheelchair, lifted him right up, and deposited him at the back entrance of the stage. He had a nasal tube in place, and he was taking oxygen.

"He was wheeled on in front of the microphone, and got up, with somebody sort of holding on to him. Maybe it was me — I don't remember. And just for a few minutes . . . he only spoke four minutes, and for the first two or three of those minutes, he was the old Bill. Fantastic! He could just mesmerize people.

"That was it. He went back into the wheelchair, and [was] wheeled off, lowered into the ambulance, and they went back to the hospital."

A.A's attending the Convention remember seeing Bill's bathrobed figure, sometimes on foot, sometimes in a wheelchair, around the hotel during that weekend. Bernard Smith and Marty M. filled in for him, giving the other talks that he had originally been scheduled to make.

He stayed on at the Heart Institute for the rest of the month, because Dr. Ed thought he could be helped there. When Bill and Lois returned North on August 1, their good friend Bernard Smith, who had so recently filled in for Bill at the Convention, was dead of a heart attack.

Upon their return, Bill promptly got pneumonia, and it never really went away. He would be taken to the Northern Westchester Hospital, where he'd be for a few days, and then he would come home. When he was able to walk a little, the pneumonia would return. In Miami, he had begun to use an oxygen tank; now, he was never without it. At first, he would use up a tank every other day; then, a tank every day; then its use became continuous.

He began to have hallucinations, hallucinations so real that he would describe them to Lois and to Nell. Occasionally, because his powers as a raconteur were so brilliant, his descriptive abilities so alive, Lois and Nell would laugh despite themselves.

By early September, Bill was totally bedridden. After November, he never came downstairs. Lois read his farewell message at his anniversary dinner that November. In his message, Bill paraphrased an Arabian greeting that had been sent to him by a member. To all A.A.'s, he wrote, "I salute you, and I thank you for your lives."

It was an exhausting, enervating period, full of effort. He would have lucid times, and in the morning when he wakened, he would say, "Oh my God, I've got to go through all this again today." To get through each day required an enormous exertion, and the strain on Lois was almost as great. Now, he had day and night nurses, too.

Bob H., who was G.S.O. general manager then, remembered:

"I was reasonably satisfied as early as late July or early August that Bill wasn't going to live very long. I didn't know how long, but we decided that we would get all the plans made ahead of time, which we did — everything. We had a list of all the people who had to be notified — those who could be notified by phone, those who had to be notified by telegram, those who could be notified by letter. All we had to do was punch a button, and the whole thing went right into gear."

In January of 1971, Dr. Ed, who was in constant touch by phone, decided that the Miami Heart Institute might be able to do something for Bill. The institute had a new breathing apparatus that might help him. He decided to bring Bill back to Miami. An old friend chartered a Learjet, and Dr. Ed flew up from Miami to accompany Bill back.

The plane's cabin was so small that a partition had to be removed for Bill's feet. Said Nell, "We had him lying in the stretcher across the back of several seats, wearing his ever-present oxygen mask. Dr. Ed had me seated towards his feet, himself in the middle, and Lois at the head." Nell, who had heard Bill counsel countless others, now used his own words of comfort. "Hold fast," she encouraged him, and Bill squeezed her hand in response. Lois whispered softly to him, holding his other hand and talking. During the flight to Miami, Bill remained conscious and in good spirits. He described his parents, his grandparents, and Mark Whalon, who all appeared to him in the cabin of the plane.

The plane arrived in Miami in the late afternoon, and Lois was near exhaustion. At eight o'clock, after dinner and after Lois had returned to Bill's room to say good night, she and Nell retired to their suite, adjoining rooms at the Holiday Inn next door to the institute. Bill was comfortable and cheerful when Lois left him.

It was January 24, and it was Lois and Bill's 53rd wedding anniversary. Bill died at eleven-thirty that night.

Afterword

On Tuesday, January 26, Bill's obituary appeared in the New York *Times*. The Traditions make no reference to posthumous anonymity; Bill's full name and his picture were prominently featured in the page one story.

At Stepping Stones, there was a private memorial service on January 27. The St. Francis Prayer, Bill's favorite, echoed through the trees around the house:

"Lord, make me a channel of thy peace; that where there is hatred, I may bring love, That where this is wrong, I may bring the spirit of forgiveness, That where there is discord, I may bring harmony, That where there is error, I may bring truth, That where there is doubt, I may bring faith, That where there is despair, I may bring hope, That where there are shadows, I may bring light, That where there is sadness, I may bring joy. Lord, grant that I may seek rather to comfort than to be comforted, To

A simple tablet in the East Dorset cemetery affirms Bill's deep belief in the spirit of anonymity.

understand, than to be understood, To love, than to be loved. For it is by self-forgetting that one finds. It is by forgiving that one is forgiven. It is by dying that one awakens to Eternal Life. Amen.''

At the General Service Office, immediately following Bill's death, the usual complaints stopped. All the combativeness and the appeals to G.S.O. to settle local disputes died down completely. For a period of about six months, there was a feeling of ''Let's get the wagons in a circle.''

On February 14, A.A.'s everywhere, now about 300,000 strong, attended memorial services for Bill. In New York City, the services were held at St. John the Divine; in Washington, D.C., they were held at the National Cathedral; in London, at St. Martin-in-the-Fields. In Montreal, they were at Notre Dame Cathedral; in Palm Beach, at Bethesda by the Sea; in Aruba, at the Sacred Heart Church in Sabaneta.

On May 8, when the Vermont ground had thawed, Bill's body was buried in the family plot in the East Dorset Cemetery. The gravestone is a simple marker of the same white marble that his father once quarried for the buildings and monuments of New York City. He is buried next to Clarence, his Griffith uncle who ''bequeathed'' Bill his violin.

The headstone reads: ''William G. Wilson, 1895-1971.''

There is a footstone. That reads: ''Vermont, 2D LT BRY C66 ARTY CAC, World War I. Nov. 26, 1895 - Jan. 24, 1971.''

There is no mention of A.A.

Significant Dates

1895	November 26: Bill Wilson born in East Dorset, Vermont
1906	Bill's parents, Emily and Gilman Wilson, are divorced
1917	The United States enters World War I, and Bill is called up Bill has his first drink
1918	January 24: Bill marries Lois Burnham
1919	Bill is released from the military; he and Lois settle in Brooklyn
1925-29	Bill's success as a securities analyst marred by a worsening drinking problem
1930-33	Bill's drinking prevents him from making a financial comeback after the 1929 crash
1933	Bill enters Towns Hospital for the first time
1934	December 11: Bill's last drink. Released from his obsession, begins thinking about a movement of recovered alcoholics who would help others Bill and Lois start attending Oxford Group meetings
1935	May: In Akron, Bill and Dr. Bob meet June 10: Dr. Bob's last drink
1937	Bill and the New York alcoholics separate from Oxford Group More than 40 alcoholics are now staying sober
1938	The Alcoholic Foundation legally established
1939	"Alcoholics Anonymous," the Big Book, is published
1941	A *Saturday Evening Post* article puts A.A. "on the map" The Wilsons buy a home, Stepping Stones
1943	Bill and Lois make first cross-country tour of the groups
1944	Onset of Bill's depression
1950	July: First International A.A. Convention meets. The Traditions are accepted. Dr. Bob makes his last appearance. November 16: Dr. Bob dies
1951	April: The First General Service Conference meets
1953	"The Twelve Steps and Twelve Traditions" published
1955	July: At the St. Louis Convention, Bill gives A.A. its "formal release into maturity"
1967	Ratio of alcoholic to nonalcoholic trustees on the board is changed to a majority of alcoholic trustees
1970	July: Bill makes his last appearance at the Miami Convention
1971	January 24: Bill dies
1988	October 5: Lois dies

The Twelve Steps of Alcoholics Anonymous

1. We admitted we were powerless over alcohol — that our lives had become unmanageable.

2. Came to believe that a Power greater than ourselves could restore us to sanity.

3. Made a decision to turn our will and our lives over to the care of God *as we understood Him.*

4. Made a searching and fearless moral inventory of ourselves.

5. Admitted to God, to ourselves, and to another human being the exact nature of our wrongs.

6. Were entirely ready to have God remove all these defects of character.

7. Humbly asked Him to remove our shortcomings.

8. Made a list of all persons we had harmed, and became willing to make amends to them all.

9. Made direct amends to such people wherever possible, except when to do so would injure them or others.

10. Continued to take personal inventory and when we were wrong promptly admitted it.

11. Sought through prayer and meditation to improve our conscious contact with God *as we understood Him,* praying only for knowledge of His will for us and the power to carry that out.

12. Having had a spiritual awakening as the result of these steps, we tried to carry this message to alcoholics and to practice these principles in all our affairs.

The Twelve Traditions of Alcoholics Anonymous

1. Our common welfare should come first; personal recovery depends upon A.A. unity.

2. For our group purpose there is but one ultimate authority—a loving God as He may express Himself in our group conscience. Our leaders are but trusted servants; they do not govern.

3. The only requirement for A.A. membership is a desire to stop drinking.

4. Each group should be autonomous except in matters affecting other groups or A.A. as a whole.

5. Each group has but one primary purpose—to carry its message to the alcoholic who still suffers.

6. An A.A. group ought never endorse, finance, or lend the A.A. name to any related facility or outside enterprise, lest problems of money, property, and prestige divert us from our primary purpose.

7. Every A.A. group ought to be fully self-supporting, declining outside contributions.

8. Alcoholics Anonymous should remain forever nonprofessional, but our service centers may employ special workers.

9. A.A., as such, ought never be organized; but we may create service boards or committees directly responsible to those they serve.

10. Alcoholics Anonymous has no opinion on outside issues; hence the A.A. name ought never be drawn into public controversy.

11. Our public relations policy is based on attraction rather than promotion; we need always maintain personal anonymity at the level of press, radio and films.

12. Anonymity is the spiritual foundation of all our traditions, ever reminding us to place principles before personalities.

Sources

The primary source for this book was material in the A.A. archives: letters, memorandums, personal notes, interviews (in tape or typed transcript form), reports, newsletters, newspaper items, magazine articles, etc. Availability of this material varies and is determined in specific instances by the archivist or by the Archives Committee of the A.A. General Service Board.

Other sources are listed on the following pages, each reference followed by page numbers in the publication concerned. The following abbreviations are used in this section:

AA   "Alcoholics Anonymous" (the Big Book, second and third editions)

Age   "Alcoholics Anonymous Comes of Age" (book)

BW   "Bill W." (book), by Robert Thomsen, published by Harper and Row; paperback published by Popular Library (page numbers refer to this more recent edition)

Dr. Bob   "Dr. Bob and the Good Oldtimers" (book)

GV   The A.A. Grapevine (monthly magazine)

LR   "Lois Remembers" (book), by Lois W., published by Al-Anon Family Group Headquarters, Inc.

N-G   "Not-God" (book), by Ernest Kurtz, published by Hazelden Educational Services

12&12   "Twelve Steps and Twelve Traditions" (book)

Pages	Lines	Sources	Pages	Lines	Sources
20	23-31	GV 3/71, 10-11	68	15-18	AA, 2
25	18-25	GV 3/71, 12	69	32-35	LR, 37
25	34-35	Age, 53	72-73	34 to 3	LR, 58
27	2-6	LR, 15-16	73	29-30	LR, 61
30	3-9	Age, 53	75	19-27	LR, 60-61
30	22-26	GV 3/71, 13-14	75-76	33 to 5	AA, 3
31	10-15	GV 3/71, 13	79	11-21	LR, 68-69
32-33	22 to 9	GV 3/71, 13	79-80	35 to 5	LR, 70
36	30-32	Age 54	80	22-24	LR, 70
36-37	34 to 3	GV 3/71, 13	81	3-9	LR, 71
39	27-31	LR, 13-14	82-83	19 to 12	LR, 72-73
40	12-18	LR, 1, 12	84	30-35	AA, 3-4
48	13-20	LR, 15	86	14-16	AA, 4
48	22-34	LR, 16	88-89	2 to 20	LR, 77-78
52	15-17	AA, 1	98	22-31	AA, 6-7
54-55	34 to 4	GV 3/71, 16-17	102	12-20	AA, xxvi
55	9-16	LR, 21	106	15-19	LR, 85-86
55	21-22	LR, 15	112	2-4	LR, 84
55	27-28	AA, 1	116-117	29 to 3	"I Stand by the Door," by Helen Shoemaker, Harper & Row, 187-191
58	15-19	LR, 22			
58	27-28	LR, 23			
59	2-8	GV 3/71, 18			
60	13-15	AA, 12	120	5-7	"Reclamation of the Alcoholic," by Dr. W.D. Silkworth, *Medical Record,* 4/21/37
60	24-26	AA, 1			
61	18-22	GV 3/71, 20			
64	7-24	LR, 29			
67	31-35	LR, 35	122	5-7	New York *Times,* 9/2/83

Pages	Lines	Sources
122	7-10	*The Journal* (Addiction Research Foundation of Ontario) 4/1/84
125	23-26	LR, 89
128-131	29 to 3	Unpublished mss. by T.W. Hunter, M. Barger; "The Oxford Group: Its History and Significance," by W.H. Clark, Bookman Associates
131-132	33 to 7	Age, 64-65
133	13-17	Age, 68
133	27-32	Age, 65-66
135	19-27	Age, 65
137	3-5	Age, 65
138	8-9	*Motor News,* 10/65
140	22-28	AA, 177
140-142	30 to 4	AA, 178
143	5-8	GV 6/73, 4
143	12-15	Age, 67
143	22-24	AA, 180
146	2-9	Age, 75-76
147	17-23	GV 6/73, 6
147	23-25	Dr. Bob, 71
147	27-34	Dr. Bob, 73
149	23-25	AA, 156
152	26-30	LR, 96
153	22-24	AA, 188, 189
154	27-30	Dr. Bob, 92
155	12-17	GV 1/51, 9
155	18-22	Dr. Bob, 107
158	4-5	AA, 154
161	29-30	LR, 101
162	5-14	AA, 17
162	25-29	LR, 102
163	2-4	N-G, 42
165	19-26	LR, 105-106
166	23-30	AA, 96-97
167-168	25 to 33	LR, 98-99
169	25-34	LR, 103
170-171	33 to 3	*In Fact,* 1/18/43
171	12-15	"People to People Therapy," by John W. Drakeford, Harper & Row, 29
175	6-8	LR, 107
176	6-11	"The Glass Crutch," by Jim Bishop, Country Life Press
176	12-14	Age, 100-101
176	24-34	Age, 101
176-177	35 to 5	LR, 107
178	8-16	Age, 76
179-181	1 to 8	Age, 144-146
183	5-6	Age, 147
185	4-14	Age, 147-150
187-188	30 to 1	Age, 151
189	16-18	N-G, 66

Pages	Lines	Sources	Pages	Lines	Sources
193-195	19 to 10	Age, 153-157	223	29-33	Age, 176
			224	15-23	Age, 177-178
195-196	23 to 34	Age, 158-161	224	24-35	Age, 21-22
197-198	14-34 3-10	Age, 160-161	229	5-7	LR, 129
			231	29	AA, 86
198-199	14 to 4	N-G, 70, 275	232-234	4 to 31	Age, 182-186
199	29-33	Age, 167	235-236	24 to 9	Age, 188-190
199-200	35 to 5	AA, 58	237	8-26	GV 1/55, 4-5
201	13-14	AA, XXV	239	1-12	BW, 282-283
201-202	24 to 2	Age, 168-169	241	8-10	BW, 301-302
			242	2-9	N-G, 98
203	17-21	N-G, 74-75	242	10-12	Age, 38
204	11-16	Age, 167	242-243	32 to 10	N-G, 99
204-205	27 to 3		243	13-15	LR, 130
205	7-21	Age, 169-170	243	16-20	Dr. Bob, 252
207-209	11 to 6	Age, 174-175	245	15-17	N-G, 101
210	19-29	Age, 175-176	245	18-29	GV 5/45, 1
213	3-9	LR, 124	245	31-35	N-G, 101
213	21-24	LR, 125	246	1-9	Age, 36
214	4-6	LR, 126	246	15-17	Age, 191
215	19-35	LR, 126	247	5-16	Age, 191
216	8-18	LR, 128	248-249	26 to 4	Age, 191
216-217	25 to 7	LR, 127	249-250	26 to 1	LR, 132
218	14-21	Age, 12	255-256	25 to 1	BW, 298
220	21-23	Age, 176			
222	8-10	LR, 130	256-257	3 to 1	Age, 193-194
223	18-28	Age, 322			

Pages	Lines	Sources	Pages	Lines	Sources
257	20-21	N-G, 78	331	21-24	BW, 36
258	18-23	*The War Cry,* 10/30/71	339- 342	10 to 1	Dr. Bob, 337-338
261- 262	1 to 2	LR, 136	342	6-31	Age, 214
262- 263	21-to 5	LR, 137	345	2-4	Age, 215
			346	13-15	Age, 216
264	14-21	LR, 130	347	18-23	"The A.A.
266	26-31	Age, 91, 93			Service Manual,"
274	10-11	GV 6/44, 5			1983-84, 5
290	28-30	LR, 143-144	347	24-32	Age, 217
293	16-18	AA, 25	349	14-34	Age, 218
295	9-17	12&12, 45	353	3-4	AA, 57
295	32-33	AA, 83	353	5-12	12&12, 105
303	24-26	"Columbia	353	21-28	12&12, 125
		Encyclopedia," 940	359	19-20	Age, 48
305	23-27	GV 8/46, 3	366- 367	30 to 4	12&12, 178-179
305- 306	29 to 9	Age, 203	368	5-6	BW, 340
307	23-24	Age, 43	372	13-19	"The Doors of
308	10-15	12&12, 184			Perception,"
308- 309	30 to 1	Age, 292			by Aldous Huxley, Harper & Row, 79
309- 310	27 to 2	GV 1/55, 9	379	7-20	BW, 332
310	26-28	GV 1/55, 6	381	20-24	BW, 332-333
313	25	GV 2/78, 6	394	24-30	N-G, 128
315	32	12&12, 130			
318- 319	17 to 12	12&12, 150-154			
324	9-12	Age, 204			
327	29-34	Dr. Bob, 319			
328	6-31	Age, 210-211			

Index

418